FEDERAL LANDS

A Guide to Planning,
Management, and State Revenues

This educational project of the Western Office, Council of State Governments was generally supported by the Lincoln Institute of Land Policy, The Western States Land Commissioners Association, and The Giannini Foundation, University of California at Berkeley. The Project was initially organized by John Thorson and has been coordinated by Nan Stockholm and Peter Sly.

FEDERAL LANDS

A Guide to Planning,
Management, and State Revenues

Sally K. Fairfax

Carolyn E. Yale

Western Office,
Council of State Governments

ISLAND PRESS
Washington, D.C. □ *Covelo, California*

ABOUT ISLAND PRESS

Island Press publishes, markets, and distributes the most advanced thinking on the conservation of our natural resources—books about soil, land, water, forests, wildlife, and hazardous and toxic wastes. These books are the practical tools used by public officials, business and industry leaders, natural resource managers, and concerned citizens working to solve both local and global resource problems.

Founded in 1978, Island Press reorganized in 1984 to meet the increasing demand for substantive books on all resource-related issues. Island Press publishes and distributes under its own imprint and offers these services to other nonprofit research organizations. Funding to support Island Press is provided by The William H. Donner, Foundation, Inc., The Ford Foundation, The George Gund Foundation, The William and Flora Hewlett Foundation, The Joyce Foundation, The Andrew W. Mellon Foundation, Northwest Area Foundation, Rockefeller Brothers Fund, and The Tides Foundation.

For additional information about Island Press publishing services and a catalog of current and forthcoming titles, contact: Island Press, 1718 Connecticut Ave., N.W., Washington, D.C. 20009.

Library of Congress Cataloging-in-Publication Data

Fairfax, Sally K.
    Federal lands.

    Bibliography: p.
    Includes index.
    1. West (U.S.)--Public lands. I. Yale, Carolyn E.
II. Council of State Governments. Western Office.
III. Title.
HD243.A17F35   1987   333.1'0978   86-27512
ISBN 0-933280-33-5

Manufactured in the United States of America

Contents

**Chapter 7   Surface Resources and Miscellaneous Revenue-
Producing Programs, 121**

Text Figures

Text Tables

Appendix Figures

Appendix Tables

Foreword

It is frequently difficult for citizens and policy makers from other regions of the country to appreciate the sheer size, scope, and impact of federal landholdings in the West. Even westerners sometimes fail to appreciate the complexity of public land issues. More than 95 percent of all federal lands are in the western states. In seven western states, federal land constitutes more than 50 percent of the total land area. Often, these landholdings are widely dispersed checkerboard-fashion among private and state-owned lands. The western states must live on a daily basis with management of the lands by federal administrative agencies and the Congress — bodies that the westerner finds geographically and politically remote.

Massive federal landholdings in the West — with their related air, water, mineral, forest, and grazing land resources — raise special federalism and intergovernmental policy questions. In addition to the theoretical and practical policy aspects of federal public lands activities, there are also significant issues of propriety and equity when supposedly sovereign state governments are routinely and substantially affected by federal agencies administering the public lands.

In recognition of this extraordinary state–federal interrelationship, a pattern of sharing monies gained from federal public lands development has evolved over the years. This is one way in which the federal government has compensated western states and communities for lost tax revenues from these lands, for detrimental impacts associated with certain public lands activities, and other factors. Fiscal and political imperatives, however, make these revenue arrangements subject to constant tinkering and thus contribute to an inconsistent, unpredictable policy environment surrounding public lands in the West.

Although most specialists are familiar with one or two resource areas, this book documents and analyzes state/federal policy and fiscal dimensions of a large number of public lands activities. It asks a consistent set of basic policy questions about each of these activities as a means of fitting the "patchwork quilt" of many public lands programs within a coherent policy framework. It also reveals the historical and programmatic context of land management decisions and issues. The major contributions of this work are its comprehensive scope in assessing public land programs, its consistent analytical framework of inquiry, and the impressive amount of fiscal data presented. This volume should be of significant value to all those who think, write, and work on public lands issues.

We are indebted to our many western state associates — governors, legislators, attorneys general, land commissioners, and a host of natural resource officials and staff — who work tirelessly to bring greater order, rationality and plain common sense to the management and planning for the public lands. We trust this work will advance those continuing labors.

Dan Sprague
Director
Western Office, Council of State Governments

The goal of this book is to help concerned citizens and state and local officials participate in discussions of revenue-producing programs on the public lands. Participation is surprisingly difficult, even for professionals in public resource management, because the programs are diverse and complex, and because general information for the concerned practitioner or citizen has not previously been available.

The research for this book began innocuously, in an effort to provide state officials with useful figures on the revenues produced for each state by each program. At the outset, that did not appear to be an unreasonable task. Five years ago it was not uncommon for state comptrollers or land commissioners to complain that they did not know how much federal money was due them or why they received the specific amounts from the Department of the Interior; they simply received irregular checks from the Department without any explanation of where, when, or from what resource the money had been generated. Improving on that situation promised at the time to be a relatively simple undertaking.

It soon became apparent, however, that obtaining adequate revenue data was not the only serious problem. The numbers do not reveal much about policy and priorities unless they are studied in context, but the context is very difficult to identify. The complexity and detail of the individual programs can be intimidating. Each resource has its own peculiar vocabulary, entrenched interests, and particular technical and economic issues. Each has a body of knowledge and a cadre of experts that are relatively isolated from the others.

Although detailed tomes on the minutiae of numerous issues are available, it is difficult to find a general introduction to any one field or an overview of all the related programs. Because the subfields are so specialized, it has been very difficult for an outsider to understand, much less to debate with, an "expert" in the law, economics, or policy in any one of these fields. It is also surprisingly difficult for the initiated from one area to discuss resource programs in general or to speak with aficionados in another subfield. Confronted with this clear need for basic information to facilitate knowledgable discussion about resource revenues, the focus of this book gradually expanded from a collection of data to an introduction to the policy debates shaping each program.

Debate is necessary because resource development on federal lands affects states, localities, and individual citizens — environmentalists, employees, and investors, as well as laypersons. The importance of competent public discussion has never been greater. Recent changes in the law and public expectations concerning management of public resources provide major opportunities for state and local officials and citizens to participate in federal land management decision making. Indeed, subsequent chapters will show that after many decades of rapidly increasing federal authority at the expense of state and local priorities, a nascent state-federal management partnership is now beginning to emerge. There is too much at stake—in terms of national economic security, environmental quality, and revenues—for interested citizens and practitioners to remain on the sidelines.

Although the history of federal resource development programs is long and complex, contrary to general misconception it is not impenetrable. Much of the apparent complexity of these issues may be simplified by understanding that the same basic questions underlie all decisions to develop public resources — from a grazing permit to an Outer Continental Shelf oil lease. All programs are grounded in common issues and the common context of evolving public lands policy: patterns emerge to guide the persistent.

This volume is organized around seven basic resource development questions and the common historical patterns. Armed with this basic information under your cap, it becomes relatively easy to ask useful, meaningful questions, and to understand and evaluate the answers.

Writing a book is a continuing lesson in humility — and this project has been particularly so. Entire careers, agencies, industries, and regions focus on the law, economics, or management of only one of the resources discussed in this volume. It is therefore impossible to write a comprehensive book on all these resources without a great deal of help from others. Recognizing that, we have imposed on many people in the last five years, and they have given us considerably more help than we had any right to expect.

This book is in many ways the product of an important community to which we wish to draw attention—people in every sector of the resources field (state and federal government, industry, public interest groups, and academia) who believe that better understanding can lead to better policy. They are willing to invest time, effort, and money in that belief. We thank them heartily for their help, and we hope that this intensely controversial field recognizes their importance. In a brokered political process like public lands policy, there are many ways to serve the public interest. Public servants can be found everywhere.

We are reluctant to conclude these lines of gratitude with the standard admission that we alone are responsible for errors of fact. Although we readily admit to being fallible, we also want to point an accusing finger at a data-keeping system so complex that it took a five-year chase to capture fairly consistent figures. Appendix D describes some of the problems we encountered in gathering data for this book. Neither democracy nor wise resource management are served by the present situation.

Although small joys abound in a project like this, the only great one, other than finishing it and learning that it is helpful to readers, is dedicating the effort to someone who helped us:

For Jan Stevens
Deputy Attorney General
State of California

We did not have to work with Jan for five years to understand that he is an extraordinary public servant and human being. We are, however, in a unique position to appreciate the enormity of his contribution and the goodness of his spirit.

PART ONE

THE PATCHWORK QUILT
OF NATURAL RESOURCE
REVENUES

CHAPTER ONE

Introduction

IMPORTANCE OF RESOURCE REVENUES
FROM PUBLIC LANDS

Like many public issues, resource revenues became a high-priority issue as a result of a series of scandals. The first major controversies concerned the energy minerals--charges and countercharges about "fire sale" coal leasing, and stolen oil production. Even with today's declining oil prices, the revenues at stake are enormous, and interest in these revenues continues to be intense. Indeed, attention to revenues has become a major aspect of public lands management debate.

Because fiscal austerity has become a major theme of the 1980s, it is not surprising that resource revenues should be a management priority and a source of contention between different levels of government. In addition, environmental groups have become increasingly sophisticated in using economic analysis as a tool for framing their priorities for the public lands. [1]

State and local efforts to obtain revenues produced on nearby public lands has, in fact, been a part of public lands policy for most of the nation's history. Much of the discussion derives from recognition that federally owned land is immune from taxation by the state and local jurisdictions in which they are located. Both the tax exemptions and resource revenue sharing are part of the various bargains [2] that states have made with the federal government through congressional compromise and other means. [3] Recent declines in the prices of resources from the public lands, combined with federal budgetary policies, have squeezed the public land states with respect to these revenues. [4] The Administration is trying to reduce the payouts while the states are trying to protect and enhance their position.

This preoccupation with revenues is, historically speaking, unusual; it reflects the pressure at both state and federal levels to cut costs and gain the most mileage out of every available revenue source. However, for most of our history, revenue production has not been a major concern in public resource management. This fact is amply illustrated with respect to the history of the current oil revenues scandal. [5]

After a decade of environmental reform, Congress and the nation are turning to public resource revenues as one way of meeting the budget crisis and of providing fiscal austerity. Extensive reform efforts have followed three principal paths—administrative reorganization [6], legislation [7], and litigation. [8] None of these avenues has proved entirely satisfactory.

RESOURCE REVENUES AS A MANIFESTATION OF CHANGING CONCEPTS OF FEDERALISM

Current preoccupation with revenues should not deflect attention away from equally significant developments in the area of management authority. Beginning in the 1970s with the Sagebrush Rebellion [9] and continuing to the present day, the states have taken an increasingly aggressive stance. Western state and local governments' capabilities to participate in land management decisions—and to challenge federal priorities—have grown dramatically in the last two decades. Congress, the courts, and the public have increasingly turned to state and local governments to play a major role in federal land management. State and local officials and their constituents are exploiting opportunities defined by Congress for participation in federal planning efforts, and through litigation and permitting processes, they are creating others. For example, states have challenged federal agency decisions not to classify oil leasing areas as "known geologic structures" (KGSs), in which oil and gas values are recognized. Leasing known areas follows procedures that produce significantly more revenues for states than leasing in unknown geologic structures. The states contend that the federal decisions cost them tens of millions of dollars in lost revenue sharing. In another case, California argued that the Department of the Interior had breached a fiduciary obligation to the states for an accounting of royalty payments. Both of these disputes show that the states are no longer bystanders who accept a share of federal revenues as a matter of federal largess, but rather are participants who have interests to protect and who have a right to be involved in the decision making.

The states' assertion of their right to involvement reflects a significant challenge to basic ideas about federal authority that have prevailed since the depression. In public lands management, as in most other fields of government, the widely held notion that the federal government is the primary, preferable, or only source of action and insight is crumbling. The brief discussion of public domain history in Chapter 2 indicates that public lands policy has always reflected major questions of federalism. The current era is no exception.

Growing state and local participation does not, however, simplify future decision making. The western states are virtually unanimous in their fight to protect and enhance resource revenue-sharing. That may, however, bring them into conflict with other groups of increasingly assertive eastern state governments. Further, western state and local positions regarding the public lands are defined by increasingly diverse and urbane constituencies that do not push consistently in a single or simple direction. Indeed, although preoccupation with revenues may be transient, choices concerning resource pricing, allocation of revenues, and foregone income in favor of other benefits do dramatize the complex and intimate relationship between the West and public resources. The western states depend upon public resources for many different, sometimes incompatible, needs and wants. We may expect that western states will frequently disagree among themselves regarding public lands issues, even compete with each other over policy priorities or for markets.

Nevertheless, the growing role for state and local involvement is appropriate. This evolving federal-state partnership is new and important and ought to overshadow the frequently hostile relationships associated with almost any family squabble over money. Finally, state and local participation in federal land management develops in a policy arena that is rich in history and complex legal and technical issues. Partnership will not be achieved automatically or without political risk. Therefore, those who would guide federal land programs should understand the basic contours of those programs and the context in which the enhanced state and local role is evolving.

CHANGING HISTORICAL CONTEXT FOR
SEVEN DURABLE QUESTIONS

Two hundred years of evolution in public domain policy have not displaced congressional reliance on private rather than government investment to develop public resources. Its effect, however, has been altered by increasing regulation of the free market and by a gradual shift toward bureaucratic planning that encourages federal land managers to negotiate conflicts in allocating resources.

Reliance on negotiation arises from congressional reluctance to set clear priorities in U.S. Forest Service (USFS) and Bureau of Land Management (BLM) mandates written during the "environmental decade" of the 1970s. This same uncertainty is reflected in congressional deference, in the same statutes, to state and local concerns.

This new role for the states in public domain policy is just the latest turn in 200 years of continual change. The initial expectation that the federal government would grant or sell all of its lands to states, corporations, and individuals [10] shifted gradually toward support for federal retention and management of one-third of the nation's land. [11]   A long period followed in which growing support for federal land retention led to erosion of state authority over those lands. [12]

This growing federal role in the West was part of a general centralization in American government in the nineteenth century. Grants of lands to the states to encourage western development have been replaced in the twentieth century by increasing federal direction of state and local economies and government expenditures. [13]   This "fiscal federalism" expanded rapidly during the New Deal and was accompanied, beginning in the late 1960s, by rapid growth in "regulatory federalism" [14], under which federal direction of state and local programs came from congressional mandate as well as from financial incentives.   Frequently associated with the federal definition of state air, water, and other environmental programs [15], regulatory federalism has also contributed to a transformation of states' management capabilities. [16]   Compliance with federal environmental mandates has given states enormous capabilities in resource management.   Western states' current efforts to align federal resource management with state programs and goals rely on these enhanced capacities and are part of nationwide redefinition of federal and state roles.

Different federal resources are managed under programs designed at different stages in this complex process; present practice, therefore, combines the concerns and strategies that were dominant when a particular resource became the focus of discussion.   The basic premise of this analysis, however, is that all public resource development decisions — from a grazing permit to an oil lease — must confront a common set of seven questions:

1. Should we charge for access to the resource, and if so, how will we determine the price?

2. Who will have access to the resource? How will we identify the players and encourage and protect their investments?

3. Which resources should be developed? Which will be reserved from development and use?

4. How can we control intensity and limit the adverse impacts of the development?   What conditions or restrictions on access are needed? What constitutes appropriate mitigation of impacts?

5. When and how rapidly should the resource be extracted? How can we assure that commodities are available in a timely fashion while protecting environmental and amenity resources?

6. Who will have a right to participate in the decision making about those key issues, and how and when will they be heard?

7. How will the proceeds from development be allocated?

Congress has tried to answer all of these questions with such devices as timber sale contracts, coal leases, and land management and planning. The states' share of receipts under these programs is shown in Table 1.

TABLE 1. State Shares of Resource Revenues (1984)

	Oil & Gas	Coal	Geothermal	Nonfuel Minerals	National Forest Revenues(a)	Public Land Revenues(b)	Payments in Lieu of Taxes	Land & Water Conservation Fund	Total
Alaska	20,424,148	0	0	483,747	1,052,096	6,837	3,197,406	633,453	25,797,687
Arizona	1,942,661	0	7,369	5,687	5,153,109	279,749	8,707,631	1,090,888	17,187,094
California	39,657,621	40	7,502,710	2,147,195	44,113,496	230,319	11,720,090	5,643,205	111,014,676
Colorado	36,257,590	10,747,134	0	47,688	2,277,289	140,413	7,643,480	1,143,260	58,256,854
Idaho	2,315,954	0	31,807	1,485,626	8,847,389	238,642	7,596,307	689,464	21,205,189
Montana	17,151,832	4,618,662	0	524,149	7,844,447	257,181	8,504,502	675,096	39,575,869
Nevada	8,013,590	0	431,615	39,536	296,103	1,318,138	5,528,402	731,052	16,358,436
New Mexico	126,160,058	3,348,523	122,839	2,313,497	1,828,665	389,576	10,071,235	770,410	145,004,803
North Dakota	9,718,962	744,124	0	1,446	96	7,069	553,728	666,629	11,722,054
Oregon	1,624,451	258	357,210	555	86,543,842	67,197,424	2,728,294	1,043,247	159,495,281
Utah	28,120,914(c)	3,788,156	99,060	75,827	767,407	190,068	8,750,225	857,704	42,649,361
Washington	510,897	69,974	16,085	99,014	25,442,985	35,333	3,001,321	1,386,574	30,562,183
Wyoming	185,838,533	16,582,930	0	2,201,651	851,466	559,978	7,706,042	628,852	214,369,452
Region Total	477,737,211	39,899,721	8,558,695	9,425,618	184,818,390	70,850,727	85,708,663	15,959,834	893,198,939
Nation Total	n.a.	n.a.	n.a.	n.a.	225,652,655	70,914,803	104,598,448	72,919,000	n.a.

(a) Includes timber, grazing, minerals leased on acquired lands, recreation, and other minor sources.
(b) Includes grazing, land and materials sales, and timber sales on BLM-administered lands.
(c) Includes $2,560 rents on oil shale leases.

7

The answers to the seven basic questions have become more complex and generally more restrictive during the transition away from grants of resources to private interests to federal retention and management of them. During the days of homesteading, any person could take title to 160 acres simply by entering a piece of land and meeting certain criteria of occupancy. Homesteading is now virtually eliminated, and the procedures for choosing among rival developers of public resources are diverse and controversial. Gone also are the days when land was sold for $1.25 per acre or given away absolutely free. Although Congress continues to avoid direct federal participation in resource extraction, early in the twentieth century it changed the emphasis in resource development: The newer programs typically do not convey full title to an entrepreneur; instead Congress uses leases or permits to grant resource development rights while retaining title and regulatory control over the resource. Assessment of public resources is usually tied to procedures for achieving "fair market value." Environmental impact statement (EIS) procedures, the National Forest Management Act (NFMA), and the Federal Land Policy and Management Act (FLPMA) all provide opportunities for identifying adverse impacts and mitigation strategies. They have also created planning processes open to participation, appeal, and litigation from all sides of the management debate.

This growing national involvement in public lands management has increased federal influence over social and economic decision making in the western states. Since the early 1900s, Congress has tried to make these changes palatable to the western states by sharing increasingly generous portions of the development proceeds. Most of the states' share in these revenues, currently almost $.9 billion annually for the thirteen western states (see Table 2, page 60), comes from minerals development. As Figure 1 shows, the revenues have increased sharply over the last decade. This same decade has also been characterized by growing pressure, at the state and national level, to reduce deficits and expenditures and achieve greater efficiency in government operations. When the popular television program "Sixty Minutes" broadcast an expose of continuing losses and mismanagement of federal oil and gas royalties, public resource revenues became a national issue.

The money involved may justify some concentration on the major energy minerals, but revenues are not the only, or necessarily even the primary, reason for state officials and citizens to become more familiar with federal resource development programs. First, although the western states' interest in the revenues is significant and must be viewed with special respect during a period of budgetary stress, it must also be kept in perspective. On the average, resource revenues contribute less than 1 percent of most western states' annual revenues (see Appendix Table 1). The total figure for western resource revenue-sharing programs, $764 million in 1980, is

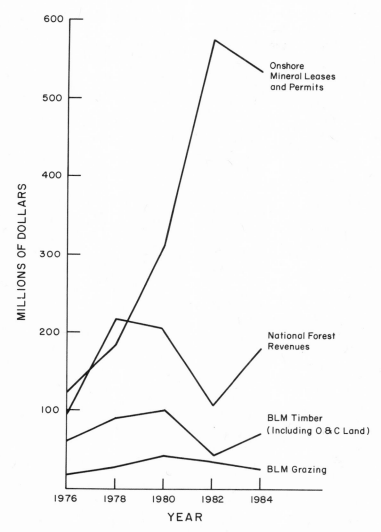

FIGURE 1. Revenue Shares to Western States of Onshore Mineral Leases and Permits, National Forest Revenues, BLM Timber, and BLM Grazing (1976-1984).

small compared to the total fiscal federalism picture: In 1980, federal aid to state and local governments constituted 20.9 percent of federal domestic outlays, $82.9 billion overall. Second, the federal government retains and manages between 29 and 89 percent of the land in western states, as can be seen in Figure 2. With or without revenues, those lands must be managed to meet the needs and goals of the citizens. In some areas, the environmental values

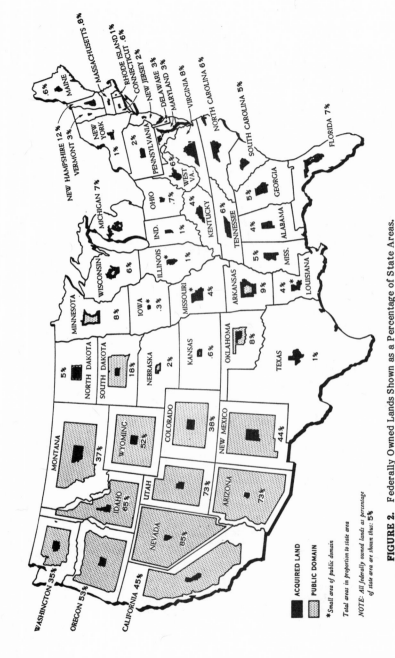

FIGURE 2. Federally Owned Lands Shown as a Percentage of State Areas.

Source: U.S. General Accounting Office, Alternatives for Achieving Greater Equities in Federal Land Payment Programs, PAD79-64. Washington, D.C., September 25, 1979.

ACQUIRED LAND

PUBLIC DOMAIN

* *Small area of public domain*

Total areas in proportion to state area

NOTE: All federally owned lands as percentage of state area are shown thus: **5%**

of the public lands may outweigh potential revenues from commodity development of some or all of the public's resources.

OVERVIEW OF FEDERAL LANDS ISSUES

Part One contains a brief overview of resource revenue issues designed to highlight: (1) the historical patterns and trends which structure our approach to resource revenues; (2) the evolving relationship between federal and state governments of which resource revenues are only a small part; and (3) the seven basic issues listed above. The general contours of environmental planning requirements, federal/state relations, public participation, and competitive sales common to most resource revenue programs are also discussed in Part One.

Part Two explores the management programs for individual resources, using the seven questions to structure each chapter. This section concentrates on the unique features of each individual program rather than repeating general discussion. Therefore, a reader primarily interested in oil and gas leasing, for example, might want to read Chapter 5 in Part Two <u>after</u> perusing the general material in Part One, but would not miss critical material by skipping the other chapters in Part Two.

Part Two begins with a brief description of the "location" system defined by the 1872 General Mining Act. The locatables or hard rock minerals produce no revenues, but the 1872 Act is a critical reminder of the evolution from land disposition to federal management and the roles that nineteenth century policies continue to play in resource programs.

The template for modern minerals management is the 1920 Mineral Leasing Act (MLA). Oil and gas and coal are the major MLA "leasables," but tar sands, oil shale, and nonfuel (sometimes called "fertilizer") minerals are also covered under MLA provisions. Outer Continental Shelf (OCS) oil and gas and geothermal resources are leased under statutes similar to but separate from the MLA. States generally receive 50 percent of the revenues gained from minerals leasing. Another 40 percent goes into a "Reclamation Fund" intended to support western water projects. Outer Continental Shelf (OCS) leasing is an exception; the states do not receive a percentage of the revenues, although a small portion of OCS receipts are earmarked for funds that are granted to all states, such as the Land and Water Conservation Fund. The final piece in public minerals management's basic trio was added in 1955 when the Surface Resources Act rendered common or construction grade minerals, such as sand, gravel, scoria, and pumice, "salable." This was done to curtail bogus location of sand and gravel "mines," which permitted the "discoverer" to take title to valuable scenic or recreation resources under the guise of a mining claim. Revenues from sales of common-grade minerals typically are distributed under the standard Forest Service (25 percent of gross to the states) or BLM (5 percent of gross to the states) formulas.

The emergent pattern in current minerals leasing policy is a shift away from industry-initiated leasing toward "programs" that rely on government estimates of future resource needs and lease sales that are timed to meet those needs while directing extraction toward the environmentally least vulnerable sites. The coal program moves in that direction and current debate suggests that an oil and gas leasing program may soon follow.

Surface resource management programs for grazing, O & C timber, National Forest timber, land sales, and special use permits are discussed separately according to which of the two major federal land managing agencies — the Bureau of Land Management or the U.S. Forest Service — is involved. National Forest programs generally return 25 percent of gross revenues to the county of origin. This varies slightly, especially regarding mineral revenues on eastern and other acquired National Forest lands. BLM revenue-sharing programs vary tremendously, from a 5 percent return to states from public land sales (a figure that originated in the 1803 statute by which Ohio joined the Union) to the 75 percent share paid from timber receipts on Oregon's O & C Lands.

Currently, 40 percent of onshore mineral revenues and lesser funding from other sources are deposited into the Reclamation Fund (see Chapter 8). This "fund" does not, however, exist as a discrete account. Instead, the money goes into the General Fund of the U.S. Treasury; it is not held in a special pool and it is not managed like a trust fund, nor does it earn interest. Accordingly, Chapter 8 merely reports the "deposits" into this fictitious account and observes that annual reclamation expenditures have vastly exceeded the amount that would have been available if the Reclamation Fund were the sole source of support for Bureau of Reclamation projects.

Finally, the Land and Water Conservation Fund (LWCF) and the Payments in Lieu of Taxes Act (PILTs), enacted in 1965 and 1976, respectively, may suggest future trends in evolving resource revenues programs. Although both provide resource-related funds to states, both are also national in scope and subject to annual congressional appropriations. The LWCF program is, moreover, specifically tied to state performance in achieving federally mandated management programs. Not coincidentally, all three of these features appear in most of the current proposals for OCS revenue-sharing programs.

Although brevity and simplicity were two major goals of this book, the revenues picture is inevitably complex in one critical regard. Revenues are only one aspect and one outcome of resource management decisions. Maximizing revenues in the short run is never the only goal of resource development, and it may not even be the optimal way to obtain economic returns from a resource. Moreover, different levels of government benefit from different aspects of resource development.   For example, under the present tax system, a major federal "share" comes from corporate income taxes rather than from rents, royalties, and bonuses associated with mineral leasing.   Similarly, localities may be interested in early returns to support local infrastructure investments required by development while the state may gain most from long-term royalty income.

One other source of complexity must be mentioned. Given the enormous importance of resource management and revenues in defining the lifestyle and environmental quality for a community, a region, and the nation, the difficulties involved in obtaining timely, accurate, and comparable data amount to a national scandal. Appendix D discusses in detail the data collection problems encountered in this project.

Except for pointing with alarm to problems in accessibility, accuracy, and uniformity of the data, this volume makes no recommendations regarding resource revenues. It is intended to provide basic introductory material that will aid and encourage concerned officials and individuals in their effort to understand the issues and to participate effectively in their resolution.

CHAPTER TWO

Historic Context of Current Issues

Current controversy over the fair market value of public resources and over the revenues that these resources generate is just one phase of a long, continuing debate over public resources. Resource development policies have been complex, and programs have been difficult to redirect: there has been no single, coherent set of strategies designed to balance conflicting priorities or to integrate opposing political and economic forces. Instead, we have negotiated a series of settlements over more than 200 years. [17] These bargains have been reinterpreted, and occasionally renegotiated, as settlers moved west, tamed the wilderness, and built cities, transportation networks, and suburbs.

The detail and vocabulary of each program is distinctive enough to justify the separate study of coal, oil and gas, timber, oil shale, and other resources. Part Two of this volume adopts that approach. Yet, it is also helpful to view the programs together, as they have evolved over time, and it is interesting to study the origins of some of the more bizarre provisions, such as severed mineral title, checkerboard lands, and the oil and gas lottery.

The literature on resource revenues often asserts tnat the entire area is without rhyme or reason. [18] Fortunately that depressing notion is quite wrong. Common patterns and questions emerge in all resource revenue issues. The general picture makes it possible to see these recurring themes in the long debate over resource revenues and their relationship to the diverse management decisions in which the states must play an increasing role. Therefore, Part One of this volume explores the common issues that underlie all federal resource development programs.

PATTERNS AND TRENDS

Two basic themes underlie all of what follows. The first is a trend toward increasing reliance on government planning and regulation. The federal land management agencies still do not produce and sell coal, timber, or forage directly. But the private entrepreneurs seeking to develop public resources have had less and less control over their investments and activities and have become increasingly subject to planning, permit, and mitigation requirements. There are some indications that this reliance on government planning in preference to market decisions has peaked. Numerous policy makers in the Reagan administration and elsewhere argue that private industry must be given a greater role in decision making about developing our federal resources. This effort may be offset by moves in Congress to bring all leasing activities into a "program" format with government targets, schedules, and plans. Nevertheless, the balance between government and market decision making is a dominant thread in public resource policy.

The second major theme is the federal government's increasing generosity in regard to revenue sharing. Federal aid to the territories started out small, but as the government and the economy stabilized, and as more and more representatives from western states were seated in Congress, the government became increasingly magnanimous. This trend may have peaked in 1976 and may be receding under pressure from budget-cutters and northeastern states. The case appears stronger for the second hypothesis, that is, that government generosity is declining, but only over time will we be able to evaluate current events.

PREVIOUS APPROACHES

Disposition to States and Private Interests

The national commitment to disposing the public domain emerged before the government did. During the American Revolution, soldiers were paid with scrip that would be redeemable for lands west of the thirteen colonies. For more than 125 years, land disposition continued, as the country continued to be short on cash but rich in land acquired from state cessions, treaty, purchase, and conquest. [19] Therefore, the federal government first sold land, and later granted it to states, corporations, and individuals to achieve national goals, primarily to encourage orderly development of the western territories. When states were admitted to the Union, they bargained in Congress for advantageous packages of land and cash grants.

The importance of revenue sharing in these early bargains between nation and state has been obscured by twentieth century debates. Current analysts often claim that resource revenue programs evolved because federal lands are immune from state taxation because of "intergovernmental immunities." It has been stated that Congress has a responsibility to compensate localities for the burdens imposed by the federal presence. This argument has an element of truth—federal lands are exempt from state and local taxation. However, those exemptions were written into state constitutions as part of the statehood bargains long before the Supreme Court discovered the intergovernmental immunities doctrine. [20] Resources revenue sharing was not part of an early recognition of burdens or tax losses imposed by federal lands because federal ownership of these lands was to be temporary. For most of the nineteenth century the federal government had no interest in holding land. During this time it was assumed that the public lands in the western states would pass almost entirely into private hands, as they did in the case of earlier public domain states (those between the Appalachian Mountains and the Rockies).

Sharing of revenues became a part of land disposition policy when the first "public domain" state joined the Union. In 1803, Ohio was granted 5 percent of the proceeds of the public lands sales within its borders. The money was a quid pro quo, to replace temporary tax losses on newly patented land. [21] As part of the statehood bargain, Ohio agreed to forego taxing these lands for five years [22] and to spend the 5 percent grant on schools and transportation. This bargain became the standard.

Later, new states also agreed to waive all future interests in the federal lands, including the right to tax them, but in return gained expanded land concessions from the federal government. This grant of lands, indeed, rapidly overshadowed the cash grants, as the government still did not have sufficient funds. As more western representatives were seated, Congress became increasingly generous with grants of land to foster western development. First one and finally four sections per township were granted as "school land sites" to the states.

The Homestead Act, probably the most familiar disposition era statute, did not pass until 1862, long after the most desirable lands had been taken. [23] Almost every acre of land between the Appalachians and the 100th meridian was granted by the federal government to a state, corporation, or individual under scores of eighteenth and nineteenth century laws and programs.

Retention of Federal Lands: Changing Federal/State Relations

As the western territories were settled and the frontier "closed," the dominant theme of public domain policy slowly shifted away from land grants and disposition toward federal retention of the public domain. [24] The year 1872 provides an interesting illustration of the gradual transition. Congress withdrew the Yellowstone area from homestead and all other entry, and established it as a federal reserve, to be used as a "park or public pleasuring ground for the use and benefit of the people." Simultaneously, in the 1872 General Mining Act, Congress reiterated its commitment to the private development of federal resources. This act promises to a prospector locating a valuable mineral deposit both full access to his discovery and almost unfettered rights to extract the mineral for his own profit without rent or royalty to the government. (Hardrock minerals are frequently called "locatables" because they are covered by the location system defined in this act.) Although the act has basically remained unchanged since 1872, its implementation has been altered by recent legislation, litigation, and administrative decisions. [25]   Hardrock minerals produce no revenues for federal or state governments. [26]

Forest Reservations.   Although land disposition endures in an increasingly circumscribed way, the system of forest reserves created a major break from congressional disposition policies. A series of congressional enactments between 1891 and 1907 authorized the president to withdraw areas from homesteading to establish forest reservations (now called "National Forests").

The concept of revenue sharing made its modern debut in connection with these forest reservations. Congress provided first that 10 percent, and later 25 percent, of the net revenues produced by the sale of National Forest timber and other forest products would be returned to the states for expenditure on roads and schools in counties where the revenues were generated. These "returns to the counties" have become increasingly generous over time: another 10 percent was subsequently made available for federal expenditure on forest roads and trails in the state.   Finally, in 1976, the base of calculation was shifted from net to gross receipts.

The original intent of this program is difficult to discern. At the time, land reservations were an unfamiliar concept.   Neither Congress nor the public was clear about the purpose of the reserves.   Whether they were to preserve watersheds or be open to timber harvest was unresolved well into the twentieth century. The appropriateness of any use fee for water, grazing, or timber was also an open question.   Finally, Congress was undecided whether the reserves should pay their own way, make money for the Treasury, or be supported by the General Fund. [27]   The exact nature of the revenue share was also unclear. At different times, it was explained as "a gift" to the states, as a compensation for the 5 percent of the sale price that the states would not receive due to the reservation, and as a compensation for the states' and localities' inability to tax the increasing acreage of reserved federal land. [28]

Mineral Reservations—The 1920 Mineral Leasing Act.   Although the Mineral Leasing Act of 1920 (MLA) constituted a further break with the land disposition policies of the previous century, it continued traditional reliance on private investment to develop public resources.   Congress rejected numerous proposals for government minerals development before establishing a leasing system for energy and fertilizer minerals.   Under the Mineral Leasing Act, however, Congress retained federal title to the land, defined authority to control exploration and production, and collected royalties and rents from private developers. Congress granted to the Secretary of the Interior enormous discretion to define most of the details of the leasing system. Revenues generated under the MLA were allocated by a 50-40-10 formula: 50 percent to the state where the revenue was provided, 40 percent to a "Reclamation Fund" to support water projects in the western states, and 10 percent to the General Fund of the U.S. Treasury. Congress was quite clear in 1920, as it had not been in connection with the earlier forest reservation revenue sharing, that the 50 percent share was to compensate for the states' inability to tax the lands.

The MLA continues to be the foundation of government mineral leasing policy.   However, secretarial discretion and occasional congressional action have introduced considerable diversity into the management of the different minerals covered, as will be discussed in Part Two.

Payments in Lieu of Taxes—New Federalism and Acquired Public Lands.   Although revenue sharing may appear to be similar to "Payments in Lieu of Taxes" (PILTs), which are received by counties in which specified federal lands are located, PILTs are quite different in origin and rationale.   These payments began in connection with acquired federal lands that were quite different from the "original" public domain. Until World War I, federal land acquisitions were neither extensive nor particularly significant. During the two world wars and the depression, however, the federal government purchased extensive land holdings for economic recovery programs and military purposes. These acquisitions removed from the local tax base lands that had previously been taxed. Many were in urban areas, and federal use of these lands frequently created extraordinary demands for local services. Others were acquired to supplement public domain programs, although they are frequently treated differently from the original public domain in regard to commodity management and revenue distribution. State and local government advocates gradually expanded public discussion of these "acquired lands" problems, such as service burdens and erosion of the local tax base, to include public domain lands. Their effort to justify federal PILTs to localities containing public domain as well as acquired lands was successful in 1976. [29]

The world wars and the depression, the same traumatic events that intensified federal land acquisitions, also altered the basic fabric of federal-state relations.   The Advisory Commission on Intergovernmental Relations (ACIR) found in 1980 that although federal regulation did not "expand greatly until fairly recently," the growth in federal aid to states has a much longer history. [30] Beginning in the 1920s and escalating during the depression, federal aid to the states expanded into a "large scale activity" during the 1960s. By 1972, with the passage of the Federal Revenue Sharing Act, virtually every state, county, and municipality in the nation was receiving federal aid. [31]   In 1978, 74 percent of state government agencies were receiving federal aid, and 26 percent were receiving half or more of their budgets from that source. [32] In 1980, federal aid to states constituted 20.9 percent of federal domestic outlays and 23.6 percent of state and local expenditures-- $82.9 billion total. [33]

This type of revenue sharing was designed to facilitate state and local support of federally defined goals. A major purpose of these programs has been to offset differences in state capabilities to implement federal goals.   It can be distinguished from revenue sharing associated with the management of natural resources on federal lands; the latter payments were justified as an effort to compensate (or "make whole") the states for growing federal control of state economic, social, and political decision making. [34]

Though the federal grant programs have been vast, even they do not fully measure the federal government's fiscal involvement in state and local economies.   "The popular calculus" includes three other categories in the "redistributed pot": federal salaries, federal public works, and federal transfer payments to individuals. [35] This enormous federal role in state and local finances does not necessarily "steer states and localities toward federal objectives." As in the case of early resource revenue sharing, "a bargaining framework fits more accurately than a superior-subordinate view of the complex intergovernmental relations involving fiscal federalism," and fiscal federalism is viewed not as "a federal master dangling a carrot in front of a state donkey," but as "a rich merchant haggling on equal terms with a sly bargain-hunting consumer." [36]

The larger revenue sharing picture puts both resource revenues and western bargaining for them into a national perspective. However, the concentration of federal lands in the western states means that growing federal control over states and localities is likely to be particularly intense and also intensely debated in the West. [37]

Federal Management and Multiple Use Planning

Growing federal control over state and local finances was exemplified by the environmental and multiple use planning statutes of the 1970s, the most recent piece in the "puzzle" of public land policy. Numerous new and revised programs clarify congressional commitment to active government management of the public lands and expand reliance on extensive federal bureaucracies to negotiate allocations of resources among competing interest groups.   Three major statutes, the National Environmental Policy Act (NEPA), the National Forest Management Act (NFMA), and the Federal Land

Policy and Management Act (FLPMA), mandate that allocation decisions be made through a comprehensive planning process. The complex mixture of data collection and analysis of impacts, alternatives, and mitigation strategies includes extensive public review of government assumptions and decisions. Although such planning has nominally been part of federal land management at least since the mid-1960s, both the Forest Service and the BLM are presently attempting to comply with statutory mandates for comprehensive multiple use planning and to include the peculiar legal and technical requirements for mineral management in the process.

It is not coincidental that 1976, the year of NFMA, FLPMA, and the Federal Coal Leasing Amendments Act (FCLAA), was also the year of expanded revenue sharing programs. The expansion of federal control over federal lands management was accompanied by diverse legislation that greatly increased the states' share of revenues associated with those lands. Congress increased Forest Service revenue sharing from net to gross, mineral leasing revenues from 37.5 percent to 50 percent of gross, and instituted the PILTs program, paying between ten and seventy-five cents per acre to all counties containing federal lands.

This negotiated settlement does not solve all problems or satisfy all participants. However, it is part of a long, diversifying trend. Affected interests negotiate, plan, and litigate to answer the basic questions of resource development: which resources should be developed; who should develop them; how the resources should be valued; when, how fast, and how intensely should the development occur; what we should do with the proceeds of development; and how we should decide all these questions.

CHAPTER THREE

Issues Underlying Resource Development Decisions

Answers to the major policy questions common to all public resource development decisions have evolved over two hundred years. Viewing the questions in a specific context also demonstrates that they sometimes merge in practice. For example, if we answer the question "who should develop the resources" with the standard "the highest bidder," concerns about the methods used to choose the players and value the resources immediately run together. Nevertheless, it is useful to discuss the basic issues separately, so as to untangle as much as possible the web of complex issues and choices.

HOW SHOULD THE RESOURCES BE VALUED?

Today's focus on "fair market value" (FMV) is unusual and probably reflects state and federal budget problems and increased prices for energy minerals during the period 1975-1985. Although not all resources are offered at competitive auction, because so many of the complexities in our current programs arise from the sales, lease, and bidding systems, it is best to start with them. In this section, a brief introduction to the theory and practice of "fair market value" is followed by a discussion of the pros and cons of frequently used lease and bidding systems. Coal and oil and gas leasing are the major reference points, although much of what follows applies to timber sales as well.

Fair Market Value

The majority of leases and sales of public lands and resources must, by law, be conducted at "fair market value." There are exceptions to this rule, as the discussion of hardrock minerals "locatable" under the 1872 Act has indicated (see Chapter 2). Further, FMV is not the only applicable criterion. Resource conservation and environmental protection are two examples of other critical management goals.

The marketing of federal resources must, therefore, meet a mix of objectives, which confuses the "fair market value" standard.

Problems Inherent in Any "Fair Market Value" Definition. A typical definition of fair market value emphasizes the securing of maximum competitive value for the commodity sold: the highest price in terms of money that a property (or resource) would bring in a competitive and open market under all conditions requisite to a fair sale.   Those conditions usually include a buyer and seller who are knowledgeable but are not compelled to make a deal. [38]

Problems with "The Market." Although the above definition is fairly straightforward, measuring FMV is frequently problematical because it requires numerous conditions, some of which may not be present. For example, it requires an open competitive market that neither buyers nor sellers are able to influence. Because the federal government holds a large percentage of many of the resources at issue, and may therefore be able to influence the price, it is not a "model" seller. "Model" buyers are rare also: because of the location and accessibility of many federal resources, only a few firms, or even a single firm, may constitute the entire relevant market. Thus, competitive conditions for federal resources are not always present.

Problems with Defining "Fair Value." The competitiveness of the market is not the only problem. When value is determined in a market context, it essentially means value to individual firms; in calculating value, each firm estimates its future income from developing the resource and subtracts anticipated costs. Value is, therefore, colored by many factors peculiar to the firm that have little to do with the resource or government resource policy: Some of the factors that affect the value of the resource but are frequently beyond the lessor's control are: the current financial situation of the particular firm; its preference for future income as opposed to present money in the pocket (or the discount rate with which the company estimates the value of future income) [39]; the availability and cost of loans; the cost associated with production technologies; start-up problems; and the future market price of the product.   Finally, as recent instability in both the timber and the energy minerals markets suggest, a firm's calculations of the value of a resource must take into account the risks it incurs in developing it. The resulting problem with "fair value" is twofold: (1) different firms will value the same resource differently and (2) none of the value estimates necessarily reflects the value to society of other uses or nonuse of the resource.

To complicate "fair value" even further, agency decisions can also affect the value of a resource. The size of the sale affects the number of bidders who can afford to participate; both the scale of the development and the type of payment required influence the amount the successful bidder has to borrow.   Transaction costs imposed by government policies also affect the value. [40] Instability in government regulations, the length of time necessary to complete the permitting process and begin production, and the time allowed to develop the resource all affect the final price.   The timing of the sale is also critical, in terms of prevailing interest rates and competitive value of the commodity. Finally, the value of the resource is influenced by stipulations on which rights and resources are being reserved by the government, and by assignment of responsibility for the environmental impacts of extraction.   For example, if the successful bidder must allow backpackers access to the site or must revegetate the land when the lease expires, it will be reflected in the amount bid.   The value of the resource is also influenced by the method and conditions of the sale (see below).

Unfortunately, these same problems afflict the process of making appraisals upon which many resource programs rely for definition of fair market value.   An appraisal is basically an estimate of the fair market value made by an expert or a computer relying more or less on data from previous or comparable sales, projected returns, and similar factors.   None reflect the particular circumstances affecting particular bidders at the time of the specific sale. When actual bids do not conform to appraised value, it can lead to concern about overbidding or failure to achieve fair market value. Appraisal practices in coal and timber sales have been particularly controversial lately.

Fair Market Value Definition Problems in the Powder River Coal Sale.   Controversy surrounding coal leasing in the Powder River Basin of Wyoming illustrates some of the factors that complicate evaluation of fair market value. Although the complete story is long and complex [41], the controversy arose primarily from the fact that actual bids on coal leases offered were significantly lower than the appraised prices.   Critics charge that the government achieved less than "fair market value" because (1) it depressed coal prices by offering too much coal for sale at one time and (2) the leases were sold in a market that had been weakened by the falling price of oil. Former Interior Secretary James Watt countered that the price of federal coal leases had been artificially inflated by a ten-year moratorium on sales. He indicated that, whether or not the market for federal coal leases (as distinct from the market for private leases or for extracted coal) was soft, the price was still "fair." Even if the government made less than it might have before oil prices fell, the sale would assure that energy would be available at prices that consumers could afford. Watt also argued that certainty and regularity in lease sales are vital to national coal and energy policy; after four years of costly planning for the sale, he could not cancel it. The idea that fair market value is not a fixed or clear amount that is inherent in the resource to be captured by appropriate government action is amply demonstrated by this aspect of the Powder River controversy.

Forms of Sales and Payments

The form of sales and payments for federal resources is the most obvious factor subject to agency control that influences the value of the resource.

Forms of Bidding. Although they are frequently used together in actual sales, there are two basic formats for resource bidding: written and oral. Debate includes complex evaluation of the information available to bidders. Recently it has centered on which format, if either, is less likely to permit collusive bidding. Feeling runs high, particularly regarding timber sales, that sealed (written) bidding—the single shot format—hurts small operators. Because small operators have limited options, it is argued, they need the opportunity to rebid inherent in an oral auction in order to compete for sales that are vital to their operations. Similarly, it is argued that when more than one parcel is being offered for sale at the same time, sequential rather than simultaneous bidding (that is, selling the parcels one at a time rather than accepting bids simultaneously on all of them) protects small businesses. Data to resolve these issues are not available.

Rentals. A rental is the fee set in the lease to charge for use of the land needed to develop the resource. This occurs primarily in connection with minerals leasing. Typically, rents have been set very low, by statute or otherwise, usually at a token sum of 50 cents to $3 an acre per year to be paid in advance of production. Rent payments may cease when production begins or they may be accepted as a credit against royalty payments. An alternate approach views rents as a burden that encourages the developer to be diligent in extracting the resource. Recent discussions have also explored using escalating rents to penalize nonproduction. Advocates of noncommodity values of the public lands have proposed a third approach that would set rent payments to reflect uses that are foregone when the area is leased. The rent would compensate the public for alternative uses of the land that are lost during the time the area is committed to private mineral development.

Bonus Bids. In addition to paying rent on the land occupied during development, the lessee must pay for the mineral extracted. Bonus payments and royalty payments are the two basic formats used in lease auctions. The system most commonly used is a combination of the two. In bonus bidding for a lease, contending firms offer to make a specified front-end, lump-sum payment. This is a familiar form of purchase. For example, lump-sum payments at the time of sale are used on most consumer transactions. It is also, in theory, the ideal way of selling a commodity. The advantage of bonus bidding is economic efficiency: bidders will be inclined to offer an amount approaching the full value of the resource. Then, once the bonus is paid, the producer will treat the expense as a "sunk cost" rather than a continuing cost that affects development and production decisions. Under ideal conditions, a bonus system does not distort the degree and timing of resource production.

In the real world, of course, the bonus bid system may seem less ideal, particularly where the sale is large, exploration and development costs are high, the time to establish production is long, or successful development is uncertain. First, high initial costs may cut out small firms. Coming up with one large lump of money is not their only problem. Useful information about the potential of mineral deposits is extremely costly to obtain; a small firm may not be able to gather enough data to justify investing in a lease that must be paid for in one swoop. Second, where uncertainty and risk are substantial, bonus bid sales may actually reduce the bid price. In this case, firms will be inclined to bid low. If the leased tract is highly productive, the government will be shorted revenues. On the other hand, if the tract proves unproductive, the lessee bears all the loss. Finally, some economists argue that bonus bidding delays production; after making the large initial payment, the lessee may be hampered by lack of production funds. Other economists claim just the opposite, however: the huge initial investment inspires prompt activity to generate returns.

Various modifications of the bonus bidding system can offset some of its shortcomings. Joint or cooperative bidding encourages participation by smaller companies. Staggered bonus payments allow the lessee to spread costs over time. "Walk-away" staggered payments permit a firm to make incremental decisions about continued development; under this system, if the tract does not prove promising, the buyer may stop additional activities and bonus payments.

Royalties. Royalties are payments based on the income received from sale of the developed commodities. There are many kinds of royalties—all of which have different advantages and disadvantages to bidders and sellers. Although they may be paid "in kind," that is, with barrels of oil or tons of coal, royalties are most frequently a fixed percentage of the market value of the commodity produced. Royalties based on net value are sometimes called "profit-sharing." Usually, however, the percentage is calculated on gross value. However, value, as we have seen, is not always easily identified. Methods for "valuation of production" for the purpose of calculating royalties are intensely controversial.

Royalties share the risk of development between seller and buyer. If the development is unproductive, the buyer owes much less to the government. Net profit royalties are particularly effective in sharing the risk of development and so may increase the selling price of the lease.

Any royalty-based program, particularly a net royalty one, is difficult and costly to administer. Record keeping and calculation of the royalties are complex procedures. Complicating the matter even further, states, localities, and Indian tribes cannot assume that private industry will deal forthrightly or that the federal administration will be effective, as difficulties surrounding the passage of the Federal Oil and Gas Royalty Management Act of 1982 (FOGRMA) demonstrated.

Finally, royalty payments may distort production decisions. The royalty is calculated as a cost on the production of each unit of output. Therefore, the point at which the cost of producing another (say) barrel of oil exceeds the selling price of that barrel will come sooner with the royalty payment than it would without the royalty. "Highgrading," that is, taking the readily accessible resource and leaving the rest, may result if the royalty makes it unprofitable for a firm to develop lower grade resources or induces it to halt production sooner than it might otherwise.

In theory, royalty payments can be modified to prevent the "choking off" of production. For example, sliding scale royalties geared to rates of extraction allow some adjustment for differences in marginal costs of production. Competitive oil and gas leases and prototype oil shale leases provide for such adjustments. More generally, the Secretary of the Interior has discretion to renegotiate royalties if they threaten the conservation goals of mineral leasing, though these modifications may not be practical because of the amount and type of data that is needed to justify them. Moreover, these accommodations are controversial: They may increase recovery of the mineral, perhaps increasing the value of the lease to the bidder as well. In addition, renegotiation of royalty rates may cause unanticipated disruptions in revenues, which in turn may place the states and localities in a vulnerable financial position. This debate is further confused by arguments that royalties are only one small cause of production cutoffs.

Bid Systems, Other Revenue Sources, and Federal-State-Local Relations. Although bonuses and royalties are the major sources of government revenue analyzed in this volume, they are not the only income items to be weighed in resource development decisions. Taxes (state, local, and federal) and "exactions" are also important considerations. Not all income sources are equally valuable to all governments. A policy at one level of government to maximize its income from development is not necessarily best served by a high bonus or a high royalty or both. Because different levels of government benefit from different revenue sources, lease sale figures may have little or no bearing on benefits to specific jurisdictions.

Taxes and exactions constitute claims on a producer's income and so influence their bid for a lease. These claims may have different impacts on production. An ad valorem tax is generally believed to accelerate development. [42] Severance taxes [43] act like royalties, adding to the marginal cost of production. Exactions [44], on the other hand, generally operate more like lump-sum, up-front bonus payments. Although it is frequently asserted that state and local taxes have a major impact on a firm's resource development decisions, resulting in highgraded development and dampening long-term production, data to prove these points are not available. Moreover, impacts on production are significant primarily to royalty recipients. A local government that shares indirectly, if at all, in royalty payments may find greatest advantage in exactions and local taxes.

Tradeoffs between bonuses and royalties highlight similar conflicts between levels of government. Particularly where major localized impacts from development are anticipated, localities may prefer early revenues (through bonuses) over deferred royalty payments, which may not show up for a decade or more. Conversely, states may have greater fiscal flexibility and, therefore, prefer the long-term royalties and the possibility of sharing in rising energy prices and future income. Where long-term income stability is important, states might go further and favor an arrangement that averages shared revenues over a period of years to avoid severe income fluctuations due to market shifts. Finally, because the federal government has less interest in the lease sale revenues, it will have a different perspective than states or localities. It will probably place more emphasis on energy production goals and environmental impacts than on returns to the Treasury from the sale. Indeed, federal interests may lie counter to state and local priorities. The federal treasury gets its major "share" not from the sale but from taxing the company's profits; thus, the federal government may oppose high lease sale prices that benefit states and perhaps localities but reduce taxable income.

WHO SHOULD DEVELOP THE RESOURCES?

The second major question, who should have access to develop the resource, is usually resolved by answering "the highest bidder," but three general considerations limit the practicality of this philosophy. First, important limits on access to federal resources are defined by the stakes and the ante: most individuals and firms do not have the legal, technical, and financial resources to enter the game. Second, because not all resources are auctioned, bidders are not always involved. Grazing permits, for example, are generally treated as integral parts of privately owned ranch operations and change hands when the private property is sold. Third, the federal government frequently defines the sale process in order to achieve social goals that conflict with maximizing economic returns from the highest bidder.

The most frequent goals defining resource sales have been to stabilize industries, to protect small businesses, and to encourage competition in resource-based industries. Large cattle operations are the principal beneficiaries of the stabilization efforts: in the original allocation of public domain grazing permits, established public range users owning nearby land (base property) were given absolute preference over all others. This ostensibly accomplished the statutory purpose of stabilizing the range livestock industry. Programs to encourage small businesses are common in the resource field, but they have not always been effective in fostering competition or protecting small businesses. For example, the purpose of the Small Business Set Aside Act, as the name suggests, is to assure that some federal timber sales are accessible to small business. The definition of "small" used in the act, however, is so large (500 or fewer employees), that all but a handful of companies qualify and the provisions have little effect. Similarly, in order to promote competition in minerals industries, Congress has developed various limits on the amount of leased acreage any individual or firm can acquire. In some cases this has been done with little regard for the technical requirements of production. (See Appendix Table 6 for a summary of acreage limitations applicable to different leasable minerals.)

These efforts are complicated by the fact that, due to the location of many federal resources and the scale of the development enterprise, the number and type of firms able to participate are frequently limited. For example, if a firm has developed an area, has installed necessary transportation facilities, and has acquired state and private rights to nearby areas, it may be the only bidder on an adjacent federal tract. Moreover, the government sometimes finds itself caught in the contradictory position of encouraging competition and access for small firms yet desiring to limit the auction to bidders with a bona fide interest in developing the resource. Efforts to modify oil and gas "lotteries" in an effort to prevent fraudulent and merely speculative participants from distorting the system are criticized by some because they exclude "the little guy."

In short, the market for federal resources is not always "open" and it is not always intended to be. At some point, the highest bidder may, in fact, win, but that result is not achieved until a variety of conditions—imposed by government policy, the location of the resource, and a host of other factors—are met.

WHICH RESOURCES SHOULD BE DEVELOPED?

As with previous questions, the routine answer to this question—"high-quality resources"—is not always useful. Discussions of "dominant use" suggest that we can develop the "high quality" sites and leave the "marginal lands" alone.

Concentration on high quality resources may make sense when efforts to recover low-grade ores or to harvest nonregenerable sites impose unacceptable environmental damage. However, many local and regional economies are dependent on management of suboptimal resources. The Forest Service is, for example, encountering increasing criticism for "below-cost" timber sales, which ostensibly lose money for the government. These sales occur primarily in the Intermountain West and are defended, in part, by their contributions to multiple use objectives and to the economies of timber-dependent communities. This dispute suggests a more general rule: different bidders will consider sites high quality for different reasons. Site quality, like resource value, is not only an attribute of the resource but also depends on other factors—distance to markets, use requirements, the availability of an appropriate labor pool, and government policies and regulations.

Land Availability

Discussions of site quality may mask what is probably the most pressing issue in public land management from industry's point of view: land availability. This issue has a number of components: the role of industry in selecting sites for development, the availability of land in which exploration and development are permitted, and the ambiguities that continue to surround development after a "decision" has been made. From the investor's perspective, the government depends on private industry but has created uncertainty and disincentives in the process of trying to achieve environmental protection and other national goals. The degree to which specific industries or firms are dependent upon access to federal lands varies considerably from resource to resource and in various regions. Nevertheless, reductions in the available land base are generally seen by resource developers as a serious problem.

One aspect of this issue is the trend toward increased government control in deciding which resources are developed. The forest products industry is accustomed to operating on sites designated by government agencies; the minerals industry is not. Whether it is more efficient and reasonable for industry or the government to select deposits for development is a matter of intense and continuing debate. Nevertheless, industry discretion in identifying areas appropriate for investment is diminishing. For example, 1976 amendments to the Mineral Leasing Act (Federal Coal Leasing Amendments Act or FCLAA) eliminated explorer-initiated "prospecting permits" [45] from the coal program. Other minerals management formats are also moving toward "all competitive" leasing on tracts identified and offered by the government. Thus far, government exploration programs mandated by the Federal Land Policy Management Act (FLPMA) have been inadequately funded due to the growing crisis in the federal budget.

The amount of land that is to be considered inaccessible to timber harvest, minerals exploration, and development is in itself a major controversy. As usual, manipulating statistics makes it possible to prove almost anything. For example, arguing that only 1.5 percent of our nation is presently wilderness ignores nonwilderness-use restrictions on federal, state, and private lands. It also conceals the fact that the proportion of wilderness designations are rapidly approaching 20 percent of the National Forests. Similarly, when the minerals industry states that only 0.5 percent of the nation has ever been mined, it understates the visual and environmental impacts of those disruptions.

The wilderness designation is the most familiar use restriction: areas identified as such by Congress on Forest Service and BLM lands are available, if at all, primarily for continued grazing of livestock. Other categories of land—areas of critical environmental concern (ACECs), endangered species habitat, travel and water influence zones, historic sites, natural research areas, dispersed recreation areas—are more or less restricted depending on the development involved.

This variability complicates the calculation of "available" areas and acres. Almost every interest group has its own set of statistics and they are different for different resources. However, the trend is clearly toward more government control and less land available for commodity development. [46]

Land-Use Planning

The trend toward bureaucratic decisions is illustrated in the growing reliance on comprehensive land use planning to allocate specific areas to particular uses. Ambiguity arises from the fact that the process for identifying land that will be available for mining or timber harvest is in continuing flux. Industry is frequently frustrated because decisions to preserve resources appear irrevocable, but decisions to develop are qualified and subject to delays and the likely imposition of future constraints. On the other hand, when consequences of development are irreversible or unknown, caution seems an appropriate priority.

Some problems have arisen because agency personnel and procedures have not been prepared to include minerals considerations in the land-use plans (minerals are explicitly excluded from coverage in the Forest Service's Multiple Use Sustained Yield Act of 1960). That situation, however, is gradually changing. The land-use planning process may eventually be the major framework for evaluation of resource allocation decisions. This will require integrating special requirements of single resource—principally minerals—statutes into multiple use, land-use planning programs. At present, much of this integration appears to concentrate on the same kind of spatial land-

use designations that the BLM and the Forest Service are accustomed to making: areas unsuitable for mining (coal); nominations
and "denominations" of areas appropriate for offshore leasing,
logical mining units (strippable minerals, now primarily coal), and
marginal lands (timber harvest).

Known and Unknown Mineral Deposits

With regard to minerals, the Mineral Leasing Act provides an interesting answer to the question of which resources to develop by
distinguishing between known and unknown deposits. (This distinction is not useful in allocating visible timber, forage, or similar
resources, which can be located and inventoried with relatively little
effort or technique. [47])   Minerals are generally obscure and increasingly so as the more obvious and accessible sites are played out
and industry looks farther and deeper for less concentrated deposits.

The known/unknown distinction was supposed to resolve one of
the thornier problems arising from our mix of market and political
decisions: how to encourage, protect, and reward the costly exploration efforts of private firms without relinquishing government
control over development decisions.   Typically, <u>known areas,</u> variously called KGSs (known geologic structures), KGRAs (known
geothermal resource areas) and the like, are accessible only in a
competitive bid process.   <u>Unknown areas</u> are to be explored under a
prospecting permit, which, if the explorer is successful, carry either
some right to development access or an advantage in the process
allocating that access.   Although the trend is clearly towards "all
competitive" leasing, there is a continuing difference between bonus
or other payment provisions for known and unknown areas in some
programs.   Moreover, the need to encourage exploration in unknown
areas persists.

Yet the distinction between the two is problematical: It is not
always clear which geologic structures are known and which are not,
although the consequences of the designation to firms, states, and
others affected by development are enormous. [48]   Exploration
costs are astronomical; it is clear that a firm's rights to information
it has gathered must be protected.   How to achieve confidentiality
while also assuring the public's right to evaluate government decisions regarding public resources is less clear.   The case of "captive"
areas, those in which location or surrounding ownerships limit the
pool of potential buyers, is particularly troubling because the most
likely bidder is also the only likely source of data on the mineralization in the area. [49]   Moreover, there is a strong feeling, especially
among opponents of development, that once a deposit is known it
will inevitably be developed.   Resolving these conflicting pressures
to identify lands appropriate for development is difficult.

TIMING

The issue of when development should begin has two dimensions: (1) timing of the sale, that is, when should the government make the resource available to potential explorers and developers, and (2) timing of the development, that is, having gained access, what discretion does the developer have regarding initiation and termination of development. The answer to the timing question differs from resource to resource.

Timing of Sale

For renewable resources such as timber, the timing-of-sale decision is the most critical because the timing-of-development decision is set in advance: the allocation of timber harvest rights is for a designated area and fixed term (usually two to five years) described in the contract. The purchaser has a limited time in which to harvest and only modest discretion to schedule activities. The intense controversy regarding relief for Pacific Northwest timber companies, which in the late 1970s bid on the probability that timber prices would rise and then could not afford to harvest in the present depressed market, underscores the point: there is so little flexibility in the contracts that it took an act of Congress for many of the companies to avoid default.

Almost without exception, major renewable resources are harvested under statutory sustained yield constraints: cut equals growth, that is, the government will not sell any faster than the resource is renewed. In theory, this strict rule may be modified by investments to increase growth. Application of the theory varies. Both Forest Service and BLM timber sales are limited to a most restrictive formulation of sustained yield: nondeclining even flow (NDEF). This formulation forbids downward variations in output and confines harvest to the level achievable in perpetuity. "Departures" from the NDEF are authorized by the National Forest Management Act but are highly controversial.

In the grazing context there is no timing-of-sale issue. Permits are granted for a ten-year renewable period. The actual use—number of animals, timing and duration of use—may be varied annually depending on market and resource conditions. Because forage yield varies annually and is not as easily measured as timber [50], sustained yield is difficult to define and difficult to impose as a ceiling on use.

The timing issues for mineral resources have been even more controversial. The Powder River controversy illustrates how critical timing of a sale can be. Depending on the market, timing can be affected by interest rates on loans, sales potential for the mineral, and a host of other factors critical to the bid price of the resource.

Moreover, questions understandably arise about the need for further leasing given the amount of land already leased.

The trend in resolving this timing-of-sale issue is toward establishing a "program" for each mineral; the program core is a set of criteria on which to base leasing targets and a schedule for leasing of specified amounts at predictable intervals. This trend is surrounded by controversy. Whether the targets should be set to meet minimally some projected need, or more expansively to meet industry's desire for flexibility and reserves, is unclear. The "correct decision" is probably based on political preference for market or government decision making. Also at issue is whether overleasing or underleasing is riskier. The Coal Commission argued that underleasing may be inadequate to meet the nation's future energy needs, and moreover, it might force industry to develop previously leased areas, which may be detrimental to the environment or the economy. The commission concluded that leasing beyond the amount ostensibly needed to meet future demand is less risky: it probably will not, as is frequently feared, lead to excessive development and will give industry the flexibility to develop the optimal deposits first. This is because, they reasoned, it is in the entrepreneur's interest to develop the most desirable leases first. The costs of development arguably provide motivation to let undesirable ones lapse. [51]

These basic questions continue to cause deep divisions. However, coal, tar sands, oil shale, OCS leasing, and timber harvesting are already nominally tied to long-term sale schedules based on government projections of future demand. Similar programs for oil and gas and nonfuel mineral leasing are being discussed and others may follow.

Timing of Development

The timing-of-development issue is basically confined to minerals management. The rapid rise in energy minerals prices during the 1970s (see pp. 67, 80) increased the value of minerals--principally coal--which had been leased but not developed. The leases were suddenly a windfall to many holders. Controversy over how to force "diligent" development of "speculatively held" leases continues to boil. Some argue that undeveloped leases should be forfeited; others counter that undeveloped leases meet a need for accessible reserves that could be brought on line rapidly in response to changes in the market. Whether leaseholders should be "forced" to develop on old, casually issued leases or in the face of unfavorable markets is also disputed. The fundamental issue is one of control: should the government or industry make basic decisions about the timing of coal production? Congress imposed strict "diligence" requirements on the coal industry in a period of rising coal prices, but the matter is less clear in a constricted economy.

INTENSITY OF DEVELOPMENT:
STIPULATIONS AND MITIGATION
REQUIREMENTS

Included in a sales contract or lease are both generic and site-specific requirements designed to impose diverse social responsibilities on the developer. This is not a recent development. The 1920 Mineral Leasing Act reflected the social concerns of the 1920s, specifying lease requirements on working conditions, child labor, and fair labor practices. Today's stipulations and conditions are usually included to express growing public emphasis on environmental protection. The current process for identifying such requirements is a public and intensely political adjunct to the land-use planning process. These requirements can, therefore, be a significant focus of conflict between federal and state agencies.

Despite the full panoply of public involvement and consultation strategies, state officials participating in the process of identifying environmental requirements sometimes perceive that persuading the federal agencies to accept their recommendations regarding stipulations or mitigations is a serious problem. Moreover, the applicability of state and local zoning and environmental regulations is not clear. [52] States and localities derive great influence over developments from programs that allow them to require permits. However, environmental mitigation requirements in those permits obviously affect the revenues returned to the states and localities under development revenue sharing programs. Whatever the developer must spend will be reflected in the bid price. The applicability of state and local environmental regulations on federal lands has become increasingly complex and controversial as federal statutes and local constituencies have expanded those regulatory efforts.

WHO PARTICIPATES IN DECISION MAKING?

The federal land-use planning process appears to invite "all comers" to provide input "early and often." However, the process, defined in NEPA, FLPMA, NFMA, and numerous other statutes, is complex and demanding. Effective participation requires considerable motivation, information, and resilience; and the rewards for effort are not always clear. For example, few National Forest plans have been completed and most of those that are done are being appealed or litigated. Moreover, Congress will probably not fund implementation of the entirety of each plan. The available plans are quite general, as opposed to site-specific, and suggest that another round of more localized analysis may precede implementation. Thus, the connection between federal land-use planning and agency action on the ground is not established. Although the plans have become the focus of much activity and debate, their significance is uncertain.

It is also true, however, that while rewards for participation are ill-defined, the consequences of nonparticipation are clear. The planning process is the only way to have voice and it is generally a prerequisite to subsequent appeals.

Institutional Confusion in Minerals Management

A major factor confusing participation in minerals programs is the complex relationships among the Department of the Interior agencies and other federal, state, and private entities involved in mineral leasing. As the successor agency to the old General Land Office, BLM has inherited major responsibility for managing minerals on all federal lands, including until recently the Outer Continental Shelf (OCS). Within the Department of the Interior, BLM shares that role with the U.S. Geological Survey, the Bureau of Mines, and, more recently, the Minerals Management Service, which now has lead responsibility for the OCS. The details of this arrangement have changed rapidly in the last two years, and the situation is not yet stabilized. Legislation granting the Forest Service full authority over minerals management on National Forest lands has been introduced as part of a major BLM/Forest Service land exchange but will probably not pass in its current form.

Forest Service participation further complicates the situation: Minerals management and revenues are treated differently on acquired Forest Service administered land, as opposed to those reserved from the public domain. In western National Forests that combine the two types of land, the situation is doubly complex.

Administrative responsibilities also differ between public domain and acquired National Forest land. BLM has the major responsibility for minerals on public domain forests; the Forest Service is technically confined to management of surface resources. Formally, the Forest Service merely consults with BLM—identifying areas unsuitable for minerals, requesting withdrawals, and suggesting lease stipulations. But the Forest Service's "advice" is normally accepted. Revenues for minerals extracted from public domain National Forests are distributed under the Mineral Leasing Act's 50-40-10 formula.

On acquired forests, BLM still plays the major role, but the Forest Service's consent is required on all decisions. Moreover, all MLA minerals, plus those hardrock deposits subject to location on public domain forests, are leased on acquired National Forests, and the revenues are distributed under the National Forest 25 percent revenue-sharing formula.

Planning Statutes

This organizational complexity is confounded by the weave of statutes and regulations that define the land-use planning process. The basic building block is the National Environmental Policy Act

(NEPA), which requires agencies to analyze "major actions ... significantly affecting the human environment" in an environmental impact statement (EIS). [53]   In addition, both the BLM and the Forest Service operate under elaborate multiple use, land management, planning mandates designed to fit with the EIS.   BLM's Federal Land Policy and Management Act (FLPMA) and the Forest Service's National Forest Management Act (NFMA), both passed in 1976, confer enormous discretion on the federal agencies. Congress relied on the planning process to control that discretion.   Lacking consensus on management priorities, Congress told both agencies to develop a process that would, through negotiation with affected interests, create support for a locally determined set of programs and allocations. [54]   The requirements on numerous specific, frequently incompatible, resource programs, defined in resource-specific statutes, are blended into a set of proposed land allocations in the plan. [55]

Both the Forest Service and BLM planning process rely heavily on public input to identify the issues to be addressed in the plan.   Both agencies also gather site-specific data about particular resources and resource potential.   Both rely on further public input to formulate management alternatives based on user preference and the data.   For most minerals proposals, planning does not end with the land-use plan.   The U.S. General Accounting Office (GAO) counted between three and five EISs required for a coal lease—from regional presale analysis to a mine development plan. [56]   Oil and gas leases are less extensively reported: an unknown but small number of EISs have ever been prepared in connection with the extant 106,152 oil and gas leases.   The Forest Service favors "phased NEPA compliance," noting that most of the leases are never explored and analysis should be focused on those that are.   The level of activity that will actually trigger an EIS requirement is not yet clear, but increasing litigation suggests that current practice is not sufficient. [57]

State and Local Role

FLPMA gives a special role to state and local governments in the land-use planning process.   The act requires that BLM land-use plans be consistent with state and local plans to the maximum extent feasible and in conformity with state and local environmental regulations.   This requirement, in theory, eases the way for negotiations between the BLM and state and local officials.   These "consistency" provisions of FLPMA have been seriously misunderstood, and recent litigation may lead state and local officials to discount the opportunities that they provide.   The Secretary of the Interior has final authority to decide what is consistent and what is not, and recent cases demonstrate this point clearly.   In Ventura County v. Gulf Oil (1979), [58] the court turned back a county effort to halt oil leasing on federal lands designated as "open space" in the county plan. A 1982 Colorado case [59] went further, voiding state plans that would have eroded rights granted under the 1872 Mining Act. [60]

The urgency surrounding conflict over consistency requirements in the context of the oil shale programs has receded due to economic and political reversals for the industry. Nevertheless, Rio Blanco County in Colorado and associated local governments in northwest Colorado precipitated an interesting issue. They objected to BLM's final resource management plan (RMP) for oil shale development in the Piceance Basin because BLM had omitted draft language stating that the lessee and local governments should develop a "mutually agreeable socioeconomic impact mitigation plan" to be submitted with lessee's detailed development plan. The local governments used a provision in BLM planning rules that allows state governors to protest a plan to the BLM director and obliges him to publish his reasons for rejecting the appeal in the Federal Register. As a result of the appeal, BLM reiterated that adding a lease stipulation requiring state and local government approval of a lessee's socioeconomic impact mitigation plan would improperly afford veto power over a congressionally approved activity on federal lands. However, the Bureau agreed to include in the RMP a stipulation that lessees must comply with relevant state and local laws insofar as they do not impermissibly conflict with the federal land use. [61]

The Supreme Court has recently agreed to review a very restrictive view of consistency, as defined by the Coastal Zone Management Act and interpreted by the Ninth Circuit Court of Appeals. The case, Granite Rock v. California Coastal Commission, involves a limestone mine located under the 1872 Act in a coastal national forest in the Big Sur area of California. It may suggest the contours of future legal approaches to consistency in general. [62]

Yet, these cases do not justify a jaundiced view of the consistency concept. Legally, congressional deference to the states is quite significant. State and local regulation must yield to the supremacy clause of the U.S. Constitution and the scope of the powers granted to Congress by the property clause. However, consistency provisions make clear that regardless of the theoretical reach of its power, Congress has in FLPMA and in other pertinent statutes chosen not to exercise it fully; instead, Congress has required that the secretary's discretion should be exercised with deference to states and localities.

Moreover, the legal issues are not the whole, or even the most important, part of the controversy. More significant, especially given the small number of administrative decisions that reach the courts, is the emerging land management partnership that the consistency provisions symbolize. The consistency provisions of FLPMA, as well as the public involvement provisions of NFMA and NEPA, give the states and localities a place at the table, and an opportunity to make their concerns and priorities known early in the process. If they prepare themselves to do so, states and localities can be very effective participants in the planning process.

Perhaps the most dramatic proof of state and local effectiveness in resource allocation negotiations comes under the heading of "exactions." Numerous localities have been extremely effective in using the planning and permitting process to force concessions from firms in return for permits and other prerequisites to development. For example, a locality typically incurs significant bond indebtedness at the outset to deal with anticipated impacts of a large development. Localities therefore have bargained directly with developers for up-front tax payments to reduce the debt burden and minimize their exposure in case the operation shuts down. [63]

ALLOCATION OF REVENUES

Justification for Revenue Sharing

Revenue sharing has been justified on a number of grounds: (1) to compensate the states for the loss of the 5 percent of the sale price of (reserved) lands not sold; (2) to recognize the extensive tax-exempt federal lands within a state; (3) to mitigate harm caused by development on federal lands; (4) to compensate for service demands generated by federal lands and federal land developments; (5) to compensate for federal acquired lands removed from the local tax base; (6) to compensate for the loss of self-determination inherent in having federal decision making dominate local, state, and regional development; (7) as a buyoff in exchange for western acceptance of increasingly restrictive federal land management. [64] The Advisory Commission on Intergovernmental Relations has made repeated unsuccessful efforts [65] to locate net financial burdens on states and localities associated with federal land ownership that require compensation. Hence, the empirical justifications for revenue sharing appear to be weak. The strongest case may be the "spoonful of sugar" argument. At critical points in public domain history when the federal government has acted on or through its lands to achieve national goals, the congressional compromise has, almost without exception, included some recognition that the western states were giving up aspirations and control over the future. Formulae for distributing revenues from public resource development amply demonstrate the states' ability to protect their interests in the congressional process. Sharing has become increasingly lucrative for the states since Ohio joined the Union in 1803. Recently, however, escalating resource values have increased attention to resource revenues and raised questions about the distribution schemes.

Problems with Revenue Sharing

Initial criticism of the revenue programs actually came from the recipients: The payments fluctuated with market and other conditions and provided an unreliable source of income to states and localities—clearly inferior to the more stable property tax opportunities foreclosed by federal land ownership; in addition, the timing of the payments did not coincide with state and local budgeting processes. Funds were earmarked to specific purposes that did not reflect local needs or self-determination.   The payments were inadequate to compensate for tax losses and burdens imposed by federal land ownership. The payments were inequitable—some areas with federal lands valuable for commodity production received substantial revenues while others with enormous federal holdings but having small commodity potential received little revenue at all. The programs were confusing and difficult for citizens or local government officials to follow. [66]

All of these complaints were summarized in the 1970 report of the Public Land Law Review Commission. The commission recommended that the entire revenue sharing program be scrapped in favor of federal PILTs; under the commission's proposal the federal government would make payments to counties equivalent to the tax rate but adjusted to account for benefits of federal land ownership and for extremely burdensome holdings.   However, instead of reforming the existing revenue sharing system [67], Congress added the PILT program to it. All of the revenue sharing problems originally identified remain.

Future Trends

Equity is beginning to emerge as a major issue in revenue sharing. The appearance of special benefits targeted to one region has invited scrutiny during a period of budget austerity. Only a small percentage of the revenues from the sale and lease of national resources appear to return to the Treasury. [68] Recent efforts to end apparent subsidies connected with federal water and hydroelectric development [69] suggest that revenue distribution will be closely scrutinized in coming years, even within the regions and states only nominally benefitting from the programs.

Traditional arguments that existing allocations are justified by the costs and burdens imposed by developments on the states are subject to dispute [70] and must be evaluated in the context of revenue-raising capabilities associated with developments on federal lands. For example, state severance taxes on coal have attracted comment because of the high tax rate. Of the states where federal coal is mined in significant quantities, only Utah does not have a severance tax.   So far, the Supreme Court has been unwilling to strike down the state taxes as an unreasonable burden on interstate commerce. [71]   On the other hand, when Congress has established clear formulae for distributing revenues, actions by OMB and other federal agencies to save money by circumventing the law are also bound to create controversy.   States have, for example, challenged the apparently improper federal efforts to fund the PILTs program with deductions from mineral leasing revenues. [72]

This debate about the equity of revenue distributions may be accelerated as coastal states attempt to procure a percentage of the royalties from Outer Continental Shelf (OCS) development.   Current proposals for sharing a small portion of OCS revenues with coastal states must be distinguished from the 8(g) issue discussed in Chapter 6. [73]   Indeed, the current OCS revenue sharing proposals suggest that, like the PILTs (1976) and LWCF (1965) programs, a significant shift may be taking place in revenue distribution programs.   The OCS shares would be subject to the annual congressional appropriations process.   Moreover, the proposed OCS shared funds would be spent on coastal protection programs that emphasize the nation's interest in the coastal zone.   These OCS proposals adopt the contours of the most recently adopted sharing programs.   Both the PILTs and the LWCF programs also require annual appropriations and meet national priorities.   Nine million dollars annually in OCS funds may be allocated to the Land and Water Conservation Fund [74] designed to encourage recreation planning and land acquisition. The Historic Preservation Fund also benefits from OCS revenues under a similar program.   The PILTs program, established in 1976, is also national in scope. [75]   These statutes may suggest new patterns in the allocation of federal resource revenues.

CONTEMPORARY EVENTS THAT COLOR THE RESOLUTION OF RESOURCE DEVELOPMENT ISSUES

Long-standing issues and patterns explain much of the vocabulary and current debate surrounding public resource development. Current events, however, both in general and in "hot" natural resource topics, also play an important role.   Bargains struck in any time period reflect both the long-term issues and the unique, but not always ephemeral, concerns and buzz words of that time.   Who cared about minute nuances of the term "sequestration" until the Gramm-Rudman-Hollings Act [76] moved to center stage in late 1985?

Broader contemporary issues must be discussed in order to understand fully the ramifications for public lands policy.   It is also useful to recognize that there will always be "wild hares" running through the debate, which complicate, confuse, and sometimes dominate the dialogue but do not alter its fundamental structure. Even neophytes can learn to recognize the basic issues beneath positions taken in fleeting conflict.

Major national issues have always played an important role in public lands policy. One has but to recall the free land/free soil [77] debate of the mid-1800s to appreciate the close relationship between durable national issues and public resource decisions. The current federal budgetary crisis may not loom as large in public resources history as does, for example, the Missouri Compromise, but it appears likely to have a significant impact on resource and revenues programs for at least the rest of the 1980s. The effects may be direct as well as indirect: In addition to potential contractions in resource management programs caused by cuts in agency budgets, state revenue shares have actually been sequestered under the provisions of the Gramm-Rudman-Hollings Act. In addition, as long-debated federal income tax reform is implemented, it could have significant impacts on the financial plans of potential developers of federal resources. Even though Gramm-Rudman-Hollings has been held unconstitutional and Congress appears to be losing momentum regarding spending controls, budget problems will be with us in some form at least for the near term. We can expect continuing administration efforts to reduce or curtail revenue sharing.

Less comprehensively, litigation could, and frequently does, alter rather well-laid plans of government and developer alike. National Wildlife Federation v. Burford [78] is one such case; it is likely to wind its way through several additional hearings, confounding diverse land exchange, access, and development sale programs in the process. Less comprehensive issues, such as the continuing saga of "quiet title," suggest that no matter how knowledgeable the interested citizen or official becomes, specialists can always unearth intriguing exotica with which to alarm the unwary and seduce scholars.

Gramm-Rudman-Hollings and the Federal Budget Crisis

The Gramm-Rudman-Hollings Act passed as an amendment to a joint resolution of Congress intended primarily to raise the debt ceiling. The Act is supposed to reduce the national debt to zero by 1991 by achieving defined debt-reduction targets each year until then. Both the Office of Management and Budget and the Congressional Budget Office prepare annual estimates of national debt. If Congress does not make spending cuts that achieve the mandated budget reduction, the Comptroller General of the General Accounting Office must prepare a report indicating across-the-board cuts that will be automatically imposed by presidential "sequestration" orders.

Authority to spend sequestered funds is simultaneously cancelled, preventing a subsequent return to previous outlays. "Special and trust funds" are exempted from automatic cancellation of budget authority. Because resource revenue sharing programs fall clearly into that category, it is possible that although state shares were sequestered in the original March 1986 orders, they will become available for expenditure in October 1986 and will not be subject to further sequestration. [79]

The Gramm-Rudman-Hollings Act requires that after 1986, 50 percent of the cuts will come from military spending, and 50 percent from nonmilitary programs. Eight specified categories of human welfare programs are exempted entirely. The act also specifies that the cuts must be on funds that are not tied up under long-term contracts or similar commitments. Because the resource management agencies in the Departments of Agriculture and the Interior constitute a major repository of these "discretionary" expenditure items, they will be hard hit in any future budget cuts. Personnel and budget reductions will curtail both the resource development programs involved in revenue production and the resource inventory planning, and protection programs that must precede and accompany development decisions.

These cuts may not take place in the manner described since the Gramm-Rudman-Hollings Act was declared unconstitutional. A District of Columbia District Court held that the Comptroller General's role constitutes an unconstitutional delegation of executive authority [80], and the decision was upheld on "expedited review" to the Supreme Court. Congress initially appeared to be prepared to reenact the bill modified to resolve the constitutional problems, but that no longer appears likely. Congress could still amend it.

It is easier to predict the outcome of continuing, diverse efforts by the Reagan Administration to reduce, redirect, or curtail revenue sharing programs. Payments in lieu of taxes allocations have never been popular with the president or OMB, and recent efforts to "zero budget" the program or to divert PILT monies [81] are not new. However, as the federal budget crisis deepened, Congress has also repeatedly defeated efforts to change the basis of Forest Service and Mineral Leasing Act revenue sharing from gross to net receipts, to fund oil and gas royalty audits with the state's share, and the like. These proposals are so uniformly unpopular in Congress that it is difficult to foresee circumstances under which they would succeed. [82]

National Wildlife Federation v. Burford

It is difficult to be precise about the meaning of current litigation brought by the National Wildlife Federation (NWF) to halt BLM classification and withdrawal review programs. [83]   The NWF charged that BLM's FLPMA-mandated efforts to reclassify lands and study (and perhaps revoke) withdrawals violate NEPA, FLPMA, and the Administrative Procedures Act.   The decision did not resolve most of NWF's claims but held that pre-FLPMA management framework plans (MFPs) did not constitute an adequate analysis of terminations of 160,000 acres of land reclassifications nationwide. Although the newer resource management plans (RMPs) were not required for withdrawal revocation (according to the judge), BLM's public involvement in those decisions was inadequate.   The court temporarily enjoined any activity on the affected properties that would have been incompatible with their status before January 1, 1981.   The defendants have asked for a stay of the order pending appeal.

Although the case was apparently motivated by NWF's concern regarding mining locations and leases on the affected lands, the decision has far broader implications.   In addition to potential effects on state revenue receipts arising from dislocations of minerals activities, a full spectrum of arduously negotiated real estate transactions have been put in limbo. These include state land selections, wilderness consolidation programs, and congressionally-ordered land exchanges, such as those in the Santa Monica Mountains.   An affidavit filed in the case by the Department of the Interior notes that 240 agricultural entries, 430 sales, and 70 land exchanges have been stopped, and approximately 7,200 mining locations and 1,000 leases are affected. Parties in the 70 exchanges include states, counties, and environmental and conservation organizations.   "The vast majority of the exchanges were," according to the Principal Deputy Undersecretary of the Interior, "proposed for actions normally considered in the public interest and/or environmentally enhancing." [84]

Quiet Title

A less widely discussed, but potentially more substantial "wild hare" is the dispute between federal and state officials over the Quiet Title Act of 1972. [85] "Quiet title" is a proceeding in which a party asks for a judicial declaration regarding title to lands for which there is reasonable or potential ownership dispute. Confusion arises from inaccurate surveys, lack of knowledge regarding the historic location of high-water lines of lakes, rivers, and tidal lands, and the like.

Until 1972, the states were unable to press their claims because the federal government claimed sovereign immunity and did not consent to be sued. That bar was eliminated by the 1972 act. The act, however, also provided a twelve-year statutory limit on state suits. A recent Eighth Circuit decision held that the statute of limitations began running from the time at which the state "knew or should have known" that there was a conflict over title. The states received such "notice" in many key instances in the nineteenth century. Despite the federal government's claim of sovereign immunity, the court has held that the states should have brought their actions in the late nineteenth and early twentieth centuries. [86] This "catch-22" is likely to remain a topic for the cognoscente. Nevertheless, it does illustrate the broad range of historical, legal, and other information that is likely to be relevant in any dispute over resource policy.

SUMMARY

Contemporary public resource management reflects 200 years of national change and congressional compromise. Congress continues to rely on private entrepreneurs and investors to develop and market most public resources; yet the incentives for private developers have been gradually but substantially modified by increasing government regulation and bureaucratic decision making. Whereas a miner or homesteader once made virtually all of the development decisions, frequently without even notifying the federal government, we now have a complex planning process that responds to a national spectrum of participants and social goals.

In the mid-1980s, new national priorities and the changing pattern of federal-state relations continue to be reflected in public lands programs. Growing concern over public expenditures and the federal deficit has spurred the search for cost-cutting and revenue-expanding opportunities. The federal administration has proposed numerous changes to make public lands revenue programs more equitable, more efficient, and cheaper for the federal government. These include basing all state share calculations on gross rather than net revenues, funding PILTs from minerals leasing revenues, and shifting National Forest revenue sharing to a tax-equivalence basis. States have also sought increased equity, efficiency, and funds through diverse claims and proposals: to give coastal states a share in Outer Continental Shelf revenues, to raise National Forest revenues to 50 percent of gross, and to give states a share of the recently increased filing fees for the oil and gas leasing "lottery." [87]

Inevitably, when budget cuts are pending, every level of government will look for new and creative ways to protect and expand their resources. Yet a cursory look at history demonstrates that

today's baby may be tomorrow's bathwater. Decisions about revenues are tied to a host of other questions about resources that also
deeply affect future state and local economies and quality of life.
Reaching these decisions is difficult, given the complex process we
have created to blend market and political decision making in public
resource management. Yet states and localities are increasingly
involved in the process for making them. Talk about a federal-state
"partnership" in federal land management seems premature rather
than unreasonable. Tight budgets may intensify conflicts which
seemed as recently as three years ago to be abating. [88] The trend
toward greater state and local participation, however, is unmistak-
able, and could increase if states and localities seize opportunities
to clarify and press their interests in public land management. It is
worth the effort for state and local officials and concerned citizens
to master the rudiments of the individual resource programs
described in Part Two.

Part One Notes

1. For example, environmental groups have challenged the Forest Service's below-cost timber sales, which do not recover the costs of putting the timber on the market. See discussion in Chapter 7.

2. Revenue sharing was expanded to include payments in lieu of taxes in 1976. See Chapter 8.

3. For example, under the Mineral Leasing Act 50 percent of lease revenues is returned to most states. See Chapter 4.

4. Balanced Budget and Emergency Deficit Control Act of 1985 (Gramm-Rudman) P.L. 99-177; legislation introduced in the 99th Congress to establish OCS oil and gas revenue distribution to states includes S1653, H3314, H3402, H3417.

5. See Chapter 5.

6. The Linowes "Commission on the Fiscal Accountability of the Nation's Energy Resources," established by Interior Secretary Watt in 1981, called for reorganization of key elements in the Department of Interior. See discussion in Chapter 5.

7. Congress enacted the Federal Oil and Gas Royalty Management Act in 1982. See discussion in Chapter 5.

8. A typical state litigation effort was California's claim that Interior had breached a fiduciary obligation to the states for an accounting of royalty payments.

9. See U.S. Department of Agriculture, Forest Service and U.S. Department of Interior, Bureau of Land Management, 1985 Grazing Fee Review and Evaluation Draft Report.

10. For example, Nebraska, part of the Louisiana Purchase, was an early public domain state in which the federal government now owns only 1.6 percent of the land. The other 98.4 percent was disposed of.

11. U.S. Public Land Law Review Commission, One Third of the Nation's Land: A Report to the President and to the Congress (1970). The figure is still startling but it is worth noting that 348 million acres of Alaskan land are

included in this figure. For the rest of the continental United States, the appropriate figure is 23.4 percent.

12. D.E. Engdahl, "State and Federal Power over Federal Property" 18 Ariz. L. Rev. 283 (1976). See also R. Cowart, L. Wilson, and S.K. Fairfax, "State Sovereignty and Federal Lands: Strategies Beyond Sagebrush," unpublished paper, Western Conference of State Governments, hereafter cited as Cowart, Wilson, and Fairfax, "Sovereignty."

13. See, for example, John Joseph Wallis, "The Birth of the Old Federalism: Financing the New Deal, 1932-1940," Journal of Economic History, vol. XLIV, March 1984, 139-159.

14. The term is taken from the title of a recent Advisory Commission on Inter-governmental Relations. Study: Regulatory Federalism: Policy, Process, Impact and Reform (A-95) Washington, D.C. (February 1984).

15. Advisory Commission on Intergovernmental Relations, The Federal Role in the Federal System: The Dynamics of Growth — Protecting the Environment: Politics, Pollution, and Federal Policy (A-83) Washington, D.C. (March 1981).

16. Advisory Commission on Intergovermental Relations, In Brief: State and Local Roles in the Federal System, B-6, Washington, D.C. (November 1981) at 2, drawing upon ACIR, The Federal Role in the Federal System (B-4) (December 1980).

17. For a fuller discussion of bargains, see S.K. Fairfax, "Federalism as if States Mattered: Resource Revenues and the Public Lands," paper presented at the annual meeting of the Western Political Science Association, Eugene, Oregon, March 1986.

18. Drawing lines is somewhat arbitrary. What follows is not, however, an exhaustive discussion of every program arguably related to the federal lands which somehow produces revenues for the states or localities. We have started with a standard concept of federal lands, encompassing those categories studied by the Public Land Law Review Commission (PLLRC). Hence, we have omitted revenue programs that are not associated with the public domain or related acquired lands, such as aid to "impacted" areas, bloc grants, and so on. Similarly, we are not analyzing herein the rent that the federal government pays or receives on office buildings and similar holdings, nor military lands. Within the public lands context, however, we have considered revenues broadly, not confining ourselves to shared receipts. This reaches Payments in Lieu of Taxes (PILTs) and Land and Water Conservation Fund (LWCF) programs. It does not reach either federal or state taxes generated in connection with those resources or federal aid to highways, which is based, in part, on total federal acreage within that state. Finally, we have mentioned revenue from water projects only to explain what happens to the ubiquitous "Reclamation Fund." Ostensibly the beneficiary of 40 to 90 percent of many public resource revenues, it turns out to be an accounting "fiction" indistinguishable for most purposes from the General Fund of the U.S. Treasury.

19. See Appendix, Figure 1 and Table 2.

20. See M.A. Binder, "Payment in Lieu of Taxes Act: A Legislative Response to Federal Tax Immunity," 85 Dickinson L. Rev. (1981) at 461, and S.K. Fairfax,

"PILTs -- A Study of the Conceptual Basis, Legal Background, and Management Implications of the PILT Program," paper, Western Legislative Conference (1983) (hereafter cited as Fairfax, "PILTs").

21. See Paul Gates, History of Public Land Law Development. Pub. Land L. Rev. Comm. Government Printing Office, Washington, D.C. (1968) at 290-91.

22. EBS Management Consultants, Inc. Revenue Sharing and Payments in Lieu of Taxes on the Public Lands, vol. II. Pub. Land L. Rev. Comm. (1970) at LA 2-4 (hereafter cited as EBS, Study for PLLRC).

23. See Appendix, Figure 2 and Tables 3 and 4.

24. See Appendix, Table 5 for a state-by-state summary of the federal lands in the western states.

25. See W. Marsh, and D. Sherwood, "Metamorphosis in Mining Law: Federal Legislation and Regulatory Amendment and Supplementation of the General Mining Law Since 1955," 26 Rocky Mtn. Min. L. Inst. (1980).

26. See Chapter 4.

27. See E. Louise Peffer, The Closing of the Public Domain. (Palo Alto: Stanford University Press, 1951), chapter 5.

28. See Fairfax, "PILTs."

29. See Chapter 4.

30. See Advisory Commission on Intergovernmental Relations, The Federal Role in the Federal System: The Dynamics of Growth. Crises of Confidence and Competence (A-77) (1980) (hereafter cited as ACIR, Crises).

31. Ibid., at 49.

32. Ibid., at 121, citing Deil Wright, "The Administrative Dimensions of Intergovernmental Relations," draft for Contemporary Public Administration, Vocino & Jack, eds. (New York: Harcourt Brace Jovanovich, 1979).

33. Ibid., at 120.

34. D. Sprague, Executive Director, Western Office, Council of State Governments, Testimony before the California State Senate Committee on National Resources and Wildlife, January 31, 1985.

35. A. Markusen, and J. Fastrup, "The Regional War for Federal Aid" 53 Pub. Interest 87 (1978) at 90. The authors note that the "geographic incidence" (e.g., what regions really pay and benefit) of the federal salaries and public works categories are impossible to determine because of subcontracting: allocating those revenues to regions on the basis of the prime contractor's location is known to be inaccurate. Yet doing so, Markusen and Fastrup point out, is an important part of the conventional wisdom that the northeast subsidizes the Sunbelt.

36. See H. Ingram, "Policy Implementation Through Bargaining: The Case of Federal Grants-in-Aid," 25 Pub. Policy (1977) 499, 501.

37. R. Lamm and M. McCarthy, The Angry West: A Vulnerable Land and Its Future (Boston: Houghton Mifflin, 1982).

38. Significantly, this concept is not "efficient" in the economic sense of allocating the resource to its most economically productive ("highest and best") use. The government does not rely on the market to allocate resources to uses; it does that in other ways, principally land-use planning. The sale is simply to allocate resources to a particular user to achieve a predetermined use. That may assure, however, that the resource will be allocated to the party that can use it most efficiently for a stated purpose.

39. It is important to note the difference between an individual firm's discount rate and a "social" discount rate, ascribed to western states and communities; these local governments may have a high discount rate due to the immediate impacts with which they must deal.

40. For example, government policies regarding minimum and maximum tract size affect the value of many mineral leases.

41. See Coal Commission, Fair Market Value. The controversy also involves last-minute changes in the Department of the Interior's rules for sales and alleged leaking of possibly significant data by government officials. See also Part Two note 86 and text accompanying it.

42. An "ad valorem" tax is based on the assessed market value of the resource or, occasionally, on the use value. Because it does not vary with production but is paid annually, it provides an incentive to develop the resource.

43. A severance tax is paid only during production. It is levied on a set amount per unit produced, on net or gross production value.

44. An exaction is a payment or action required of the developer as part of procuring permits from local government. Its intent is to mitigate development impacts by shifting costs to the project sponsor. See Cowart, Wilson, and Fairfax, "Sovereignty."

45. And thereby eliminated so-called "preference right" or noncompetitive leasing as well. See Chapter 5.

46. See U.S. Office of Technology Assessment, Management of Fuel and Nonfuel Minerals in Federal Lands: Current Status and Issues (1979) at 215-20.

47. But see National Research Council/National Academy of Sciences, Developing Strategies for Rangeland Management: A Report Prepared by the Committee on Developing Strategies for Rangeland Management (Boulder, Colorado: Westview Press, 1984) (hereafter cited as NRC/NAS, Strategies) for a discussion of the problematical techniques available to the range manager.

48. See note 41 above and text accompanying it.

49. The Federal Coal Leasing Amendments Act of 1976 required the Department of the Interior to do its own drilling prior to selecting tracts for lease sales, but the effort has never been adequately funded.

50. See NRC/NAS, Strategies. But see also Part Two note 214 and text accompanying it regarding lack of precision in timber volume estimation.

51. See generally Coal Commission, <u>Fair Market Value</u>, for fuller discussion of these issues. See Appendix, Table 8 for a quick summary of lease period provisions for fuel and nonfuel minerals.

52. See <u>Ventura County v. Gulf Oil</u> 601 F.2d (9th Cir. 1979). See also discussion on State and Local Role below.

53. The EIS must contain a description of alternatives to the proposed action, adverse impacts of each, and mitigation strategies. NEPA does not require that the agency select the least damaging alternative, but it does require a "hard look" at the "worst case" arising from any proposal. It also emphasizes review of agency assumptions and decisions, and requires agencies to structure early and frequent comment opportunities throughout draft and final EIS preparation. Commenters include affected interest groups, the general public, and other federal agencies with related responsibilities.

54. The major structural difference between the two procedures is that the Forest Service land management planning is tied into a rigidly scheduled cycle of decennial national inventories (the "Assessment") and production target-setting (the "Program") every five years; the BLM process, after the first set of plans is done, will not repeat itself except "as needed." The national level of the Forest Service system is mandated by the Resource Planning Act, passed in 1974 (hence the RPA). The RPA process emphasizes economic analysis of alternative investment opportunities and national demands for national forest outputs. Although the Forest Service portrays the national RPA plan and the local land management plans mandated by NFMA as an integrated unit, they deal with significantly different issues and utilize almost wholly different kinds of data that are collected so differently on different forests that they cannot be aggregated. See S.K. Fairfax, "RPA and The Forest Service" in Conservation Foundation, <u>A Citizens Guide to the Resources Planning Act and Forest Service Planning</u> (1980).

55. These special statutes include the Endangered Species Act, the Wild and Free Roaming Horse and Burro Act, the Wilderness Act, the Wild and Scenic Rivers Act as well as the Coal Leasing Act Amendments of 1976, the Surface Mining Control and Reclamation Act, the Geothermal Steam Act and numerous others. See Nelson, "Re the Public Lands" in Paul R. Portney, ed., <u>Current Issues in Natural Resource Policy</u> (Washington, D.C.: Resources for the Future, 1982) for a chart and full discussion.

56. <u>Sierra Club v. Peterson</u> (Palisades Case) 14 ERC 1449 (D.D.C. 1982); <u>Conner v. Burford</u>, No. CV-82-42 BU (D. Mont. March 8, 1985).

57. <u>Ibid.</u> See Part Two, notes 32, 44-46 and text accompanying them.

58. <u>Ventura County v. Gulf Oil</u> 601 F.2d (9th Cir. 1979).

59. <u>Brubaker v. El Paso County</u>, No. 81SA86, Slip Op. (Colo. September 13, 1982); 652 P.2d 1050 (1982). See also <u>Elliott v. Oregon International Mining Co.</u> 654 P.2d 633 (1982).

60. Consistency is not, of course, unique to FLPMA. A recent Supreme Court decision, <u>California v. Watt</u> 464 U.S. 312 (1981), regarding OCS oil leasing, is widely interpreted as undercutting consistency provisions in the Coastal Zone Management Act. However, because the Supreme Court never reached the consistency argument, the result is still unclear. It decided that the exploration, development, or production stage of oil development, but not the leasing stage would have "direct effects" on the coastal environment.

The court concluded that, in any event, the Coastal Zone Act explicitly did not affect activities on the Outer Continental Shelf.

61. W. Morck, U.S. Department of Interior, letter to Richard Pond and Tim Evans, Associated Governments of Northwest Colorado, April 25, 1985.

62. Granite Rock Co. v. California Coastal Commission 590 F.Supp. 1361 (N.D. Cal. 1984), 768 F.2d 1077 (1985), cert. granted 106 S.Ct. 1489 (March 31, 1986). We discuss "consistency" throughout generically, making little distinction among the various statutory, political, and administrative definitions of the term. However, readers needing the precise wording of pertinent statutes, such as FLPMA, C2MA, OCSLAA, NFMA are referred to the table of statutes in Appendix Section A for appropriate U.S. Code and Code of Federal Regulation citations. Readers may also be interested in noting the difference between the rights of federal lessees, under the MLA or similar statutes, and the rights of mining claim holders, under the 1872 Mining Act. By statute, mineral lessees do not gain access with the lease and have no implied right of access to the lease site. Access is defined apart from the lease. Claimants under the 1872 Act have property rights that carry with them implied rights of access. Granite Rock involves consistency requirements under the federal Coastal Zone Management Act as it applies to a mining claim under the 1872 Act. That might be viewed differently in Court than a case involving FLPMA's consistency provision as applied to a coal lessee. Moreover, readers should also take care to distinguish preemption cases in which federal law is found to override conflicting state law, such as Ventura County, Brubaker, and Elliott, from consistency cases, in which the preemption question is viewed in the context of consistency provisions evincing congressional intent to defer to state law.

63. Cowart, Wilson, and Fairfax, "Sovereignty."

64. Fairfax, PILTs.

65. Advisory Commission on Intergovernmental Relations, The Adequacy of Federal Compensation to Local Governments for Tax Exempt Federal Lands (A-68) Washington, D.C. (1978) (hereafter cited as ACIR, Adequacy).

66. EBS, Study for PLLRC.

67. Congress was reluctant to fight the beneficiaries of established programs. It did not want to pay for a tax assessment of the federal lands; and it was equally wary of trying to calculate burdens and benefits accruing to localities from federal land holdings.

68. The federal government actually loses money on mineral leasing programs. This is because state shares generally are taken out of gross revenues; the 10 percent of gross going to the General Fund does not cover the leasing program expenses of the lead agency. In fiscal 1983, ignoring all agency costs except the BLM's, the federal government lost more than $17 million on the coal leasing program alone. Coal Commission, Fair Market Value at 329. It is important to reiterate, however, that there is more to resource revenues than revenue sharing discussed in this book. A few lines about tax revenues will give an added perspective to the problems of equity. The Coal Commission (Linowes II) points out that a full accounting of the distributional impacts of mineral leasing programs must include the federal tax treatment royalties and bonuses, which are used in computing federal corporate income taxes. To illustrate, each dollar of coal leasing revenue collected by the federal government is partially distributed to the states and gives the cor-

poration a writeoff on their federal taxes. How one evaluates the Reclamation Fund (see Chapter 8) is critical in assessing the states' benefits. If the Reclamation Fund portion of the revenue share is treated as a benefit to the states, and the corporate tax rate is assumed to be 46 percent at the margin, every dollar of revenue collected winds up losing the federal government 36 cents. If one assumes that the corporation pays no taxes at all and treats the Reclamation Fund allocation as a benefit to the federal government, then the federal government makes 50 cents per dollar of revenues collected, not including the administration costs noted above. See Coal Commission, ibid. at 328.

69. See K. Kroese, "Legal Aspects of the Upcoming Reallocation of Hoover Dam Energy: The Conflict Between Arizona, California and Nevada," 24 Ariz. L. R. 927 (1982).

70. See ACIR, Adequacy.

71. Commonwealth Edison Co. v. Montana 453 U.S. 609 (1981).

72. See Fairfax, PILTs.

73. Sharing of revenues from OCS development should not be confused with the ongoing dispute over Section 8(g) (of the OCSLAA) funds. Congress provided in 1978 that revenues produced from development within three miles on either side of the federal/state boundary (Three Mile Limit) should be shared. See Chapter 6.

74. Annual apportionments to states have rarely amounted to a third of this figure, however. See Chapter 8.

75. This was accomplished by including national parks in the "entitlement lands" despite extensive evidence indicating that they were an overwhelming tax benefit to proximate localities. It was clearly a device to garner national support for the measure.

76. Balanced Budget and Emergency Deficit Control Act of 1985, Pub. Law No. 99-177, 99 Stat. 1037.

77. Free land summarizes the "land for the landless" theme of pre-Civil war politics; free soil was the slogan of those opposed to extending slavery into new states.

78. Civil Action No. 85-2238 (D.D.C. February 10, 1986).

79. James C. Miller, III, Director, Office of Management and Budget, letter to Honorable Malcolm Wallop, United States Senate, April 21, 1986.

80. Synar v. United States (D.D.C. Civil Action No. 85-4106, February 7, 1986).

81. In the past, the administration has proposed funding PILTs with oil and gas royalties. See notes 82, 251 and text accompanying them.

82. See Public Land News, February 7, 1985, at 4; March 7, 1985, p. 7; October 3, 1985, p. 5; February 20, 1986, p. 6.

83. National Wildlife Federation v. Burford, Civil Action No. 85-2238 (D.D.C., February 10, 1986).

84. Joseph J. Martyak, Principal Deputy Undersecretary of the United States Department of the Interior, affidavit in <u>NWF v. Burford,</u> April 11, 1986.

85. 28 U.S.C. § 1346 (F), 1402(d) and 2409(a).

86. <u>Block v. North Dakota</u> 461 U.S. 274 (1982).

87. See Chapter 5.

88. Cowart, Wilson, and Fairfax, "Sovereignty."

SPECIFIC RESOURCES AND PROGRAMS

CHAPTER FOUR

The Acts of 1872 and 1920

MINERALS LOCATED UNDER THE 1872 GENERAL MINING ACT

The purpose of the 1872 Mining Act was to encourage private individuals and corporations to locate and bring to market the minerals of the western territories. No rent for the land used or royalty for the minerals was charged to the prospector or miner. This continues to be the basic pattern of the much-discussed 1872 Act, but implementation of the statute has been altered considerably in recent decades by subsequent statutes and administrative and judicial action.

As originally passed, the Mining Act of 1872 provided that whoever discovered and developed a "valuable" mineral deposit on federal land may mine that deposit free of charge and without competition. The miner was normally allowed to take title to an unlimited number of twenty-acre parcels in connection with the deposit and up to five additional acres per parcel for a mill site. Mill sites have traditionally been available in connection with mining operations on patented land as well. In the original scheme, mining on federal land was controlled almost totally by the entrepeneur, and the miner needed no federal license or other grant of permission either to prospect or to mine. Until the Federal Land Policy and Management Act (FLPMA) introduced federal "recordation" requirements in 1976, the prospector or miner was not even required to inform the federal government of his presence.

Although the 1872 Act still covers hardrock or metallic minerals such as gold, silver, lead, and copper, it has been considerably limited by subsequent congressional and agency action. [1] "Leasables," sometimes described as sedimentary deposits and/or fertilizer minerals, were removed from the 1872 Act by passage of the Mineral Leasing Act of 1920. The Common Varieties Act of 1955 also provides for the sale of sand, stone, gravel, pumice, cinders, and other "common" or construction-grade minerals. Moreover, the Wilderness Act and attendant studies, and a plethora of programs protecting air, water, wildlife, and endangered species have limited the areas open to exploration and discovery. Land classifications, withdrawals, and regulations, and programs designed to protect surface resources on federal lands have also restricted hardrock operations. [2]

Nevertheless, the 1872 rules of discovery continue to govern the "locatables." In order to have a valid mining claim under those rules, the prospector must (1) discover a "valuable deposit;" (2) locate the claim by placing boundary markers on the ground; (3) give notice of his location in the appropriate local jurisdiction; and (4) perform annual work, called "assessment work," to develop the claim. A prospector is protected from rival claimants by the doctrine of pedis possessio, or "toehold." In 1976, Congress modified those rules slightly; following the passage of FLPMA, the claimant is required to record the claim with the BLM and also certify annually to the BLM that the assessment work has been done. BLM efforts to invalidate claims that were not properly recorded or that failed to certify the annual assessment, have been challenged in court. In a key case, the Supreme Court supported the BLM programs. [3]

Claimants are, under the 1872 Act, allowed to obtain deeds or "patent" their claims. To do so requires that they "prove up" their discovery, that is, demonstrate to the U.S. Geological Survey that a "valuable deposit" of a mineral covered by the act has been discovered. Initially, miners were obliged to patent their claims because eastern banks were not convinced that rights of pedis possessio constituted a solid basis for an investment. More recently, the rules of discovery have been tightened, and the management agencies have worked to eliminate ancient and bogus mining claims. Whereas the "prudent man rule" originally defined "valuable deposit" in terms of physical workability, the threshold was raised in the 1960s to require that the deposit produce ores that could be sold at a profit. Miners unwilling to risk invalidation of their claim do not attempt to "go to patent." However, a valid mining claim is subject to federal environmental controls applicable on federal lands. Because a patented claim becomes private land that is frequently subject to less stringent state and local regulation, it may be worth risking the challenge to discovery. [4]

For present purposes, the 1872 Act is important for what it does not require; these hardrock minerals can be located and developed without paying the government any royalties or rent. Simply staking a claim—literally driving stakes into the ground and reporting their location to appropriate officials—is sufficient to establish an exclusive right to the minerals and the surrounding land. Thus, the mining of hardrock minerals on the federal lands provides no revenue sharing for states or localities, though such mining is subject to state and local taxes—such as severance, production, or property taxes. In light of this arrangement, states and localities should evaluate the tradeoffs between tax receipts and revenue shares.

INTRODUCTION TO THE MINERAL LEASING
ACT OF 1920

The Mineral Leasing Act (MLA), enacted in 1920 after a decade of debate, constituted a major redirection of public lands policies. The MLA removes major energy and fertilizer minerals from the 1872 "location" system and makes them "leasable." [5] The new system set up systems for leasing in <u>known</u> and <u>unknown</u> minerals areas. Firms were encouraged to explore in unknown areas by a "prospecting permit" that would ripen into a lease involving no bonus payment if valuable deposits were found.   In areas of known mineral value, competitive auctioning of leases would assure a fair return to the Treasury.   The Secretary of the Interior was granted extremely broad discretion to design auction systems, lease terms and conditions, rents, and royalties that would assure both conservation and timely development of the minerals.

Under the original Mineral Leasing Act, states and localities have limited influence over mining activities. The statute contains very standard "savings" language protecting state laws and authorities, but the courts have not interpreted them consistently to sustain state programs. [6]   Other, more recent statutes, such as the National Environmental Policy Act (NEPA), the FLPMA, and the Federal Coal Leasing Amendments Act (FCLAA), give states and localities a significantly larger role.   Nevertheless, they still may not interfere with the implementation of any federal law, policy, or regulation.   Likewise, the extent of state police powers on federal lands is mixed. Although long-standing state oil and gas conservation programs were woven into MLA implementation and are generally accepted as controlling, other state programs may be vulnerable to federal preemption under the MLA. [7]

Although western states lost considerable control over their own economic future during debate on the Mineral Leasing Act, they were able to gain some advantages from revenues distribution. As shown in Table 2, western states theoretically benefit from 90 percent of the lease revenues: 50 percent of the revenues is distributed to the state where the development is located and another 40 percent goes into the "Reclamation Fund," an account established in 1902 to provide start-up money for irrigation projects in western states.   The remaining 10 percent goes to the General Fund of the U.S. Treasury.   None of the revenues are directly earmarked to support the federal minerals management program. [8]

However, the 90 percent state benefit may be more apparent than real. Although receipts are logged in and out of a "Reclamation Fund," this is basically a bookkeeping exercise.   There is no separate "fund" administered for the benefit of western irrigation projects; rather, the money goes into the General Fund of the U.S. Treasury.   Annual federal expenses for water projects typically

TABLE 2.   Major State and County Entitlements under Federal Resource Programs

Program	Formula
National Forest Revenues Act (NFRA)	25 percent of gross revenues to states
Mineral Leasing Act (MLA)	50 percent of gross revenues to states other than Alaska; 40 percent of gross revenues to Reclamation Fund; 10 percent of gross revenues to Federal Treasury
	90 percent of gross revenues to Alaska (includes oil, gas, coal, tar, sands, oil shale, and various fertilizer minerals, such as sulfur, potash, and phosphorus)
National Petroleum Reserve (NPR)	50 percent to state 50 percent to U.S. General Fund
Outer Continental Shelf (OCS) (a)	No sharing off federal lands — states received "marginal sea" instead
Geothermal	Follows MLA formula
Grazing (BLM)	12.5 percent of grazing district revenues to state; 50 percent of Section 15 revenues to state; 50 percent of revenues to district for range improvements
Land and Materials (BLM)	5 percent of gross revenues to states
O & C Grant Lands Coos Bay	75 percent to county 25 percent to U.S. General Fund (mineral leases, timber, surface materials, land sales)
Payment in Lieu of Taxes (PILT)	10 cents to 75 cents per acre of entitlement land depending on (1) population of county and (2) county receipts under six resource revenue programs designated in statute
Land and Water Conservation Fund (LWCF)	Apportionment to states based on fixed share and population

(a)   Does not reflect the recent dispute over allocation of revenues from development of "common" pools at the federal/state boundary in Section 8(g) of the Outer Continental Shelf Leasing Act Amendments.

exceed the fund's 40 percent "share" of minerals revenue by a considerable amount. However, the appearance of having a fund arguably makes it easier for Congress to justify annual appropriations for
those programs. [9]

Congress justified this revenue sharing formula, which was
considerably more generous to states than previous programs [10],
chiefly by noting that valuable mineral lands within western states
had been withdrawn from private development at a time when there
was acute industry interest in developing the resources. The states
anticipated substantial economic activity and population growth
once the resources were available for development.   With that
growth would come need for public services, particularly roads and
schools, which would be financed in many jurisdictions through
property taxes. Although the Mineral Leasing Act and subsequent
statutes preserve the states' right to tax lessees of federal minerals,
this was deemed inadequate to meet the requirements of the growing West.

Although the MLA leasing system was a major change in public
policy, the act was neither comprehensive [11] nor precise as initially passed.   Three kinds of changes have extended the act to
include (1) more minerals, (2) additional categories of federal lands,
and (3) more specific directions regarding congressional priorities to
the Secretary of the Interior. First, the original, official title of the
MLA was "An Act to Promote the Mining of Coal, Phosphate, Oil,
Oil Shale, Gas and Sodium on the Public Domain." Subsequently,
potash, sulfur (in some states), asphalt, and bitumen were added.
Second, coverage has been extended from public domain lands to
include rights-of-way granted by the United States (1930) and lands
acquired by the federal government (1947). [12] When acquired lands
are managed by agencies not in the Department of Interior, such as
the U.S. Forest Service, the revenues are not always distributed
under the MLA standard 50-40-10 formula. For example, revenues
from minerals developed on acquired national forests are distributed
according to the Forest Service formula, which requires that 25
percent of gross revenues be distributed to states for use by the
counties in which forest lands are located. [13]

Third, and most significantly, Congress has given the Secretary
of the Interior new authority and specific directions for implement-
ing the MLA.   Key statutes related to the MLA or specifically
amending it include the 1976 Federal Land Policy and Management
Act (FLPMA), the 1976 Federal Coal Leasing Act Amendments
(FCLAA), and the 1977 Surface Mine Control and Reclamation Act
(SMCRA). Other leasing programs for public minerals are defined in
statutes similar to, but separate from, the MLA. [14] The Geothermal Steam Act of 1970 and the Outer Continental Shelf leasing
program build on MLA experience.

The MLA, therefore, is not a single minerals management program. There is a common core, but the separate treatment of each

mineral reflects the period in which management of the mineral became sufficiently problematical to require action. Moreover, the emphasis on legislation does not mean that controversy has always been resolved in Congress. The Secretary of the Interior has frequently reinterpreted his enormous discretion to adjust and redirect programs. [15]

At different periods, Congress has emphasized different goals in the management of minerals: encouraging exploration and development of public resources; increasing returns to the treasury or maximizing revenue production on the public lands; protecting the environment; protecting surface owners; protecting rights of states and localities to self-determination; promoting competition within industry and preventing monopolies; discouraging speculation; and assuring energy independence for the nation. For example, although the phrase "fair market value" is ubiquitous when discussing the sale of public resources, financial returns have not been viewed as a priority until relatively recently. For many programs, revenues continue to be an insignificant consideration. For example, because Congress was eager to encourage development of oil shale technologies, oil shale lessees may credit development expenditures against 40 percent of their bonus bid and their annual rent. Although this may encourage development, it does not maximize returns to the Treasury. Obviously, some of these goals are compatible but some are not. This has meant that over time answers to our basic questions—valuation, access to the resource, and so forth—have varied considerably for the different minerals.

Because the leasing programs are both complex in their history and provisions and critical in their financial, environmental, and resource availability impact, the MLA and related programs dominate the discussions in Part Two.

CHAPTER FIVE

Minerals Leased Under the Mineral Leasing Act of 1920

OIL AND GAS

The Resource

The nation's extensive "known" [16] onshore oil and gas reserves are concentrated in five subregions of the western states, as shown in Appendix Table 8. Although the demand for oil and gas increased rapidly between the early 1920s and 1972, only recently have federal lands become important sources of domestic oil and gas production. [17] In fact, production from federal oil and gas leases has been concentrated in just a few states. California and Wyoming dominate federal oil production while New Mexico dominates in gas (see Figure 3). Although extensive conservation efforts and high prices [18] have combined to decrease reliance on oil for fuel, development of recent discoveries in the "Overthrust Belt" (which includes parts of Idaho, Montana, Colorado, and Wyoming; see Appendix Figure 3) is expected to be significant in the future.

Although federal oil and gas production was limited until a short time ago, the acreage under lease for oil and gas is surprisingly large—123.8 million acres at the end of 1984, as shown in Figure 3. [19] This figure is large, especially in light of controversy over areas leased for coal, which cover under a million acres (see Figure 4).

Most oil and gas leases are noncompetitive. In 1982, "over-the-counter" and simultaneous filings—the two noncompetitive programs—accounted for 52.9 million out of a total of 53.9 million acres leased in that year and 97 percent of the leases. Typically, about 3 percent of the leases issued are competitive. [20] Given the concentration of leasing in unknown areas, it is perhaps not surprising that only 11 percent of all leases (covering 8.6 million acres) were producing or "producible" (likely to produce). Thus, a substantial portion of the revenues collected from oil and gas leases (approximately 38 percent) [21] are from rents paid by leases that

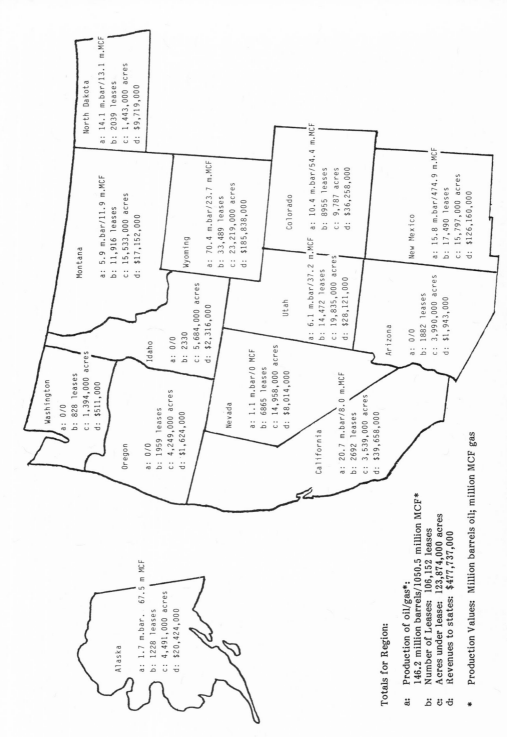

Alaska

a: 1.7 m.bar. 67.5 m MCF

b: 1228 leases
c: 4,491,000 acres
d: $20,424,000

Washington

a: 0/0
b: 828 leases
c: 1,394,000 acres
d: $511,000

Oregon

a: 0/0
b: 1959 leases
c: 4,249,000 acres
d: $1,624,000

Idaho

a: 0/0
b: 2330
c: 5,684,000 acres
d: $2,316,000

Nevada

a: 1.1 m.bar/0 MCF
b: 6865 leases
c: 14,958,000 acres
d: $8,014,000

California

a: 20.7 m.bar/8.0 m.MCF
b: 2692 leases
c: 3,539,000 acres
d: $39,658,000

Montana

a: 5.9 m.bar/11.9 m.MCF
b: 11,916 leases
c: 15,533,000 acres
d: $17,152,000

North Dakota

a: 14.1 m.bar/13.1 m.MCF
b: 2039 leases
c: 1,443,000 acres
d: $9,719,000

Wyoming

a: 70.4 m.bar/23.7 m.MCF
b: 33,489 leases
c: 23,219,000 acres
d: $185,838,000

Colorado

a: 10.4 m.bar/54.4 m.MCF
b: 8955 leases
c: 9,787 acres
d: $36,258,000

Utah

a: 6.1 m.bar/37.2 m.MCF
b: 14,472 leases
c: 19,835,000 acres
d: $28,121,000

Arizona

a: 0/0
b: 1882 leases
c: 3,990,000 acres
d: $1,943,000

New Mexico

a: 15.8 m.bar/474.9 m.MCF
b: 17,490 leases
c: 15,797,000 acres
d: $126,160,000

Totals for Region:

a: Production of oil/gas*:
146.2 million barrels/1050.5 million MCF*

b: Number of Leases: 106,152 leases

c: Acres under lease: 123,874,000 acres

d: Revenues to states: $477,737,000

* Production Values: Million barrels oil; million MCF gas

FIGURE 2. Oil and Gas Production and Revenues from Federal Lands (1984)

64

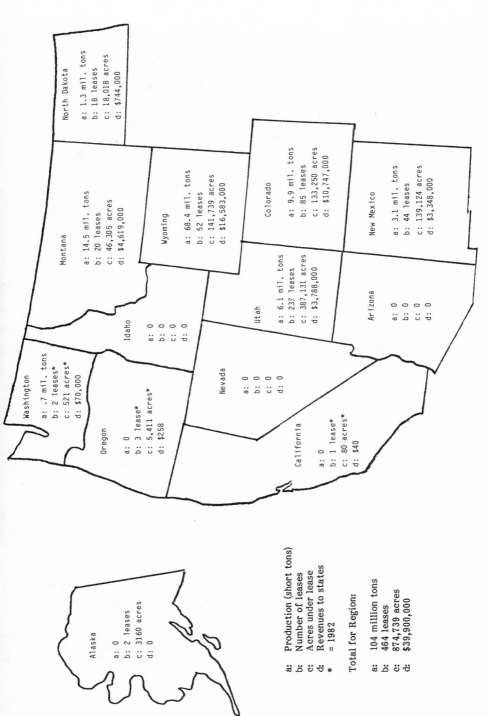

FIGURE 4. Coal Production and Revenues from Federal Lands (1984).

Washington
a: .7 mil. tons
b: 2 leases*
c: 521 acres*
d: $70,000

Oregon
a: 0
b: 3 lease*
c: 5,411 acres*
d: $258

Montana
a: 14.5 mil. tons
b: 20 leases
c: 46,305 acres
d: $4,619,000

North Dakota
a: 1.3 mil. tons
b: 18 leases
c: 18,018 acres
d: $744,000

Idaho
a: 0
b: 0
c: 0
d: 0

Wyoming
a: 68.4 mil. tons
b: 52 leases
c: 141,739 acres
d: $16,583,000

Nevada
a: 0
b: 0
c: 0
d: 0

Utah
a: 6.1 mil. tons
b: 237 leases
c: 387,131 acres
d: $3,788,000

Colorado
a: 9.9 mil. tons
b: 85 leases
c: 133,250 acres
d: $10,747,000

California
a: 0
b: 1 lease*
c: 80 acres*
d: $40

Arizona
a: 0
b: 0
c: 0
d: 0

New Mexico
a: 3.1 mil. tons
b: 44 leases
c: 139,124 acres
d: $3,348,000

Alaska
a: 0
b: 2 leases
c: 3160 acres
d: 0

a: Production (short tons)
b: Number of leases
c: Acres under lease
d: Revenues to states
* = 1982

Total for Region:

a: 104 million tons
b: 464 leases
c: 874,739 acres
d: $39,900,000

65

most likely will never produce. The breakdown on those revenues—total collections by state and the state share—is shown in Table 3 for the years 1976, 1978, 1980, and 1982.

Although the basic MLA concepts define federal oil and gas leasing, their application to oil and gas is altered by unusual properties of the resource that affect development. Oil is found in pools or reservoirs that migrate underground without regard to surface ownership, and is sometimes under pressure from accompanying gas reserves. [22] Because oil migrates, the earliest pumper can capture all the oil unless others who own the land above the same pool begin to pump or otherwise move to protect their rights in the pool. However, if overlying owners pump competitively, the result is that any natural gas pressure present may be dissipated and the oil becomes difficult, or even impossible, to extract. More generally, a supply glut caused by competitive pumping usually drives prices down. Almost inevitably, the result of unregulated pumping is waste. Therefore, although the oil and gas program reflects the MLA's emphasis on competition and opposition to monopolies, Congress adjusted the law to make room for some form of cooperative development of oil pools. [23] The complexity of these agreements makes monitoring production from a specific federally leased portion of the pool difficult.

This cooperative pool development situation is complicated by the patterns of landholdings in oil fields. A federal lease rarely grants access to a developable pool of oil because land ownership is sufficiently fragmented in a way that the federal government does not usually own all the land overlying the entire underground formation.

Pricing of Oil and Gas Leases

Despite the unusual physical properties of oil and gas, the process for pricing oil and gas leases begins with the familiar distinction between known and unknown geologic structures mandated in the MLA. [24] There are actually three systems: (1) known areas are allocated competitively; (2) leases for unknown areas never previously leased are available "over the counter" to the "first qualified applicant"; (3) terminating leases in unknown areas are reoffered by lottery under what is frequently called the "SIMO" or "SOG" system.

All of these leasing systems have become increasingly controversial. Two principal criticisms of noncompetitive leasing are that it frustrates development by fragmenting ownership and diverts revenues from public beneficiaries to speculators, gamblers, and crooks. The major criticism of the competitive system is that current methods for defining a "known" area are inaccurate. As a

TABLE 3. Oil and Gas Receipts and State Revenue Shares (1976-1984)

	1976		1978		1980		1982		1984	
	Total Collections	State Allocation	Total Collections	State Allocation	Total Collections	State Allocation	Total Collections	State Allocation	Total Collections	Payment to State
Alaska	$2,283,624	$2,055,262	$1,624,249	$1,461,824	$2,942,044	$2,647,840	$80,343,566(a)	$44,467,505	$29,375,669	$20,424,148
Arizona	628,748	235,780	1,272,799	636,223	3,969,698	1,984,849	9,692,717	4,846,358	3,858,047	1,942,661
California	15,795,265	5,757,092	20,267,533	8,687,913	43,912,984	20,935,528	59,096,686	28,180,504	59,872,939	39,657,621
Colorado	25,380,964	9,514,501	29,170,098	14,582,005	36,749,019	18,342,465	68,200,696	34,081,402	66,852,615	36,257,590
Idaho	743,084	278,656	2,090,251	1,045,126	3,072,487	1,536,244	7,828,250	3,914,125	4,632,230	2,315,954
Montana	10,911,016	4,086,108	12,876,176	6,434,989	17,443,607	8,715,408	27,282,282	13,566,827	30,226,549	17,151,832
Nevada	1,984,579	744,217	7,786,768	3,893,384	13,018,793	6,509,396	23,213,741	11,606,870	16,043,397	8,013,590
New Mexico	68,955,027	25,855,992	105,910,062	52,954,502	198,318,751	99,152,732	275,269,506	137,572,428	250,979,373	126,160,058
North Dakota	1,958,993	718,568	1,321,588	649,854	8,305,834	4,081,489	12,881,532	6,377,946	14,874,078	9,718,962
Oregon	78,607	29,478	78,409	39,204	65,174	32,587	8,426,394	4,213,197	3,234,053	1,624,451
Utah	14,481,954	5,345,255	21,182,869	10,513,364	29,035,861	14,460,410	54,518,821	27,189,084	55,400,581	28,118,354
Washington	710	266	64,524	32,262	67,414	33,707	1,147,954	573,977	1,021,794	510,897
Wyoming	91,636,179	34,363,538	123,940,852	61,970,384	213,923,786	106,959,473	313,282,283	156,611,751	352,390,521	185,838,533
Regional Total	$234,838,750	$88,984,712	$327,586,178	$162,901,033	$570,825,452	$285,392,129	$914,184,428	$273,201,976	$888,761,846	$477,734,651
National Total	$240,645,422		$340,330,950		$583,496,310		$1,146,117,340		$905,416,826	

Note: Like the other leased mineral tables in this report (see Tables 5, 8, 9 and 11), this table reports revenues from leases on public domain lands, whether the lands are administered by the BLM or other agencies. Consequently, revenues from leases on public domain land in national forests are included here; mineral revenues from leases on acquired forest lands are included in Table 12. (There are no acquired military land leases in the thirteen western states.) The state share columns through 1982 and the BLM component of 1984 are based on estimated allocations to the state, taking 37.5 percent of adjusted total receipts for 1976, and 50 percent of adjusted total receipts for 1978-1982. The formula for Alaska is 90 percent of receipts, except for National Petroleum Reserve revenues (50 percent). Adjustments were made for nonshared oil and gas revenues, based on data provided by the BLM. For further information on data and methods, see Appendix E.

Source: 1976-1982: Public Land Statistics, 1976-Table 112, 1978-Table 117, 1980-Table 108, 1982-Table 105. 1984 Collection Data: Public Land Statistics (published August 1985), Table 103 ("Receipts from Mineral Leases, Licenses and Permits on Public Lands and Acquired Military Lands," preliminary data); Table 103A ("Receipts from Oil and Gas Right-of-Way Rentals and Mineral Leases, Licenses and Permits on Public Lands"). Table 103 represents Minerals Management Service receipts only. Table 103A shows Bureau of Land Management receipts. 1984 Payments Data: Minerals Management Service (actual payments made in fiscal year 1984, including oil and gas royalty audit findings and windfall profits tax reimbursements). Allocations of BLM receipts have been estimated from Public Land Statistics, Table 103A.

(a) Indicates over $69.6 million from the National Petroleum Reserve, which is shared 50 percent.

result, many valuable areas are leased as unknown areas, thus shorting the state governments. These criticisms will probably lead to redefinition of oil leasing in the very near future. Moreover, the question of the appropriate time for environmental impact assessment has been raised repeatedly in recent litigation.

Competitive Leasing in KGSs. Leases for known geologic structures (KGSs) accounted for less than 3 percent of all leases in 1982. Competitive leases are issued completely at the discretion of the Secretary of the Interior. A KGS is defined in the statute as land with "proven production." Once a "producible well is completed," the surrounding land (generally about one square mile), is designated by the U.S. Geological Survey as a KGS. [25]

It is important to note that this KGS definition is based on proven rather than potential production. Although it is arguable that oil reserves, unlike other minerals, cannot be known until they are actually in production [26], basing the KGS designation on certain knowledge rather than probability of success or site potential has created widely acknowledged problems. For example, controversy in the Fort Chafee (Arkansas) and Amos Draw (Wyoming) oil fields arose because tracts widely recognized as valuable, but not meeting the statutory criteria for a KGS, were leased as unknown areas, severely reducing returns to the states. This conflict led to a long-promised overhaul of the department's KGS identification system prompted by the Arkla case. [27] The department's new procedures were designed to assure that competitive leasing takes place where oil reserves are likely to be valuable, but the controversy continues nonetheless. The Eighth Circuit Court of Appeals recently upheld the Arkla trial court. The court directed the department to weigh "competitive interest" and "all geologic data" regarding a tract when categorizing an area as "known" or "unknown." Department officials argued that those requirements are difficult or impossible to implement and are also beyond their statutory authority. [28] However, the Supreme Court declined to review the Arkla decision.

New legislation may be required to resolve the issue, and Congress is currently considering numerous proposals. The most typical provide a two-tier system: new leases would first be offered competitively; if there are no takers, the lease would later be reoffered noncompetitively. This would have the effect of eliminating the need to make the troublesome known/unknown distinction.

Under the current system, once the KGS is identified and is available for leasing, a bonus bid competitive sale is advertised for two to five weeks. Sales are preceded by a tract evaluation to determine an acceptable minimum bid or "fair market value." The utility of these evaluations is in dispute, given limited geologic information on which they are based and the costs that would be incurred in conducting a thorough assessment. [29] Leases for a maximum of 640 acres are offered at an annual rental of two dollars per acre. Royalties are also set in advance and stated in the sale notice. They vary from 12.5 to 25 percent of market value for oil and from 12.5 to 16.66 percent for gas. The higher rates correspond to higher rates of production once the lease is developed. However, as noted below, determining the value of oil or gas production against which to compute the royalty is controversial indeed. Once a discovery is made, minimum royalties of one dollar per acre in lieu of rental are due annually. [30]

Noncompetitive Leasing in Unknown Areas. Lease tracts outside of a KGS are offered on a noncompetitive basis. Tract size ranges from 640 acres (unless in a unitized field) to 2,560 acres. Rent is fixed at one dollar per acre annually. Royalties on producing, noncompetitive leases are set at 12.5 percent of production. There are two kinds of noncompetitive leases. Areas that are not in a KGS and have never been leased before are offered "over the counter." Leases that have expired or terminated are reoffered under a "simultaneous" bidding or lottery system.

New Leases: Over the Counter. Though the name might imply otherwise, over-the-counter leases cannot be purchased like a grocery item. An interested party identifies an area and submits a lease application, a seventy-five dollar filing fee, and the first year's rent. Although the Secretary of the Interior clearly has the discretion to grant the lease or not, in practice the department treats leasing to qualified applicants as nondiscretionary. [31] The Forest Service format for processing oil and gas lease applications shown in Appendix Figure 4 confirms that most of the work on the application is done by low-level federal land managers, located near the area in question. Typically, decisions are based on the land-use planning process. Areas for which other uses are identified are designated specifically unsuited to leasing; other lands are presumed acceptable for leasing unless proven otherwise.

Such a system requires little information on the minerals resources. On the other hand, a lease application creates a need to assess alternatives and potential impacts and to design stipulations for the lease. Increased interest in leasing in recent years has collided with escalating data requirements in environmental protection programs. Both the Forest Service and the BLM have large backlogs of lease applications waiting to be processed.

The agencies have argued that because so few leases are ever explored or developed (about 20 percent and 5 percent, respectively) the specific environmental impacts of a lease are difficult to identify and thus to analyze. It is more effective and efficient to do the analysis when a company has made a firm, specific proposal, at the "APD" (application for permit to drill) phase. The Sierra Club has successfully argued that such an approach precludes the analysis of cumulative effects and postpones consideration of environmental costs of leasing until after irrevocable decisions have been made.

Recent litigation required that the Forest Service complete an environmental impact statement rather than rely on a less extensive environmental analysis whenever a lease permitting surface occupancy was issued. The question of whether lease stipulations such as "nonsurface occupancy" (NSO) stipulations or "contingent right" stipulations (CRS) are being used in lieu of timely environmental analysis has intensified controversy surrounding land-use planning for oil and gas leasing. [32]

Reissuing Terminated Leases: The Lottery. The simultaneous filing system known as "SIMO" or "SOG" is even more controversial even though it simply reallocates terminated or expired leases. To avoid the effort (and occasional violence) involved in determining which of the many applicants filed first, the secretary long ago decided to presume that all the applications were filed simultaneously and the successful applicant is selected in a drawing. The result is a lottery, open to virtually anybody who can pay the mandatory seventy-five dollar filing fee. In 1982, 37 percent of the 19,762 noncompetitive leases were issued via the lottery. [33] A common scam is for a "service" industry to purport to offer assistance—for as much as $200 to $500 per application—in filing for oil leases. Unsuspecting citizens are often misled by these unsavory but enormously profitable operations. A number of western attorneys general have concentrated enforcement efforts against this fraud.

Resource management problems arise from the fact that terminating leases are frequently attractive to speculators as well as to bona fide operators. BLM estimates that fewer than 5 percent of all lease applicants engage in actual oil development. More commonly, successful applicants resell their leases to bona fide operators within two years. This practice suggests that there is in fact a highly competitive market for the noncompetitive leases.

It is frequently argued that the government could capture additional revenues with a competitive lease allocation system. The sevently-five dollar filing fee, raised recently from ten dollars, cut the number of lottery participants in half, but problems with speculation and fraudulent filing "services" continue. Moreover, the increased revenues raise the possibility that the lottery fees could exceed the potential revenues from bonus bids in a competitive system. In February 1984, the Secretary of the Interior announced that SOG applications, like over-the-counter applications, must be accompanied by a deposit of one year's rent. [34] Congressional advocates of all-competitive leasing have urged cutting the department's funding for the lottery, but the program continues. Controversy is likely to persist as some state officials are demanding that revenue sharing formulas apply to the increased filing fee receipts as well as to production revenues.

Access: Who Should Develop Oil and Gas Resources

Noncompetitive leasing is defended primarily as needed protection for small independent operators. Independent producers argue fervently that they would be eliminated by an all-competitive leasing system. They also argue that if they were cut out, exploration and revenues would be reduced while oil and gas development on federal lands would be turned over to "the majors." Advocates of all-competitive leasing argue just the opposite. Data to resolve the conflict are not available.

Acreage limitations also bear on the question of who has access to the resource. A 640-acre limit on competitive leases is designed to permit smaller companies to buy into the system, and in fact, approximately 85 percent of the competitive leases do go to "independents." [35]   For over-the-counter noncompetitive leases, the acreage limit is 2,560 acres; 10,240 is the maximum size for a SIMO lease. [36]   For all leases, there is a statewide limit of 246,080 acres for any individual or firm. However, acres held in a unit or cooperative plan are not counted against the limit, which severely reduces their import. During discussions of lease policy the need for acreage limits to sustain smaller "independents" is balanced against the need for larger tract sizes to facilitate exploration.

Which Lands Should Be Developed

Land-use planning is nominally the major focus in identifying lands for development. Other factors--the noncompetitive lease system, acreage limitations, and the costs of minerals information—are probably just as important.

Determining which lands should be developed is partially restricted by difficulties in assembling fragmented rights to a promising site. The problem of mixed ownership—federal, state, and diverse private holders of rights in the same field—is exacerbated by brokering of noncompetitive leases. Because the SIMO system is open to such broad participation, it is not difficult for unsavory operators to obtain speculative leases, subdivide them into forty-acre parcels, and resell them to the general public at inflated rates "with the representation that they contain valuable energy resources." [37] This fraud subdivides ownership to the point that if oil is discovered it becomes costly and difficult to assemble rights to develop an area from the dispersed owners. In March 1984 the Interior Secretary halted further subdivision of federal oil and gas leases. [38]

Acreage limitations also influence which lands will be developed. According to the Master Report on Mineral Leasing for the PLLRC, acreage limits prevent the major oil firms from exploring lands in which the independents are not interested. [39] That, in turn, may lower the bonus bids and also create an incentive for abandoning a mediocre well when a more promising one comes along. [40] The acreage limits may also inhibit secondary and tertiary recovery, which may require more land than the initial development. [41]

The high cost of minerals information undercuts the role of planning in selecting sites for oil and gas development. In many areas outside KGSs, where minerals information is limited, the government relies chiefly on private enterprise for exploration. Therefore, a high degree of uncertainty exists as to the promise of particular locations for minerals development that cannot be resolved by data gathered during land planning. Therefore, industry argues, oil and gas exploration becomes a residual use. Lands are open to exploration and leasing unless they are ruled out as too environmentally sensitive or appropriate for other uses.

Timing of Oil and Gas Development

The "fugitive" nature of oil and gas limits the secretary's control over diligence and other timing-of-development issues. Any rights holder in a pool can, by initiating extraction, create an incentive for others to go into production or into a cooperative or "unitization" agreement to exploit the reserve. Federal onshore oil and gas resources are interspersed with state and private lands, and federal regulations are sufficiently general to accommodate specific state requirements. Thus, timing of production from onshore federal leases is largely "guided by state law—for instance in the realm of well spacing, pooling, and proportionate production of gas and oil in oil-and-gas reservoirs." [42]

There are, however, applicable federal criteria. Competitive leases are for five years primary term; noncompetitive leases are for ten. Either can be extended for two years by paying "delay rentals" in lieu of royalties from development, as long as drilling is in progress. After that, the lease simply expires. Leases producing commercial quantities or capable of commercial production but being reworked or redrilled are extended automatically.

Given present agitation to develop a comprehensive—or all-competitive—federal oil and gas program, it is worth noting that the federal system may have relatively little impact on the timing of production of oil and gas for national needs. The small market share of federal onshore production and the intermingling of federal, state, and diverse private holdings afford the federal administration relatively little leverage. Regulating production levels is presently a state function. Some states—among them New Mexico—have statutes that regulate the production of oil relative to "market demand." In New Mexico, a regulatory commission makes monthly estimates of demand for two producing areas in the state and allocates output per well. In recent years, high demand has allowed production at well-capacity or the maximum efficient rate of a reservoir. [43]

Intensity of Development

No statutes specifically regulate oil and gas development. The four-stage process established by administrative action (shown in Appendix Table 5) suggests that oil and gas leasing is less complex procedurally than coal leasing. No surface occupancy (NSOs) and contingent right stipulations (CRSs) are a peculiar and increasingly controversial feature of the process. The government has granted CRS leases in advance of the mandatory environmental analyses. The agency is freed to meet its numerical goals for reducing the backlog in applications, by provisionally granting the lease, "contingent" upon identification of stipulations, restrictions, and mitigation requirements. Those are identified subsequently, as part of the planning and environmental assessment process surrounding the APD (application for a permit to drill). Obviously, these CRS leases are not wholly satisfactory to industry, which in effect pays rent to secure its place in line for a "real" lease later. In the Forest Service, applicants refusing a lease with CRSs lose their priority. BLM managers let the applicant choose between a CRS lease or delay.
    Another source of controversy is the use of NSO stipulations. Like the CRS, a NSO provision expedites lease processing by granting a lease that allows the holder limited access or requires slant drilling. Recent litigation suggests that the Forest Service's "phased NEPA compliance" is not acceptable. It will not, however, be easy to define what is acceptable because so much is at stake. [44] Industry and environmental groups both have reservations about the CRS and NSO "stips" and their current role in leasing. Although the stipulations do speed up the processing of lease applications, they may also short-circuit timely environmental impact assessments. It is also not clear what kinds of rights are conveyed to the successful applicant. [45] Some of these concerns are expressed in environmentalists' efforts in shaping a new oil and gas program: a "suitability" test to identify lands appropriate for leasing has been suggested. [46] This concept is borrowed from timber harvest and coal-leasing programs.

Participation

Participation in the oil and gas program has two unusual components, beyond the normal elements indicated by reference to NEPA, FLPMA [47], and NFMA in Chapter 3. The first is related to the historic role of states in oil and gas conservation. The second is the more current, less defined role of states in minerals royalty accounting.

States were first to act to regulate oil and gas production. Generally, state statutes establish a regulatory body with broad discretion to conserve resources by control of drilling and production practices, spacing of wells, and reporting of output. State authority, generally speaking, controls drillers on the public domain. State and federal authorities have historically worked together in relative harmony to achieve similar goals. However, the potential for conflict and for federal preemption of state programs is always present. [48]

States seek a role in federal minerals auditing to ensure that the payment and collection of royalties has been proper and complete. The Federal Oil and Gas Royalty Management Act of 1982 (FOGRMA) did not incorporate state proposals that they be allowed to take over accounting and collecting, deducting their share of the revenue due prior to turning the remainder over to the federal government. Nevertheless, significant state participation is authorized at critical points: a state role in defining information revenue reporting requirements; agreements for cooperative inspections, audits, investigations, and enforcement procedures; and delegating to the states authority for inspections, audits, and investigations. Eight states previously participated with the Minerals Management Service (MMS) in a Cooperative Audit Program authorized under FOGRMA. Currently, eight states and one Indian tribe have petitioned successfully for a delegation of authority to take over the audit program. Funds to compensate states for that effort, also authorized by FOGRMA, have been included in the fiscal year 1985 and 1986 budgets. [49]

Distribution of the Revenues

Oil and gas royalties, rents, and bonuses derived from most leases are distributed 50 percent to the state of origin, 40 percent to the Reclamation Fund, and 10 percent to the U.S. Treasury. Except for National Petroleum Reserve lands, 90 percent of revenues from leases in Alaska go to the state; the Petroleum Reserve formula is 50 percent. Leases on acquired lands do not follow this pattern. The funds on acquired lands are distributed according to the distribution of revenues collected by the surface management agency. Table 3 shows states' shares of oil and gas revenues.

Oil and gas royalty management was completely redefined by FOGRMA, which was enacted following prolonged public outcry regarding abuse in the program and the publication of the Linowes Commission Report on Fiscal Accountability of the Nation's Energy Resources. [50]   Principal provisions of FOGRMA authorize the cooperative federal-state audit program described above and require the Secretary of the Interior to establish a comprehensive data collection and production monitoring system, to set up information requirements for lessee and operator reporting, and to provide for enforcement, including annual site inspections.

All of these provisions present complex and controversial issues. The MMS is now required to develop administrative programs and computer capabilities under intense time pressure and without a consensus on basic concepts. Implementation has been further retarded by lack of personnel, budget cuts, and administrative confusion. The MMS was only recently established and shares record-keeping responsibilities with BLM. BLM programs are, however, in flux due to a recent reorganization in which the Conservation Division of the U.S. Geological Survey (long responsible for key aspects of lease evaluation) was moved to BLM. [51] MMS estimates that full development of regulations and information management systems could take a decade. [52]

Although the problems of revenue distribution are wide-ranging, three specific areas of confusion merit discussion: accounting, auditing, and key definitions.

Royalty Accounting. Royalty accounting presents special problems in the onshore oil and gas field. Record keeping and production monitoring is complicated by the minutiae of cooperative development ("unitization") agreements, and assignments of subdivisions of those agreements to heirs or others indicated by the lessee. [53] The accounting has been further complicated by the (presently discontinued) brokering of noncompetitive leases. These factors do not justify continuing fraud and malfeasance in accounting programs, but they suggest one reason why resolving the problems has been difficult.

Three information management systems have been under development since 1981 to handle the accounting problems: PAAS, a production accounting and auditing system; AFS, an auditing and financial system to process, account for, and distribute royalties; and BRASS, an accounting system for bonuses. The basic idea is that PAAS, the production accounting system, will interface with AFS, the royalty system, to assure that royalties are being properly paid on the oil and gas produced. [54] However, the PAAS system was designed without input from industry, which must supply the pertinent data. Both the General Accounting Office and the House Interior and Insular Affairs Committee recommended that MMS delay contracting for the computer system until major problems could be resolved. [55] One major problem is that the financial data system (AFS) is set on a thirty-day cycle while the production data system (PAAS) is set on a forty-five-day cycle, and it is not at all clear when—or if—the two will mesh. [56] The system is costly and complex. Recently, there have been indications that the computer is not secure and is subject to outside manipulation. However, MMS has proceeded amidst great controversy and criticism. In May 1985, MMS contracted with Martin Marietta to provide the mainframe computer to process all the information. At that time, Robert Boldt, MMS Associate Director for Royalty Management, stated that the agency's June 1986 target for bringing the full system into operation was reasonable. [57] Subsequently, a decision to implement PAAS for all onshore leases was deferred until late 1986.

Auditing. States are also concerned with ongoing audits to collect lost revenues from previous underpayments and monitor future payments. FOGRMA provided for two kinds of state participation in the auditing process. States may initiate negotiation of cooperative audit agreements for an extendable three-year period. States are nominally to be reimbursed 50 percent of their contribution, but funding to reimburse states is dependent on annual appropriations. Alternatively, the state can present a plan of operations and petition for delegation of audit authority. Again, although the Royalty Management Act authorizes 100 percent reimbursement of state expenses, appropriations are not guaranteed. Rules to implement those programs emerged slowly over many months, and funding of the state efforts has been a continuing source of frustration. The states argue that the federal government, acting under the 1982 Royalty Act on behalf of western revenue recipients, should pay administrative expenses. [58] The Reagan administration has responded by proposing to deduct the cost of royalty management from onshore revenues before distribution of the states' revenue shares. Figures shown in Appendix Table 9 suggest that this method could cost an estimated $12.9 million, while payments to the states (without the deduction) are around $715 million. [59] States, of course, do not generally support the administration's proposal. They also oppose a Linowes Commission proposal to set up a fund for audits and inspections largely from offshore leasing revenues. [60]

Implementation of these state audit programs has been difficult. Negotiating the initial cooperative audit agreements was slow; nevertheless, joint audit programs with eight states netted almost $34 million as of June 1985, according to MMS calculations (see Table 4). In January 1984, $10.7 million had been distributed to the states. [61] Currently all eight affected states (Wyoming, Montana, Oklahoma, Colorado, North Dakota, California, Nevada, and Utah) have successfully petitioned for a delegation of audit responsibilities. [62] Continuing dispute focuses on efforts to get federal funds appropriated for the state auditing programs.

Although most of the problems that the cooperative audit program has encountered thus far reflect differences between state and federal perspectives, industry has also expressed concern. If individual states with delegated audit authority decide to disregard

TABLE 4. Delinquent Oil and Gas Royalties Collected through the Joint Federal-State Audit Program

	Total Collected to Date (6/85)	Collections 1/1/84 to 12/31/84
California	$ 458,417	$ 57,405
Colorado	7,755,347	1,059,390
Montana	477,692	600,089
Nevada	328,454	276,267
New Mexico	1,131,568	38,759
North Dakota	749,920	142,596
Utah	365,037	45,886
Wyoming	22,678,532	5,042,542
Total	$33,944,967	$7,262,934

Source: Minerals Management Service, Royalty Compliance Division.

secretarial determinations regarding royalty management, industry could be caught in the middle. [63] Industry is also concerned that in addition to the MMS and the states, the Office of the Inspector General also has authority to audit federal royalty payments; industry fears a three-ring circus.

Definitional Problems. In addition to these pervasive accounting and auditing problems, the oil and gas revenue sharing program is confounded by disagreement on fundamental concepts. Two examples are windfall profit taxes and product valuation. The states contend that present accounting practice for calculating windfall profits tax unfairly reduces their share. The tax is presently deducted from gross royalty receipts before calculating the states' revenue shares. Approximately 13 percent of total onshore oil and gas revenues, or about $163.6 million annually, is at issue. This procedure has been challenged, and in New Mexico v. Regan a federal district court found in favor of the state. On appeal the case was remanded to the U.S. Court of Claims, and the Supreme Court declined to review the matter. [64] While the states continue to await a court of claims decision, MMS took partially remedial action. An audit of the windfall profit tax program proved that there had been significant overwithholding from the states and the excess was returned in 1984.

A second definitional problem, one underlying all of the above issues, is the question of valuation. Royalty payments and therefore revenue sharing are ostensibly calculated based on the "value of production." However, determining the value of production is complex, and valuation errors are the biggest cause of royalty under-payment. [65]   Some industry experts favor valuing production in terms of the contract price for which the lessee sells the oil or gas. Critics point out, however, that many of the contracts were signed in the 1960s when prices were lower than today and that many of the contracts were made between subunits of vertically integrated enterprises or in other settings not constituting "arms length nego-tiations." States and other beneficiaries of the revenues advocate valuing production based on current well-head prices.

Marathon Oil recently lost a major controversy with the Depart-ment of the Interior over valuation. The court ordered Marathon to calculate the value of liquified natural gas by deducting transporta-tion and liquifaction costs from gross sale proceeds, in accord with Interior's royalty orders. Marathon had agreed to establish the value by comparison with "other gas sold from the same field." [66]

The long awaited MMS guidelines for valuation have still not been completed.   Their publication will probably not, however, resolve the issue and further litigation appears inevitable. [67] The states' concerns about a recent MMS effort to define valuation criteria under FOGRMA [68] were summarized in a recent memo from the Chair of the Conference of Western Attorney Generals to Interior Secretary Hodel. Challenging Interior's proposal to replace the current valuation scheme (NTL-5 [Notice to Operators and Lessee) with four to six options among which a producer could choose, the conference queried pointedly, "Is there any reason to believe that companies will not choose the cheapest alternative and MMS will support that choice?" [69]

Tar Sands: Close Relative of Oil and Gas

Beginning in the early 1960s, the Department of the Interior declined to grant tar sands leases for development because the government could not differentiate between tar sands and oil and gas. [70] However, the push to develop alternative energy sources after the oil embargo in the mid-1970s focused renewed congres-sional attention on the elusive resource.   The Utah congressional delegation has led this effort, as 90 percent of the estimated 30 billion barrel tar sand reserves in the U.S. are located in that state.

The Combined Hydrocarbon Leasing Act of 1981 redefines oil to include tar sands. It provided: (1) for converting existing oil and gas and other appropriate leases in areas identified as special tar sand areas (STSAs) to include tar sands, and (2) for noncompetitive leases to be issued conveying rights to develop all hydrocarbons in the lease area except coal, oil shale, and gilsonite. [71]

In order to convert an existing lease, the operator must file a plan of operation for development of the tar sands. The Department must respond within fifteen months. [72] Because the price of oil has fallen considerably since 1981, tar sands leasing has returned to the back burner.

COAL

The Resource

The Arab oil embargo and federal air pollution regulations enhanced utilization of low-sulfur western coal, which was used sparingly prior to 1974. [73] During the 1970s oil prices skyrocketed and it became cheaper to transport low-sulfur western coal to eastern markets than to build scrubbers required by the Clean Air Act to burn high-sulfur eastern coal. [74] Wyoming, Montana, and New Mexico, as shown in Table 5, account for the major share of the growing coal production from federal lands.   Alabama and Kentucky contribute miniscule amounts. Increased production from western lands during the 1967 - 1983 period compared to eastern coal production is noted in Table 6.   The dropoff in total coal production for 1983 suggests that the 1970s coal boom slowed in the generally weak economy. [75]

BLM management of federal coal parallels this history of coal use: Table 7 reflects a forty-year period in which a small number of leases were granted fairly casually, followed by rapidly increased leasing during the 1960s, still without a coal program. The Secretary of the Interior halted coal leasing in 1971 so the department could evaluate the situation.   Increased leasing combined with declining production led to criticism of speculatively held leases and charges that the government was not getting a fair return for its coal.   Throughout the early 1970s, Congress and the department competed with each other to devise a federal coal program responsive to environmental pressures and then to President Ford's "Project Energy Independence."   The moratorium and controversy over program design have continued, with brief respites, to the present.

In 1976, Congress passed the Federal Coal Leasing Amendments Act (FCLAA), which made major changes in coal leasing.   It is therefore important to be aware, when discussing a lease or applicable regulations, whether it is a pre- or post-FCLAA lease. In 1979, the Carter administration promulgated regulations to recast the Ford coal regulations, which had been hastily redrawn to comport with FCLAA. Although leasing was proceeding on a limited scale in 1982, the Reagan administration promulgated another new set of regulations.   Litigation and congressional irritation with policies of former Secretary Watt followed. In October 1985, yet another draft EIS on yet another revised set of coal program regulations was issued and met with predictable dismay from most observers. However, softness in the coal market and a growing consensus that sufficient coal is already under lease may relieve the pressure on the program.

TABLE 5. Coal Receipts and State Revenue Shares (1976–1984)

	1976		1978		1980		1982		1984	
	Total Collections	State Allocation	Total Collections	State Allocation	Total Collections	State Allocation	Total Collections	State Allocation	Total Collections	Payment to State
Alaska	$39,399	$35,459	$3,350	$3,015	$2,475	$2,228	$2,320	$2,088	0	0
Arizona	0	0	0	0	0	0	0	0	0	0
California	80	30	0	0	80	40	80	40	80	40
Colorado	776,783	291,294	1,158,467	579,234	5,797,536	2,898,768	16,557,718	8,278,859	21,867,541	10,747,134
Idaho	0	0	0	0	0	0	0	0	0	0
Montana	1,531,889	574,458	1,556,905	778,452	1,555,239	777,620	7,609,160	3,804,580	9,397,645	4,618,662
Nevada	0	0	4,031	2,016	0	0	0	0	0	0
New Mexico	326,622	122,483	800,297	400,148	1,524,095	762,048	9,689,104	4,844,552	6,697,047	3,348,523
North Dakota	70,936	26,601	115,558	57,779	295,503	147,752	1,257,191	628,596	1,488,247	744,124
Oregon	3,411	1,279	0	0	2,429	1,214	9,916	4,958	15,362	258
Utah	948,902	355,838	1,165,171	582,586	3,974,484	1,987,242	9,601,866	4,800,933	7,722,148	3,788,156
Washington	1,727	648	0	0	280	140	12,996	6,498	139,947	69,974
Wyoming	3,287,157	1,232,684	6,529,667	3,264,834	8,726,530	4,363,465	24,455,978	12,227,989	33,803,452	16,582,930
Regional Total	$6,986,906	$2,613,774	$11,333,446	$5,668,063	$21,878,651	$10,940,317	$69,196,329	$34,599,012	$81,131,389	$39,899,721
National Total	$7,184,132		$11,908,915		$22,348,846		$70,851,507		$81,420,750	

Source: Public Land Statistics: 1976–Table 112; 1978–Table 117; 1980–Table 108; 1982–Table 105; 1984–Table 104 was used for total collections. State payment data for fiscal year 1984, Minerals Management Service. State allocations for 1976–1982 are estimates (see Table 3 note).

TABLE 6. Coal Production from Federal and Other Lands 1967-1983 (Millions of Tons)

	1967	**1976**	**1980**	**1983**
Total West	29.0	135.4	251.0	281.8
Federal Lands (a)	n.a.	33.4	71.9	105.1
Total East	522.4	542.4	578.7	503.0
Total U.S.	551.4	677.8	829.7	784.9

Sources: Total U.S.: U.S. Department of the Interior, Bureau of Land Management, Final Environmental Impact Statement, Federal Coal Management Program (April 1979); U.S. Department of Energy, Energy Information Administration, Coal Data: A Reference (October 1982). 1983 data supplied by Coal Division, Energy Administration Agency. Adapted from Coal Commission, "Fair Market Value," p. 15.
Federal Lands: Public Land Statistics: 1976-Tables 73, 74; 1980-Tables 67,68; 1973-Table 70. Figures for 1980 and 1983 are fiscal year.

(a) Includes public domain and acquired lands administered by the BLM. In 1983 no production was reported for acquired lands. Virtually all federal land coal production is in Colorado, Montana, New Mexico, North Dakota, Utah, and Wyoming.

TABLE 7. Past Federal Coal Leasing

Year(s)	Number of Leases Issued	Total Acres Leased	Total Recoverable Reserves Leased (millions of tons) (a)
1920-1949	85	45,889	659.0
1950-1959	77	89,858	1,172.0
1960-1964	115	154,893	1,738.0
1965-1969	215	411,236	10,043.0
1970-1980	66	99,131	1,837.0
1981	22	48,895	405.0
1982	36	70,549	1,488.0
1983 through Oct. 1, 1983	18	25,696	815.1
TOTAL	634	946,147	18,160.93

Source: U.S. Department of the Interior, Bureau of Land Management, Automated Coal Lease Data System, November 7, 1983.

(a) Data may not add to totals shown due to independent rounding. Tonnage shown is for leases issued in that year. Final lease issuance often occurs several months after a lease sale, so tonnages shown do not necessarily correspond to lease sales in that year.

Regardless of these uncertainties of federal management, federal coal will be a part of the future American energy supply. About 50 to 70 percent of the nation's remaining coal deposits are in the western states and Alaska, and an estimated 60 percent of those deposits are on federal lands (see Appendix Figure 6 for a map showing coal fields in the lower forty-eight states). [76] The federal government does not control access to all federal coal, however. Approximately 58 percent of federal coal, particularly in Colorado, Montana, North Dakota, and Wyoming underlies privately owned surface. Under the requirements of the recent Surface Mine Control and Reclamation Act (SMCRA, 1977), it cannot be leased without consent of the qualified surface owner. [77] A brisk market in surface owner consents has developed, which predictably redirects most of the value of the federal coal to the surface owner.

As of the end of 1982, there were 641 federal coal leases [78], almost all of them in the seven western coal states. Ranked by recoverable leased reserves, these states are: Wyoming (9.6 billion tons), Utah (8.2), Colorado (2.2), Montana (1.6), New Mexico (.45), North Dakota (.27), and Oklahoma (.2). [79] Federal coal leases cover more than 1 million acres, or 9 percent of the 11.5 million acres presently known to contain coal deposits. As shown in Table 5, coal revenues to western states steadily increased from $2.64 million in 1976 to $40 million in 1984 (figures not adjusted for inflation). [80]

About 75 percent of the coal now under lease (18.1 billion tons of recoverable reserves) were leased before 1970. In addition, although the FCLAA abolished noncompetitive leasing for coal, there are still about 120 noncompetitive lease applications pending, which, if approved, convey a right to leases involving another 6.8 billion tons. These pending leases will produce no bonuses if they are granted, but will affect the amount of coal available for development and, therefore, the amount that ought to be leased.

Pricing of Coal Leases

Federal coal leases are sold at auction to the highest bidder. Because both the rent and the royalty rate are set prior to the auction by the secretary, it is typically the bonus that distinguishes among bidders. Bids for competitive coal leases must be accompanied by a check for 20 percent of the bonus offered. If the bid is accepted, the lessee normally pays the remaining 80 percent of the bonus in annual installments over the next four years.

In addition to the bonus, the lessee must pay a rental per acre on the lease tract. Annual rental payments continue whether coal is being mined or not. The three-dollar per acre minimum rent established by FCLAA is the normal charge for post-1976 leases, although some especially sensitive lands have been priced as high as seven dollars per acre per year. Before FCLAA passed in 1976, one dollar per acre was the normal rate for rentals, and lessees could credit rental payments against anticipated annual royalty payments on production--terms that still hold for pre-1976 leases. For leases written or adjusted after August 1976, FCLAA eliminated the practice of accepting rentals in lieu of royalties in an effort to encourage development of leaseholds. [81]

The coal royalty is based on a fixed percentage of the gross value of coal produced on the leased area. Pre-1976 leases set the royalty at a cents-per-ton charge; the minimum in the MLA was five cents per ton, but the actual rate, set at the discretion of the appropriate BLM state office, varied from five to twenty cents per ton. The customary price on pre-1976 leases was 17.5 cents per ton. Under the new FCLAA rules, the royalty is set at a minimum of 12.5 percent of the gross value of strip-mined coal. For underground coal (there is no statutory minimum) the secretary has set the royalty at 8 percent. [82] As pre-1976 leases come up for renegotiation, typically twenty years after they were signed, the Department of the Interior is trying to change the old cents-per-ton royalty provisions to a percentage of gross value. Because many leases were acquired in the 1960s, some expect that federal coal royalties may rise markedly during the 1980s when the new and presumably higher royalty requirements start taking effect in old leases. However, it is not clear what constitutes a "reasonable" readjustment to the old lease royalty rates, nor when the adjustment must be made. Industry argues that "reasonable" adjustments must be gradual and justified by the economics of the specific operation. [83]

Royalty payments are likely to produce about 90 percent of revenues over the life of a lease. [84] However, the royalty is paid only during production. Figure 4, showing the extent of coal leasing and coal production from the leases, demonstrates that in states where there is relatively little federal coal development but large areas under lease--primarily Utah and Colorado--the rentals can provide significant revenues. This suggests that there may be some revenue advantages in nonproductive leases. [85]

The basis on which the secretary decides whether or not to accept a bid is currently a thorny issue. The secretary is authorized to reject bids that do not constitute fair market value. The government does a presale appraisal of the tracts offered. That estimate, approximate and qualified as it may be, provides a benchmark on fair market value. Nevertheless, determination of minimum acceptable bid is subject to error and enormous exercise of discretion. Believing that market value ought to reflect the price that potential buyers are willing to pay, the Department of the Interior officials made allowance in the Powder River sale for post-auction adjustment of the minimum acceptable bid, based on what the department learned from the auction about the value of the property. [86]   This action led to the charge that the department accepted bids that were less than the appraised value of the tracts.

Who Should Develop the Coal Resource

Difficulties encountered in assembling a workable tract limit the market for federal coal.   In the Surface Mine Control and Reclamation Act (SMCRA), qualified surface owners were given absolute discretion to bar the leasing of any federal coal underlying their land that will be surface-mined.   That provision affects approximately 58 percent of federal coal.   The amount of federal coal in "split estates" or "severed mineral title" varies from region to region as shown in Appendix Table 10. Obtaining surface owner consent is just one step in the arduous task of putting together a developable collection of leases from all rights holders.   Land ownership is fragmented among federal, state, and diverse private owners around most of the coal fields where the federal government has holdings. Therefore, the federal government rarely offers for lease a tract or combination of tracts that would be a "stand alone" new coal mine. Most federal tracts are assembled into an aggregation of developable leases.   The market for a given federal parcel, therefore, is frequently limited to the entrepreneur who has accumulated the neighboring rights.

This does not necessarily mean that there is a monopoly. Although there may be a limited number of bidders for any particular federal tract, the coal developers compete intensely for markets for the coal they extract.

Which Lands Should Be Developed

In terms of coal, four aspects of the "which lands" question require special discussion.   The first two are variations on familiar MLA features—the distinction between known and unknown deposits and acreage restrictions.   In addition, environmental protection measures in SMCRA and FCLAA introduce two terms—"areas unsuitable" and "logical mining units" (LMUs)—unique to the coal program.

The familiar known-unknown distinction for coal leasing was eliminated by the 1976 FCLAA so that all post-1976 leasing is to be competitive.   Still pending, however, are 133 lease applications arising from prospecting permits issued between 1955 and 1971. The "preference right lease applications" (PRLAs) cover 307,881 acres and an estimated 5.8 billion tons of recoverable coal. They are, as shown in Appendix Table 11, widely spread throughout the western coal fields.   In some areas they are quite significant.   In the San

Juan coal fields for example, PRLAs cover an estimated one-half to two-thirds of the surface minable coal. [87] Which leases will be granted and what will become of the areas on which the applications are rejected is a matter of intense debate.

The PRLA debate centers on two questions. First, it is not clear what a "right" to a lease conveys. Under the 1920 MLA system, a "successful" prospector had an absolute right to a lease. In the 1970s, however, changes in the definition of prospecting success put the PRLAs in limbo. [88] Second, the applicability of post-1976 regulations to the pre-1976 applications has been fiercely debated. [89] The new definition of success requires that the deposit be marketable at a profit rather than simply technically workable. The post-1976 regulations impose additional, costly responsibilities on the developer. The effect of applying these new provisions to long-pending lease applications could be to raise the costs of development sufficiently to eliminate the likelihood of profit and hence successful prospecting and the right to a lease. Falling coal prices, of course, make meeting the new definition of success all the more difficult.

Acreage restrictions for coal lands are notable because they are more liberal than for other types of deposits: 46,080 acres in one state or 100,000 acres nationally. There is no limit on the acreage per lease, although leases cannot be combined to form a "logical mining unit" in excess of 25,000 acres. Existing coal leases include sixty covering under 100 acres each and four over 10,000 acres.

Designating "areas unsuitable for mining," a process roughly outlined in SMCRA, has become a critical and controversial aspect of lease tract selection. Section 522 of SMCRA required the Secretary of the Interior to determine whether lands with certain characteristics were unsuitable for any mining at all, and if so, under what circumstances. The Carter administration promulgated a list of twenty criteria for "unsuitability." The administration defended its considerable expansion of the SMCRA criteria as an effort to blend the SMCRA requirements of other federal programs (such as the Endangered Species Act) into a single review procedure. The lengthy list generated both industry complaints and efforts to expand the list even further. [90]

Implementation of the designation is also controversial. The Office of Technology Assessment (OTA) found, not surprisingly, that criteria involving lines of maps [91] are readily applied while other more qualitative concerns [92] are not used. [93] Key terms in the criteria are ill-defined and data for evaluating them are sparse. BLM therefore is inclined towards using the designation process as a source of "red flags" for further analysis and "excludes" from mining a troublesome area within a leased tract rather than designating it "unsuitable." Excluded areas can be changed while unsuitable areas cannot. [94] Included in the "unsuitability screening" is the controversial evaluation of "alluvial valley floors."

Logical mining units (LMUs) are also unique to the coal program. FCLAA authorizes the Secretary of the Interior to consolidate leases by requiring any post-1976 lessees to form a "logical mining unit." An LMU is an area of not more than 25,000 acres in which the coal resources "can be developed in an efficient, economical and orderly manner as a unit with due regard to conservation of coal reserves and other resources." It can include one or more federal leaseholds and/or nonfederal coal, but the holdings must all be under the effective control of one operator.

Timing of Coal Development

In the coal program, both timing of sale and timing of development are extremely controversial. Sale timing is usually examined in conjunction with "lease targets" or "leasing levels." Development timing discussions are dominated by the concept of "diligence." These two timing issues are tightly interwoven but will be discussed separately in an effort to clarify the major focus of dispute in the coal program: Is coal leasing necessary and if so, how much?

Secretarial determination of leasing "targets" has two components: (1) determination of how much land will be leased and (2) determination of the pace at which leasing will occur. [95] Although the Secretary of the Interior has final responsibility for determining leasing targets, Regional Coal Teams (RCTs) play an important role. Composed of federal and state government representatives, RCTs are to advise the secretary regarding tract rankings and regional leasing goals. Under newly proposed rules, the secretary would accept RCT recommendations unless they contravene the national interest.

The Reagan administration reoriented the target setting. It discarded the Carter administration's effort to evaluate future coal demands and lease coal to assure that adequate amounts of federal coal would be available to meet projected needs. The new Reagan targets are based on the theory that reserves of coal under lease will permit numerous coal companies to become active competitors in each regional coal market. Because it takes about four years to get a lease sale proposed, and another eight to twelve years to get a leased area into production, they argue that reserves are necessary. [96] Reagan administration officials have stated that they want market competition, rather than government energy planning based on wildly varying government estimates of future needs, to be the driving force in determining production locations and rates for federal coal. [97] The Reagan program orientation has sharpened debate over whether, given the number of outstanding nonproductive leases, any leasing is needed to satisfy industry's need for reserves. [98]

The concept of diligence has been central to the timing of development issue. The length of a coal lease is not in itself controversial. Pre-1976 leases did not specify the primary period (initial period of the lease), and the lease terms were to be adjusted every twenty years; post-1976 leases have a twenty-year primary period and are adjusted every ten years thereafter. Both old and new leases continue for as long as coal is in production. [99] So-called "speculative" holding of federal coal leases is the controversial issue. Many believe that it is undesirable for firms to hold undeveloped leases, presumably hoping to profit by "assigning" (selling) the lease to another company or developing it themselves when coal prices rise. Critics argue that the government loses revenues and loses control over the timing, location, and environmental impacts of federal coal development when firms simply hold onto undeveloped leases. They also argue that if one firm cannot or does not develop the coal, the lease should, at a clearly defined point, become free for study and possible releasing by another firm.

Congress agreed with this argument [100] and in the 1976 FCLAA imposed two kinds of diligence requirements on lessees. First, lessees are required to begin production of commercial quantities within a specified period; second, they are subject to requirements for "continuing production." The general rule is that within ten years of lease issuance, the lease must be producing "commercial quantities" of coal, and it must produce continuously thereafter. "Commercial quantitites" was defined in the regulations to mean 1 percent of the reserves within ten years. For a new lease included in a "logical mining unit," the operator must submit a mining plan that would exhaust the coal deposit in forty years. [101]

When these two new diligence requirements may be imposed on pre-1976 leases is unclear. The terms of the old leases are readjusted every twenty years and they could be imposed at that time. Or, if the department so chose and the courts agreed, they could be imposed at the time stated in the Ford administration's reinterpretation of the MLA—1986. However, the Carter administration's 1979 diligence regulations granted the Secretary of the Interior discretion regarding pre-1976 leases; he could extend for five additional years the ten-year period in which 1 percent of the reserves must be produced. This authority was not included in the 1982 Reagan revision of the program. All of these issues are in litigation, and the meaning of these requirements for pre-1976 leases will not be clear for some time. [102]

The penalties for failure to achieve diligent development are also controversial. The basic provision is that nondiligent developers lose their leases. However, Section 3 of FCLAA also provides that any pre-1976 coal lessee not diligently producing on a coal lease by August 1986, will become ineligible for other onshore federal mineral leases. Whether that includes just other <u>coal</u> leases or <u>all</u> other leases is not entirely clear. Because many firms holding nonproductive old coal leases are also active in other federal mineral leasing programs, this provision has become the focus of industry lawsuits and lobbying efforts in Congress.

Senate efforts to resolve the Section 3 dispute have become tangled in efforts by the railroad industry to alter restrictions in Section 2(c) of FCLAA on railroad leasing of coal. [103] The House has passed legislation that would allow lessees to continue to hold nonproviding leases by paying a fee (HR 1934). [104] Congress did agree to extend the deadline for complying with Section 3 from August 4 to December 31, 1986, but the final resolution is still stalled. [105] In evaluating these diligence requirements, it is worth noting that no coal lease has ever been canceled for failure to develop diligently.

However, the heart of both timing issues is whether to lease more coal. In part, the answer depends on how much coal is already leased. It is not easy to determine that figure. The answer depends on how one assesses the likelihood and desirability of diligent development of the existing undeveloped leases.   Moreover, both the pending preference right lease applications and changing regulations complicate the calculation of how much coal already leased will be developed. [106] Collapse of the coal market spurred by ten-dollar-per-barrel oil, however, relieves the urgency to engage in further leasing.

The issue also involves the appropriate criteria for setting federal lease targets. High lease targets are in order if the government aims to make enough federal coal available (1) to enhance competition in the industry, (2) to allow for having developable coal reserves at the ready, or (3) to rely on the market for decisions about the extent of coal development. If, on the other hand, targets should be set for leasing the amount of coal necessary to meet projected future demands, then too much coal is probably already under lease. [107] Choosing lease targets rests ultimately on a definition of the appropriate role of government planning, as opposed to industry planning, in coal leasing. If returns to the Treasury are a high priority, a larger role for industry in identifying tracts is arguably correct.   If environmental protection is a major goal, carefully regulated government exploration and planning may be more appropriate.

Intensity of Development

Probably because the coal leasing planning process is the most recently and extensively defined in statute [108], the planning procedure for defining the location and intensity of coal development is by far the most complex of federal resource management programs.   The recent OTA study, <u>Environmental Protection in the</u>

Federal Coal Leasing Program, summarizes the process. [109] Rather than describe the current planning process in detail, the following discussion highlights four factors that seem to result in the general complexity of the procedure.

Insignificant distinctions in planning sequencing and terminology employed by the BLM and the Forest Service constitute one complication. For example, both agencies are operating under comprehensive land-use planning statutes passed in 1976. Although the nomenclature varies [110], the basic pattern is familiar. Both agencies are supposed to complete their initial round of land-use data-gathering, analysis, public involvement, and planning by the mid-1980s [111], but the chance of that occurring is slim, according to many observers. BLM appears to be simply amending its existing plans (MFPs) rather than preparing new ones (RMPs).

A second reason for the complexity is that coal planning occurs in two supposedly distinct phases: (1) multiple use land planning for all resources, including coal, and (2) coal "activity" planning. The multiresource, long-range planning, which evaluates coal in the context of "multiple use tradeoffs," is supposed to precede activity planning. [112]   Specific coal activity planning (identification of lease levels, rates, sites, and appropriate mitigation measures, and the like) follows comprehensive land-use planning in the agency schematics of their planning procedures.   Planning delays and the priority given to coal in national energy planning under the Carter and Reagan administrations has collapsed the process considerably, and coal activity planning, coal development, and multiresource planning activities are all occurring simultaneously. [113]

A third source of complexity is the "tiering" required in the EIS regulations issued by the Council on Environmental Quality. Both the land-use plans and the coal activity plans are tiered. The process cycles, focusing on smaller and smaller areas, with the idea that more data will be used in increasingly site-specific analyses. For example, broad analysis is done for national and regional coal activity programmatic EISs (and must be redone every time the basic program is altered). [114]   Then, more detailed analyses are prepared for the coal lease sale and for the issuance of each lease. Further analysis accompanies the operation and reclamation plan required by SMCRA.

As the land-use and activity plans cycle and focus on increasingly specific sites, the federal government cooperates [115] with state agencies and the public to design the "lease stipulations" that impose environmental protection and mitigation measures on the development. Some of the "stips" and mitigation measures are identified prior to sale of the lease while others are attached to the lease prior to lease issuance.

A fourth source of complexity in the coal planning process arises from the fact that a lease does not convey a right to mine. The leasing process is essentially a federal planning process and must be distinguished from the permitting process, in which states and localities deal directly with the leaseholder. After a specific area is leased, the most intense environmental analysis occurs, and the permit to mine may be conditioned by the state, which has authority to approve mine permit applications pursuant to SMCRA and to enforce air and water quality regulations. Localities also become involved working with and through the state to grant necessary permits. Although no tract has failed to receive a permit due to economic or technical infeasibility of reclamation [116], areas within the lease have been withdrawn [117] and the conditions placed on the permit may alter the economics of the development. [118]

The GAO has suggested that the many repetitions in this process may be excessive. [119] The costs have two components: (1) the direct cost of planning for all involved and (2) reductions in the value of a lease caused by the risk and ambiguity inherent in the long and contentious process. It is not clear that the planning generates benefits to offset the costs. However, the issues may be complex and significant enough to justify a sequential and even repetitive planning process during which states, localities, and citizens can gain skills requisite to effective participation.

Participation

The complexity of the planning process suggests a corresponding proliferation of opportunities for participation. The general public and other federal agencies are most likely to find formal opportunities for comment during the land-use planning process of the BLM and for the Forest Service and during EIS preparation on coal activity planning. State and local governments have those same opportunities, in addition to their participation in RCTs and in the permitting process. The general public's ability to participate in state and local review of plans depends on local programs and interest. [120]

State efforts to influence federal coal policy have been contentious and largely unsatisfactory for all concerned. The RCTs were intended to involve state officials at the earliest stages, thereby reducing the conflicts that tended to arise at the last minute. Although the governors had some success in forcing former Interior Secretary Watt to reconsider his decision to ignore the recommendations of the Regional Coal Teams [121], the RCTs functioned only briefly as a route to federal-state cooperation. State officials generally believe that their suggestions on appropriate leasing levels and rates and lease stipulations are frequently given short shrift in day-to-day federal decision making.

However, the pivotal role of the states in SMCRA implementation, and the importance afforded state and local environmental regulations in FLPMA, assure that during the attenuated process the states and localities will be able to negotiate from a position of some strength. Although under the MLA the secretary's discretion is broad and likely to override state and local positions in a litigated conflict [122], it rarely comes to that. Moreover, the states and localities have ample opportunity to garner allies and deal directly with the developer, who frequently does not wish to become embroiled in protracted litigation. [123]

Distribution of Revenues

Coal revenues are distributed under the standard MLA formula: 50–40-10. The major exception to this rule is that acquired lands that are not managed by Department of the Interior agencies but instead are leased under the Acquired Lands Leasing Act of 1947 follow the pattern for distribution of revenues collected by the appropriate agency. For example, coal leases on acquired lands managed by the Forest Service return the standard 25 percent to the states for expenditure on roads and schools in the county of origin plus 10 percent for forest roads and trails in the state. Money distributed to the states is not earmarked although priority in state allocation of the funds is to be given to areas affected by minerals development. Disbursement of the funds to the states should occur within the month that the U.S. Treasury receives the funds.

OIL SHALE

The Resource

Oil shale leasing and development is nearly dead on federal lands and appears unlikely to revive in the near future. However, because oil shale was such a controversial part of the 1970s energy crisis, the resource is discussed here.

Although oil shale is covered by the Mineral Leasing Act, uncertainties regarding development led the Secretary of the Interior to withdraw oil shale lands from entry in 1930. That order is still in effect. However, it was altered to permit an experimental "prototype" leasing program in the mid-1970s. BLM spent several years during the energy crisis establishing a leasing "program" in case future interest should warrant renewed development efforts. Their regulations, proposed in February 1983, were withdrawn in September 1985 due to lack of interest. [124]

Oil shale was used in the 1800s by early Appalachian settlers as a lubricant, for lamp oil, and for medicinal purposes. Since then, oil shale has enjoyed several periods of intense speculative attention, but it has never been widely developed as an energy source. In the 1850s and again between 1915 and 1930, lift-off in the industry seemed imminent. Both times, discovery of more easily exploited oil fields scotched oil shale development. In the 1960s, interest was piqued by an improvement in the extraction process called "retorting," but no bids were made on leases offered by the department in 1968. [125] Once again, in the 1970s and 1980s, oil shale boomed, only to bust when the price of oil fell sharply.

Oil shale becomes useful as an energy source when the organic matter, kerogen, is extracted from the shale. This process, known as "retorting," is accomplished either (1) by in situ retorting, which uses steam injection or explosions underground to extract the kerogen without removing the shale, or (2) in a furnace on the surface, typically after the shale has been stripped or mined in an open pit (aboveground retorting). For aboveground retorting, the choice of extraction methods depends on the depth and quality of the shale deposit. Although surface mining requires enormous development because the shale is low in BTU value, it also can lead to 90 percent recovery of the resource. Underground mining typically results in less than 60 percent recovery. [133]

Aboveground retorting is typically associated with air pollution and extensive surface disturbances and requires disposal of massive quantities of spent shale. In situ techniques generally avoid those pitfalls but present ground-water contamination problems instead. Technical problems with both methods abound.

In the West, oil shale is concentrated in Colorado, Utah, and Wyoming (see Appendix Figure 7). Perhaps because it has not been consistently regarded as valuable, the tracts are less broken up than in most other energy resources. It is almost totally in federal ownership. There is a slight severed title problem, with Uinta and Ouray Indians holding the surface and some lands within deposits in Utah and limited state and private holdings in all three states, but the federal government holds most of the mineral rights. [126] The limited private holdings result from early homesteads and pre-MLA claims "located" under the 1872 General Mining Act. However, they are presently held primarily by oil companies and therefore will not be a barrier to development. [127]

The oil embargo of the mid-1970s led to a flurry of oil shale activity. In 1974, as part of an effort to generate "alternate" energy sources, the Department of the Interior offered six experimental or "prototype" oil shale leases in Colorado, Wyoming, and Utah. Two each in Colorado and Utah were sold. In 1980, the federal government again moved to encourage oil shale development by establishing the Synthetic Fuels Corporation (SFC), a quasi-governmental corporation that was to invest $17.5 billion to develop synthetic fuels. Since then, the SFC appropriations were drastically reduced and then eliminated. For several years presidential appointments to the Board of Directors were not made. The clearly intended result was that the board lacked a quorum and could not make loans. A 1984 call for expression of interest in leasing one additional tract in

Colorado produced no response [128], and Congress froze $500 million of SFC's funds in late 1985. [129]

Activities on the prototype leases never met expectations, and commercial production is nonexistent. Development at the two Utah sites was delayed by litigation and questions involving Indian water rights. Although some construction was initiated, it has been halted. In Rio Blanco and Cathedral Bluffs, Colorado, progress has also been considerably slower than originally planned. Development at the Rio Blanco site was slowed pending results of retort testing and finally halted. Of the four prototype leases, only one was operating in 1986. On April 1, 1986, Occidental Oil Shale paid its annual rental on its Cathedral Bluffs site.   When asked to justify the expenditure of over $1.7 million, an Occidental spokesperson commented that CEO Armand Hammer "is an advocate of oil shale." [130]   A month later, the company sought a suspension of the lease. Oil shale diehards have advocated using the four moribund prototype leases as the core of a subsidized oil shale R & D center. [131] There has been no commercial production thus far on any of the leases. [132]   The Department of Energy has also decided against development of 50,000 acres of low-grade Naval Petroleum Reserve oil shale, which it manages in Wyoming and Utah.

The inconsistent interest in oil shale arises in part from fluctuations in oil prices. It is difficult to estimate future income from oil shale development with oil prices so volatile. Recent concerns for environmental quality, particularly ground-water quality and air pollution, have further burdened the risky business.   States have been particularly active in seeking to control these economically and environmentally uncertain developments.   However, the major problem with oil shale is that extraction is uncertain and costly. Although the deposits are extensive, rich, well known, and concentrated primarily on federal lands in the West, other resources continue to be easier to exploit.

Pricing Oil Shale

Because of the uncertainties of production technology, including environmental impacts, costs, and prices, and, therefore, the timing and economics of oil shale development, the terms of the prototype leases were set at the discretion of the Secretary of the Interior. The prototype leases issued in 1974 were awarded through competitive bonus bidding, although that procedure is not specified in the law.   Likewise, royalty rates are not fixed by law. The 1974 sales settled on a royalty of twelve cents per ton of processed shale; this royalty is adjusted according to whether the yield is more or less than thirty gallons per ton, and to reflect change in the price of crude oil. Rentals were fifty cents per acre per year. Data on these prototype leases appear in Table 8 and Figure 5, but they are probably not a good basis for evaluating future programs.

TABLE 8. Oil Shale Receipts and State Revenue Shares (1976-1984)

	1976		1978		1980		1982		1984	
	Total Collections	State Allocation	Total Collections	State Allocation	Total Collections	State Allocation	Total Collections	State Allocation	Total Collections	Payment to State
Alaska	0	0	0	0	0	0	0	0	0	0
Arizona	0	0	0	0	0	0	0	0	0	0
California	0	0	0	0	0	0	0	0	0(a)	0
Colorado	65,618,720	24,607,020	0	0	0	0	0	0	0	0
Idaho	0	0	0	0	0	0	0	0	0	0
Montana	0	0	0	0	19,660	9,830	0	0	0	0
Nevada	0	0	0	0	0	0	0	0	0	0
New Mexico	0	0	0	0	0	0	0	0	0	0
North Dakota	0	0	0	0	4,522	2,261	0	0	0	0
Oregon	0	0	0	0	0	0	0	0	0	0
Utah	0	0	0	0	0	0	129,420,000	48,532,428	n.a.	2,560
Washington	0	0	0	0	0	0	0	0	0	0
Wyoming	0	0	0	0	136,219	68,110	0	0	0	0
Regional Total	$65,618,720	$24,607,020	0	0	$160,401	$80,201	$129,420,000	$48,532,428	n.a.	$2,560
National Total	65,618,720		0		$160,401		$129,420,000		n.a.	

Source: Public Land Statistics: 1976-Table 112; 1978-Table 117; 1980-Table 108; 1982-Table 105; 1984-Table 103 for collections; payment data from Minerals Management Service. (See Table 3 note of this text.)

(a) In 1984, Colorado's mineral revenues were adjusted for ($3,228) in oil shale royalties.

94

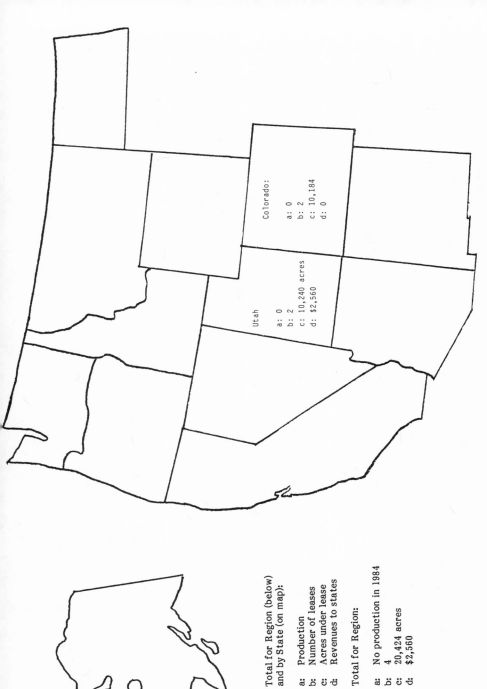

Total for Region (below)
and by State (on map):

a: Production
b: Number of leases
c: Acres under lease
d: Revenues to states

Total for Region:

a: No production in 1984
b: 4
c: 20,424 acres
d: $2,560

Colorado:

a: 0
b: 2
c: 10,184
d: 0

Utah

a: 0
b: 2
c: 10,240 acres
d: $2,560

FIGURE 5.   Oil Shale Production and Revenues from Federal Lands (1984).

95

BLM proposed and later rescinded proposals for an all-competitive program should leasing become feasible in the future. That is consistent with the fact that the extent and quality of oil shale resources are generally believed to be known. However, it presently appears that they may never be developed.

Who Should Develop Oil Shale

Because the technologies are developing and the profits uncertain, prototype leasing was dominated by familiar names with extensive experience in the petroleum field: Standard Oil of Indiana, Gulf, Union, Phillips, Exxon, Chevron, and Mobil. However, the MLA provides that no firm or individual can have more than one 5,120-acre lease, nationwide. These limits were criticized by industry, which argued that because the whole operation is so experimental, a developer ought to have an opportunity to use the experience gained in an initial operation in subsequent ventures. [134] This possibility also appears unlikely.

Which Lands Should Be Developed

One of the unique features of oil shale is that exploration is not really an issue; the consensus is that most of the developable sites are familiar. BLM's program proposed using the land-use planning process, in conjunction with industry nominations, public comment, and "Regional Oil Shale Teams" to identify tracts for leasing.

FLPMA explicitly forbids leasing of lands beyond the 5,120 acres allowed in an oil shale lease by the MLA for disposing of spent oil shale. This provision was controversial when enacted because it appeared to hamper the struggling developments. Congress altered this provision in 1983 (by amending ILPMA) to provide one off-site shale disposal site of not more than 6,400 acres for just one tract only. [135] However, the lessee relinquished the lease soon thereafter.

After a year of negotiations with industry and environmental groups, state and local officials from the three affected states proposed extensive amendments to the MLA that would have removed the constraint on the number of leases, allowed larger leases, imposed diligence requirements, and defined extensive environmental protection keyed to the cumulative impacts of development on federal and private lands. Legislation was introduced in 1984, but the coalition broke apart. [136] The bill is unlikely to be revived in the current economic climate.

Timing of Oil Shale Development

In the program proposed by the BLM, leasing would have been done "as needed." This term was not defined, but the reliance on "Regional Oil Shale Teams" similar to Regional Coal Teams may indicate that the format will become a feature of future development programs. Leasing targets were to be based on some estimate of future need for oil shale development and reserves.

Diligence requirements were not spelled out in the BLM proposed program. If there was no commercial development within twenty years, the lease was to be terminated. In the prototype sales, diligence "requirements" were manifest in up-front royalties and rent payments. Minimum royalties were to be paid beginning in the fifth lease year, and increased in the sixth through twentieth years. However, as with geothermal resources, development expenses on the prototype leases could be credited toward minimum royalties due. Also, lessees were allowed to withhold 40 percent of the initial bonus bid if they invested this amount in developing the lease.

Intensity of Development

BLM was planning to include oil shale leasing in its regular Resource Management Planning (RMP) process. However, BLM officials treated prototype oil shale leases like coal, conducting an EIS on the oil shale leasing "program" and then proceeding with detailed analysis of individual lease sales. The Surface Mining Control and Reclamation Act was intended for eventual application to stripped minerals other than coal, but it was not applied to oil shale development. A National Academy of Sciences Committee formed to study the issue recommended against extending SMCRA's provisions beyond coal.

Participation

Participation occurs through FLPMA and NEPA formats and certain specially formed groups at the regional and state levels. Oil shale development presents special problems with respect to land reclamation and water impacts. Finally, a major aspect of oil shale debate was fear of "boomtown" growth in rural areas. Because of potentially severe impacts, state pressure to influence federal policy was unusually strong. At one time, Colorado had a joint legislative task force dealing with oil shale policy. The more typical pattern was for states to act through a Regional Oil Shale Team (ROST) similar to the Regional Coal Team, supplemented by an Oil Shale Environmental Advisory Panel.

Distribution of Revenues

Oil shale follows the standard MLA formula, with states currently paid 50 percent of revenues. Bonuses from the prototype lease sales have accounted for almost all revenues to date and have been paid by companies over a period of years (see Table 8). Because of litigation, distribution of bonuses from Utah leases was withheld until 1982, after which it was distributed using the pre-1976 formula of 37.5 percent to the state until the leases were relinquished.

NONFUEL MINERALS LEASABLE UNDER THE MLA

The Resources

Nonfuel leasable minerals—among them the "fertilizer minerals"—include phosphate, potash, native asphalt, sodium, solid and semi-solid bitumen, bituminous rock, and sulfur in Louisiana and New Mexico. [137] The same nonfuel minerals leasing rules also apply to minerals on acquired National Forest lands that would be locatable under the 1872 Act if they were on the public domain lands. [138] Although many western states produce nonfuel leasable minerals, the most important, based on the revenues they generated in 1982, are potash in California and New Mexico, sodium in California and Wyoming, phosphate in Idaho and Montana, and sulfur in New Mexico (see Figure 6).

Access Rules

Nonfuel leasable minerals are subject to all the basic provisions of the MLA. They vary only slightly for different deposits. Because they have not, generally speaking, created great controversy since 1920, the statutes concerning nonfuel leasables have generally remained the same as when they were passed. Under the Carter and first Reagan administrations studies and program reviews were conducted to provide the basis for design of a "program" for the nonfuel leasables, but Congress took no action. Therefore, in 1984 and 1985 the Department of the Interior proposed minor amendments to some of the regulations covering "leasing of solid minerals other than oil shale."

The known-unknown deposit distinction is critical. In unknown areas, nonfuel leasables are still subject to "preference right" leasing, which has been abolished for coal. In unknown areas, the secretary is authorized to issue prospecting permits for phosphate, potash, sodium, or sulfur. Like the pre-1976 coal "preference right"

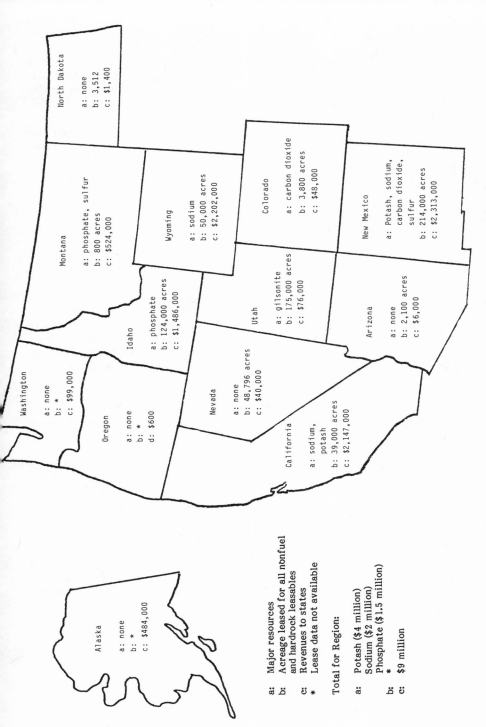

FIGURE 6. Nonfuel Mineral Production and Revenues from Federal Lands (1984).

99

leases, the permittee has a right to a lease if a valuable deposit is found. However, unlike coal PRLAs, the secretary in 1984 has redefined "valuable deposit" to return to the "prudent man" rule. Therefore, preference right lease applications will not, unlike coal, be subject to the "marketability test"; the less demanding workability rule is used. [139] Moreover, the same rulemaking defined the term "chiefly valuable" as it applies to sodium, sulfur, and potash discoveries. For those deposits, the area containing the "valuable deposit" must, according to the MLA, be in an area "chiefly valuable" for the mineral. That definition appeared to give the secretary discretion to deny leases for environmental reasons. However, the new regulations restrict assessment of the "chiefly valuable" term to a "significant conflict" with minerals development, thus rendering it almost redundant. [140]

These changes are reflected in a reorganization of the regulations for the "leasable solids other than oil shale" proposed in April 1985 and made final April 22, 1986. The proposals included elimination of noncompetitive leasing for gilsonite. They also proposed switching phosphate, sodium, potassium, and sulfur to an exploration license system, which would convey no right to a lease. [141] The final regulations provide for both prospecting permits, which ripen into leases upon location of a valuable deposit in unknown areas, and for explorative licenses for assessment of known areas with no right to a lease. This applies to gilsonite and phosphate, sodium, potassium, and sulfur. [142]

In areas of known mineralization, the secretary is authorized to advertise and auction leases through competitive bidding or some other method to be defined in regulation.

Following the general MLA pattern, maximum acreage is specified for individual leases and permits and for holdings by an individual or firm within a state and nationwide. Rentals and royalties are also specified; some are set in the act as minimums, others are set at a flat rate. For phosphate and sulfur, the royalty is 5 percent; for potash and sodium, 2 percent, and so on. Leases are generally limited to twenty years, and prospecting permits are issued for two years, extendable for up to four more years.

The secretary has nearly total discretion to establish diligence and other appropriate rules for individual leases. [143] The revenues for some states are substantial, as shown in Table 9. They are divided according to the standard 50-40-10 MLA formula.

TABLE 9. Nonfuel Mineral Receipts and State Revenue Shares (1976-1984) (a)

	1976		1978		1980		1982		1984	
	Total Collections	State Allocation	Total Collections	State Allocation	Total Collections	State Allocation	Total Collections	State Allocation	Total Collections	Payment to State
Alaska	0	0	0	0	0	0	0	0	0	483,747(b)
Arizona	13,912	5,217	206,091	103,046	11,360	5,680	10,854	5,427	11,375	5,687
California	2,968,092	1,113,034	3,390,299	1,695,115	4,838,139	2,419,072	8,411,277	4,205,638	4,293,435	2,147,195
Colorado	106,738	40,026	140,898	70,449	100,955	50,478	877,303	443,651	88,921	47,688
Idaho	1,342,389	503,396	1,734,642	867,321	2,577,338	1,288,669	1,940,927	970,464	6,112	1,485,626
Montana	81,020	30,383	85,616	42,814	107,742	53,871	562,544	281,272	2,191,632	524,149
Nevada	115,263	43,223	152,117	76,058	96,935	48,468	95,048	47,524	79,071	39,536
New Mexico	6,256,208	2,346,078	11,960,685	5,980,342	9,901,034	4,950,518	7,810,547	3,905,274	4,643,429	2,313,497
North Dakota	34,880	13,080	21,402	10,701	2,157	1,078	25	12	2,892	1,446
Oregon	0	0	3,583	1,792	508	254	1,188	594	1,108	555
Utah	138,388	51,896	91,229	45,614	580,009	290,004	290,552	145,276	183,893	75,827
Washington	0	0	1,248	624	0	0	0	0	198,028	99,014
Wyoming	5,803,163	2,176,185	7,881,104	3,940,552	7,471,653	3,735,827	6,499,176	3,249,588	4,631,001	2,201,651
Regional Total	$16,860,053	$6,322,518	$25,668,844	$12,834,428	$25,687,380	$12,843,918	$26,499,441	$13,249,720	$16,330,897	$9,425,618
National Total	$16,883,451		$26,235,981		$25,725,731		$26,510,751		$19,995,294	

Sources: Public Land Statistics: 1976–Table 112; 1978–Table 117; 1980–Table 108; 1982–Table 105. Collections Data for 1984: Public Land Statistics (to be published August 1985), Tables 104 & 104A. Payments in 1984: Minerals Management Service and estimates from BLM collections. (See notes to this table and Appendix, "Methodology.")

(a) The resources included in this table are potash, sodium, phosphates, sulfur and other nonfuel minerals located on public domain lands, including public domain in the National Forest system. State shares in 1984 are for the most part actual distributions made by the Minerals Management Service. In addition, the Bureau of Land Management makes non-Mineral Leasing Act payments on oil and gas right-of-way rentals and some nonfuel leasables (approximately $9 million in fiscal year 1984). The method for allocating these revenues to states is explained in Appendix E.

(b) There is an apparent discrepancy between reported 1984 collections and disbursements for Alaska. See Appendix E.

101

CHAPTER SIX

Resources Leased Under Other Statutes

OUTER CONTINENTAL SHELF

A Brief History

From many perspectives germane to resource management and revenue sharing, the Outer Continental Shelf (OCS) appears to be a unique case. The money involved almost defies imagination. The federal government receives more revenues from OCS—about $9.16 billion in 1983—than from any other funding source except income taxes. And although a small portion of the funds are earmarked to support several national resource-related programs [144], no program has been established for sharing OCS revenues with the states (see Figure 7). [145] Numerous distinctions may explain this different treatment. First, the OCS does not lie within the boundaries of any state and is not a part of other state, federal, and private lands. (The Section 8(g) belt, an arguable exception, is discussed later in this chapter under Distribution of Revenues. [146] See Appendix Figure 8 for a map showing the location of OCS resource areas.) Therefore, the spillover effects, planning requirements, impacts on established users, and loss of self-determination are arguably less than with onshore federal resources. Similarly, the OCS was never part of the states' taxable land base and so has not been removed from it. And although the state taxing powers exercised with respect to private operations on federal lands onshore are, by statute, not applicable on the OCS, the state has complete jurisdiction over OCS-related development within its borders.

OCS resources are among the most difficult to locate and exploit. Development of the vast oil and gas deposits in deep water did not become technically feasible until after World War II, long after subsidies for western settlement and development had receded as a high-priority congressional goal. Disputes regarding title to tidal wetlands arose early in the 1800s [147], but OCS resource extraction did not become a focus of national concern until after the

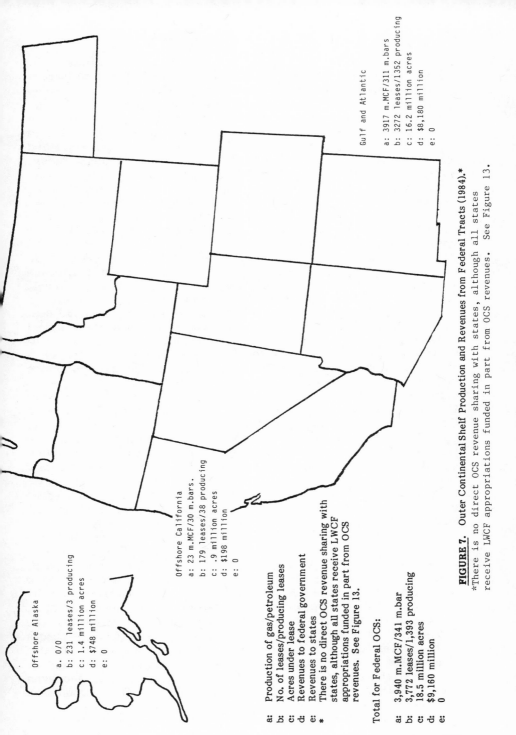

FIGURE 7. Outer Continental Shelf Production and Revenues from Federal Tracts (1984).*

*There is no direct OCS revenue sharing with states, although all states receive LWCF appropriations funded in part from OCS revenues. See Figure 13.

Offshore Alaska

a. 0/0
b: 231 leases/3 producing
c: 1.4 million acres
d: $748 million
e: 0

Offshore California

a: 23 m.MCF/30 m.bars.
b: 179 leases/38 producing
c: .9 million acres
d: $198 million
e: 0

Gulf and Atlantic

a: 3917 m.MCF/311 m.bars
b: 3272 leases/1352 producing
c: 16.2 million acres
d: $8,180 million
e: 0

a: Production of gas/petroleum
b: No. of leases/producing leases
c: Acres under lease
d: Revenues to federal government
e: Revenues to states
* There is no direct OCS revenue sharing with states, although all states receive LWCF appropriations funded in part from OCS revenues. See Figure 13.

Total for Federal OCS:

a: 3,940 m.MCF/341 m.bar
b: 3,772 leases/1,393 producing
c: 18.5 million acres
d: $9,160 million
e: 0

Arab oil boycott of the mid-1970s. OCS issues arise, therefore, slightly apart from the "normal" pattern of public resource history and management.

After a century of resting obscurely in state ownership (as may befit the repository of unknown and unexploitable resources), the OCS became a focus of federal-state jurisdictional conflict in the 1930s and remains so to this day. The balance between state and federal roles in OCS management has shifted several times in recent decades [148], but the basic pattern is clear. Up to three miles from the shoreline [149], states have title to the land and control over resource development. From three to 200 miles, the federal government has "paramount powers," which Congress has chosen to exercise, to an ill-defined and intensely controversial degree, "consistently" with state programs and priorities.

Following an early line of Supreme Court cases, the states' title to the "marginal sea" extending to three miles from shore was virtually unquestioned for almost a century. This state title did not, however, limit federal power to regulate commerce, provide for the national defense, or exercise eminent domain in the marginal sea. [150] Secretary of the Interior Harold Ickes spearheaded the initial federal challenge to state title. He persuaded President Truman to bring suit against California to declare the federal government's rights in the marginal sea and enjoin California's leasing of offshore oil tracts. [151]   Both the state's and the federal government's arguments in the case focused on <u>title</u> to the marginal sea. Nevertheless in deciding <u>United States v. California</u> [152], the Supreme Court ignored that issue and sweepingly declared that the federal government had "paramount powers" over the marginal sea. Unlike title, which would be constrained by the Constitution, the Supreme Court concluded that "paramount powers" were virtually limitless. [153]

Under intense pressure from both the coastal states and advocates of national control, Congress acted to undo part of the Supreme Court's decision through the Submerged Lands Act and the Outer Continental Shelf Lands Act (OCSLA), both passed in 1953. The Submerged Lands Act returned to the states title to the marginal sea. Although it reasserted the federal government's paramount powers over the area, Congress specifically excluded resource development from the scope of those powers and granted to the states the "right and power to manage, administer, lease, develop, and use" the marginal sea. [154] A strong minority position that the Submerged Lands Act constituted a "giveaway" of national resources to the states [155] was "compensated for" in the companion legislation. [156] The OCSLA gave the states no role in development of the OCS, the area beyond the three-mile marginal sea, and even provided that any state law affecting the OCS would be administered by the <u>federal</u> government. [157]

The Coastal Zone Management Act of 1972 (CZMA) softened the

edges of that singleminded commitment to federal control. The act encourages states to plan to protect coastal resources (1) by making grants to defray planning and administrative costs and (2) by authorizing the states to require that certain federal actions "directly affecting" the coastal zone be consistent "to the maximum extent practicable" with plans that had been approved by the federal government. [158]

In 1978, Congress took another step in the same direction. It amended the OCSLA to define a "program" to encourage expeditious leasing of OCS oil and gas resources. A significant feature of the program was an expanded state role in OCS leasing. When developing a mandatory five-year leasing schedule and when making specific lease sale decisions, the secretary must demonstrate that views of governors and local officials have been given appropriate weight, and that the decision provides for a proper balance of state, regional, and national concerns.

The combination of the CZMA and the OCS Leasing Act Amendments (OCSLAA) provides the basis for asserting a state role in OCS resource management. However, a recent Supreme Court decision upholding Secretary Watt's decision to lease in the OCS in the face of objections from California has cast some doubt on the foundations of the state position. [159]

Although consistency between federal and state governments has been the major focus of the dispute thus far, consistency cannot be presumed to exist within either the federal or state government. For example, in California, the Coastal Zone Commission and the attorney general work at considerable cross-purposes with the governor. The attorney general has sued to oppose a consistency determination negotiated by the Department of the Interior with the governor on OCS Lease Sale 73 under the previous five-year OCS lease schedule. [160] Under the proposed program [161], the governor and the attorney general both want areas north of Morro Bay deferred, but the governor has requested deferral of a smaller area than has the attorney general. [162]

Coordination of "the" federal position is complicated by division of responsibilities among a variety of federal agencies and departments. The Department of the Interior, the National Oceanic and Atmospheric Administration (NOAA), the Department of Energy, the Coast Guard, and the Environmental Protection Agency (EPA) also have significant responsibilities for OCS management. Some confusion exists even within the "lead" leasing agency, the Department of the Interior. Prior to May 1982, OCS activities were conducted jointly by the Conservation Division of the U.S. Geological Survey and the BLM. After that date, all OCS-related activities of the Departments of the Interior and Energy were consolidated and assigned to the newly created Minerals Management Service in the Department of the Interior. The CZMA continues to be administered by NOAA in the Department of Commerce.

The Resource

Using the Department of the Interior's definition, the OCS is composed of an area of approximately 1 billion acres.   Although 56
percent of the shelf lies off the coast of Alaska, Louisiana has
historically been the major OCS oil and gas producer (see Appendix
Figures 9a and 9b).   Although the area is vast and largely unexplor-
ed, its oil and gas potential is impressive.   The OCS is estimated to
contain somewhere between 26 and 41 percent of the nation's undiscovered recoverable crude oil reserves and 25 to 28 percent of the
undiscovered, recoverable, natural gas reserves. [163]   This amounts
to between 17 and 44 billion barrels of oil and between 117 and 230
trillion cubic feet of gas.   Although these estimates are variable and
likely to change, OCS production currently accounts for a significant
proportion of our national totals.   Since the inception of leasing in
the 1950s, OCS natural gas production has been rising at a rate of
roughly 1 percent annually.   The OCS share of domestic output
totalled 12 percent in 1981, down from a peak of 24 percent in 1971
(see Appendix Figure 9).

Pricing of OCS Leases

All OCS leasing is competitive, using sealed bids.   Although bonus
bidding with a fixed royalty is the convention in OCS leasing, the
OCSLAA requires the Department of the Interior to experiment with
alternative procedures in 20 to 60 percent of the total lease sales
offered. [164]   A royalty rate of 16.67 percent on production is
normal.   The statutory minimum 12.5 percent may be applied to
leasing in deep waters or in harsh environments.   Firms also have
some flexibility on timing payment of the bonus bid, which the
secretary has authority to defer up to five years.
    Experimentation with bidding forms was initially authorized for a
five-year period, ending in 1983.   However, the results thus far have
been inconclusive and the General Accounting Office has recently
recommended a continuation of the trial period. [165]
    The department is required to achieve fair market value in the
sale of OCS leases.   However, because OCS resources are totally
controlled by the federal government, estimating FMV has been
complex.
    In 1982, a revision of the leasing procedures changed the method
of making FMV estimations.   Previously an appraisal was made for
each tract prior to sale.   Now, MMS relies upon a combination of
appraisal data and bids resulting from the auction process. [166]
Secretary Watt's effort to accelerate leasing elicited criticisms
similar to those raised in the coal program.   Critics charged that the
department accepted bonus bids well below anticipated value, and,
indeed, that in some cases the department accepted bids for leases

at prices lower than those rejected as too low for the same tracts under the previous administration. [167]

The courts, however, upheld the secretary's approach to FMV and held that it was not necessary to restrict the rate of leasing to maximize revenues in order to comply with the FMV test. [168] Concerns about fair market value also take the opposite position. If the allocation system forces the royalty rates to rise to an unreasonable level, the resource may be inefficiently developed, causing the apparently lucrative royalties to go unpaid. [169]

Who Should Develop OCS Resources

Access to federal oil and gas resources is limited directly by the systems of competitive bidding used in lease sales and indirectly by such factors as size of sale tracts and technologies required for resource exploration and development. Congress required the alternative procedure bidding system to encourage the participation of smaller firms that might be excluded from leasing by high initial costs and risk.

Which Resources Should Be Developed?

Because of "paramount powers" over the OCS, the federal government faces few legal barriers in deciding which lands to lease. Moreover, because the federal government owns the entire OCS, unlike the fragmented federal ownership onshore, practical limitations on OCS leasing are fewer. However, decisions as to which areas will be leased must include adequate consideration of state and local interests. The OCSLAA requires that the secretary develop a five year oil and gas leasing schedule. The present schedule runs from January 1982 through December 1986, and the department is currently seeking comment on its proposed 1987-1991 schedule. However, the schedule as of summer 1986 (see Appendix Table 13), which was a revision of a schedule adopted in 1980 for the period from 1980-1985, has been interrupted due to litigation and congressional budget action to halt OCS leasing expenditures.

The department's proposed 1987-1991 OCS leasing schedule was released for comment in February 1986. It retains the familiar "wide area" leasing focus of earlier Reagan administration proposals, meaning that it allows industry numerous options from which to select lease areas. This shifts much of the initiative for final selection of development sites to industry, which is supposed to incur most of the exploration costs in choosing the final development sites from the areas offered. Neither the states nor the federal government concentrates planning and environmental assessment efforts until after the lease sales. The schedule also removes fifteen areas from consideration, designates thirteen more as needing "further study," and slows the pace of leasing by extending the period between leases from two to three years. [170] The proposal has, however, caused controversy in California because it includes areas that Secretary of the Interior Hodel had previously agreed, in a bargain with the California congressional delegation, were off limits. Adopting a schedule is not a commitment to actual leasing because the administration may subsequently revise the plans, omitting or modifying sales.

Basically the OCS leasing process is an iterative exchange of information. It begins with a "call for information" relating to the larger planning areas. [171] The goal is to elicit information from industry, states, and other parties regarding areas where leasing interest is focused and to eliminate areas of significant environmental conflicts. The 1986 proposal adds an additional "request for interest" regarding further areas. Following the call for information comes an "area identification" delimiting locations that will be considered for leasing (this replaces tract selection under the previous process). A third winnowing of areas eligible for leasing comes at the stage of selecting tract offerings under the "final sale notice." Finally, individual firms decide on what areas to bid and how much to offer.

The areawide offerings do not necessarily increase the amount leased (see Appendix Figure 10). To illustrate, between 1954 and December 1981, under the tract offering system, 42.9 million acres were offered, of which 48 percent (20.7 million acres) received bids. In the following two years, with more sales using the areawide procedure, 184.2 million acres were offered, with only 7 percent (13.5 million acres) receiving bids. [172]

A principal difference between the two approaches lies in who - industry or the federal government--selects the tracts for actual leasing. And, regardless of the size of the area initially put up for evaluation, tract size in OCS sales is statutorily set at a maximum of 5,760 acres (unless more area is needed to make up a reasonable economic unit). The average size of tracts offered to date is 5,314 acres. [173]

Because of emphasis in the areawide leasing program on encouraging exploration and development of frontier area resources, Alaska is particularly affected. Half of the planning area acreage scheduled for lease offering and 60 percent of the promising geologic structure acreage lies off the Alaskan coast.

Timing and Intensity of Development

OCS "diligence" requirements have recently been relaxed. It used to be standard to issue leases for a five-year primary term, with drilling expected within four years. However, ten-year leases are now standard with drilling expected within nine years. Leases may be extended one year if drilling is underway. Once a well is producing the lease continues as long as economic production continues.

For those tracts that are drilled, the average time from the lease date to the drill date is well below the statutory limit. It ranged between 6.2 and twenty-six months in the 1974-1981 period. [174] For leases that eventually go into production—almost all of which have been in the Gulf of Mexico—the average time has decreased from 52.9 months in 1974 to ten months in 1981. [175]

Stipulations regulating the intensity of oil and gas activities are developed before lease sales and then proposed for attachment to leases so that potential lessees, states, and other parties can participate in definition of the terms of operation. Typically, stipulations have been used to protect cultural and environmental resources or to mitigate geologic hazards. Stipulations may pertain to an entire tract or to portions. [176]

Participation

Involvement of states and communities in federal OCS development occurs in two contexts: at the five-year program-planning stage and at the lease sale stage. State authority to participate in planning for an area under the theoretically unlimited paramount powers of the federal government comes primarily from two statutes [177] in which Congress has explicitly directed that states and localities should have a significant role in OCS development.

The OCSLAA directs the Secretary of the Interior to solicit state and local recommendations regarding the size, timing, and location of a proposed lease sale and must accept these recommendations if "they provide for a reasonable balance" between state and national interests." [178]   It also directs that "the rights and responsibilities of all States and, where appropriate, local governments, to preserve and protect their marine, human and coastal environments through such means as regulation of land, air, and water uses, of safety, and of related development and activity should be considered and recognized." [179]

This brings into play the second critical statute, the 1972 CZMA, which requires that "to the maximum extent practicable" federal actions "directly affecting" the coastal zone must be consistent with federally approved state plans for the area.

As noted above, considerable controversy and ambiguity surrounds the question of how much leverage these provisions actually grant to the states. Both the programmatic OCS scheduling and individual lease sales have been challenged by states contending that federal compliance with participation requirements has been deficient.   For example, the programmatic schedule set out by Secretary Andrus and Secretary Watt's subsequent revision was contested in court by California, Alaska, and other parties as inadequate in its treatment of states' interests. [180] California has also argued lease sales must conform to its approved CZM program, including policies precluding lease of certain areas. The Department of the Interior asserts that OCSLA authorizes oil and gas development as long as lease stipulations achieve environmental program goals.

Thus far, the courts have dealt with the OCSLAA requirements by treating state and local opinions as "relevant factors" that the secretary must weigh. If the secretary can demonstrate that he has given adequate consideration to state and local recommendations—or to use the standard Administrative Procedures Act formulation, if the administrative record demonstrates that the decision was neither "arbitrary nor capricious" but based on an appropriate assessment of the relevant factors—the courts have found a "reasonable balance" of state and national interests. [181] The meatier issues have involved the CZMA's consistency requirements. In the key case thus far, the Supreme Court reversed the district and appeals courts' holding that Secretary Watt had violated the CZMA's consistency requirements. The reversal turned on a very narrow reading of the phrase "directly affecting" the coastal zone. The Court held that the lease phase, as opposed to other facets of OCS development, does not "directly affect" the state's coastal zone. This strongly suggests that state participation in subsequent phases, that is, exploration, development, and production, will be viewed differently by the Court. Nevertheless, the narrowness of the "direct affect" interpretation is worrisome to state advocates.

Meanwhile, Congress has acted in Department of the Interior appropriations bills to support the states' position. For several years in the early 1980s, expenditures for leasing in some or all of the disputed areas of California's coast were banned. [182] Congress has also considered, but not enacted, revisions to the CZMA to require a broad definition of "directly affecting" and strictly specify maximum possible (rather than merely practicable) consistency. [183]

Distribution of Revenues

The growth of OCS revenues over recent years has been dramatic, as can be seen in Table 10. States and localities are anxiously seeking ways to expand their access to this enormous source of revenues. Congress has earmarked portions of OCS revenues for contribution to the Land and Water Conservation Fund and to implementation of the Historic Sites Preservation Act. [184] Nevertheless, there has never been any formal program for sharing OCS royalties with the states.

One justification for this policy is that in 1953 Congress established a different kind of sharing with the states than in the past.

TABLE 10. Outer Continental Shelf Production and Federal Revenues

	Calendar Year				
	1976	1978	1980	1982	1983
Gas Production (in thousands of MCF [millions of cubic feet])					
Offshore Alaska	0	0	0	0	0
Offshore California	3,475	3,472	3,107	17,751	23,160
Other Regions (b)	3,966,449	4,381,589	4,638,350	4,661,760	3,916,666
Total Federal Offshore	3,595,924	4,385,061	4,641,457	4,679,511	3,939,826
Oil Production (in thousands of barrels) (a)					
Offshore Alaska	0	0	0	0	0
Offshore California	13,979	12,086	10,199	28,434	30,169
Other Regions	302,941	280,179	267,190	292,777	310,534
Total Federal Offshore	316,920	292,265	277,389	321,211	340,703
Revenues (in thousands of dollars; not adjusted for inflation)					
Offshore Alaska	561,063	2,813	111,788	2,057,598	748,408
Offshore California	11,892	13,686	21,265	296,397	198,481
Other Regions	2,394,905	2,924,613	6,229,605	5,469,209	8,212,934
Total Federal Offshore	2,967,860	2,941,112	6,362,658	7,823,204	9,159,823

Source: Minerals Management Service, Federal Offshore Statistics, September 1984,
Tables 16, 19, 20, 21, 31, 32.

(a) Includes oil and condensate.
(b) Includes offshore Louisiana and Texas.

Rather than share OCS revenues with the states, Congress simply gave them the three-mile marginal sea. Another justification is that, unlike federal lands, no tax losses or service burdens are imposed by federal use of the OCS for which states can claim they ought to be compensated.

However, at the beginning of accelerated OCS leasing in the mid-1970s, Congress allocated $1.2 billion in loans and grants to aid coastal states in dealing with environmental risks concentrated in the coastal zone. Cuts in this program have led some in Congress to advocate a form of OCS revenue sharing aimed at earmarking funds to revitalize the program.

The Coastal Energy Impact Program (CEIP), launched as a 1976 amendment to the Coastal Zone Management Act, is composed of three separate parts. The first establishes OCS "formula grants" for new and improved public facilities and services or for preventing or reducing the loss of any valuable environmental or recreational resource required as a result of OCS and coastal energy activity. The second part of the CEIP contains various grants that can be made by the Secretary of Commerce to any coastal state that requires assistance to carry out its responsibilities under the OCSLA, as amended, and provides funds to plan or to prevent or reduce loss of any valuable environmental or recreational resource in the coastal zone associated with certain energy-related activities. The third part of the program is the Coastal Energy Impact Fund, from which loans, bond guarantees, and grants are provided to states that are affected by OCS-related activities. (See Appendix Table 12.) The CEIP was authorized for ten years (1976-1986). Appropriations, which have never approached the authorized level, have been cut during recent budget reductions, and the program may not be renewed.

In September 1984, the House of Representatives overwhelmingly adopted a measure to authorize appropriation of 4 percent of OCS revenues to fund block grants to aid coastal states in coastal planning, research, and management activities. The bill died in the Senate.

Another less direct approach to OCS revenue sharing may result from litigation of Section 8(g) of the 1979 OCSLAA amendments. Section 8(g) gives coastal states a right to a "fair and reasonable share" of OCS revenues generated from federal leases that develop pools of oil underlying both federal and state lands within three miles of the states' marginal sea. The department was directed to put those revenues in escrow until either the states and the department agree as to what is "fair and equitable" or a federal court allocates the money. Approximately $6 billion has ultimately gathered in the account.

Two district court opinions supported arguments made by Texas and Louisiana that the states' share should be based on revenues, including federal taxes and any increase or "enhancement" of the value of federal leases caused by discoveries on nearby state leases. The Department of the Interior has argued that the "fair and equitable" share is confined to reimbursement to the state for oil drained from state lands by federal lessees.

Congress recently approved a settlement that will give coastal states 27 percent of bonuses and rents (plus interest) in the escrow account. Congress also agreed to pay an additional $600 million to states over the next fifteen years for monies that were not in the account. Finally, Congress directed that 27 percent of future revenues from the 8(g) strip, prorated to conform to the proportion of federal and state ownership in the actual oil pool in the strip, be shared with the states. This amount would include only rents, royalties, and bonus monies, and not the tax and "enhancement" payments Texas initially demanded. [185]

OCS Minerals Other than Oil and Gas

Although the major controversy surrounding OCS leasing has thus far focused on oil and gas, MMS has claimed authority to lease other "nonenergy" OCS minerals under the OCSLA and has proposed a standard lease form for such minerals.   Environmental impact statements are presently being prepared on leasing of (1) polymetallic sulfide minerals in the Gorda Ridge area, (2) sand and gravel in Alaska, and (3) cobalt-rich manganese crusts surrounding the Hawaiian Archipelago and Johnston Island.   In a recent "call for information" MMS requested comments regarding the kinds of minerals and leasing areas that were of interest to industry. [186]

GEOTHERMAL

The Resource

Geothermal energy is "derived from the intrinsic heat of the earth." [187]   Although geothermal resources have been known and utilized in some parts of the world (most notably, Larderello, Italy) for over 150 years, geothermal development for the purpose of generating electricity is virtually a post-World War II phenomenon.   Major projects are located in Reykjavik, Iceland; Japan; the Soviet Union; and the Geysers area in California.   In 1985, the total, installed, geothermal electric-generating capacity worldwide was 5,000 megawatts. [188]   The field is developing, but major technical questions are unresolved.   An optimistic assessment is that early in the twenty-first century as much as 25 percent of the electric energy utilized in the western United States could be geothermally generated. [189]   The Department of Energy estimates total U.S. geothermal potential at about 20,000 megawatts, approximately equivalent to 40 medium-sized coal-fired plants. [190]
Technology for large-scale geothermal energy varies with the form of the resource; drystream is least problematical, but in recent years significant advances have been made in using hot brines in California's Imperial Valley.   The major commercially producing leases on federal lands are located in the California Geysers area and rely on natural steam; other producing federal leases may be found in the Imperial Valley.   Initial developments focused on natural steam or hot brine near the earth's surface, frequently causing geysers.   However, two other types of earth heat are the focus of current exploration: hot dry rocks found within 20,000 feet of the surface in the western United States, and deep zones of "hot pressurized water with widely varying salinity" found along the Gulf Coast of the United States and Mexico. [191]   Five basic technologies exploit these different types of resources. [192]   Each has different by-products, advantages, and environmental costs.   Typically the by-products and environmental impacts include some combination of hot mineralized water, sulfur gas, noise pollution, and waterborne minerals deposited in the pipes and casings that can be recovered and sold.

Another constraint on geothermal energy is the fact that there are well-known alternatives in most areas where geothermal resources abound. Because heat dissipates during transport, it must be used, directly or indirectly, close to where it is extracted. Nevada, for example, contains geothermal resources but continues to rely on readily available coal. Reluctance of utility companies to embark on geothermal projects when alternatives are available stems in part from uncertainty as to the time over which a geothermal development can be expected to produce. They cannot become dependent upon short-term or intermittent sources.

Confusion as to whether the geothermal resource is mineral, water, or neither has also slowed the development of public resources. If it is a mineral, was it reserved to the government when surface title passed reserving the minerals? The answer is not clear, nor, therefore, are the rights of overlying surface owners. Is it water? If so, the state water allocation systems in the West may be particularly significant, but their role is not clear either. These ambiguities caused the Department of the Interior to protect geothermal resources in 1967 by withdrawing 86 million acres of public land from mineral entry under both the 1872 and 1920 Acts. Congress was outraged by the withdrawal, and within months it was reduced to 1.1 million acres under the 1872 Act. However, the fracas inspired Congress to consider special legislation for geothermal resources. [193]

The Geothermal Steam Act, which governs the development of public geothermal, was passed in 1970. [194] Its great flexibility testifies to the ambiguous status of the resource, the technology, and the industry. The act does not clarify the definition of geothermal, but it does set up a leasing system for geothermal that is similar in structure to the familiar MLA. Leasing began in January 1974, with interest concentrated in California. Nevada, New Mexico, and Oregon account for most of the public geothermal activity outside California, although some geothermal areas are known to exist in most of the western continental United States, Alaska, and Hawaii. Figure 8 shows the extent of leasing.

Pricing of Geothermal Leases

Geothermal resources are leased in much the same way that oil and gas are leased. Competitive bonus bidding for known areas reflects congressional desire for fair returns to the Treasury. Noncompetitive leasing on unknown areas ostensibly encourages exploration. Unique features in this scheme reflect the numerous unknowns confronting Congress during the design of the act. The Geothermal Energy Research, Development, and Demonstration Act of 1974 establishes a coordination and management project within the National Aeronautics and Space Administration (reorganized into the

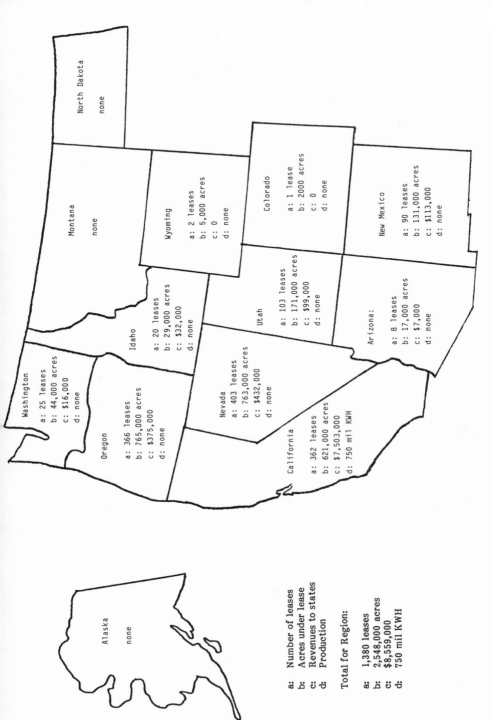

FIGURE 8. Geothermal Production and Revenues from Federal Lands (1984).

North Dakota
none

Montana
none

Washington
a: 25 leases
b: 44,000 acres
c: $16,000
d: none

Oregon
a: 366 leases
b: 765,000 acres
c: $375,000
d: none

Idaho
a: 20 leases
b: 29,000 acres
c: $32,000
d: none

Wyoming
a: 2 leases
b: 5,000 acres
c: 0
d: none

Colorado
a: 1 lease
b: 2000 acres
c: 0
d: none

Nevada
a: 403 leases
b: 763,000 acres
c: $432,000
d: none

Utah
a: 103 leases
b: 171,000 acres
c: $99,000
d: none

California
a: 362 leases
b: 621,000 acres
c: $7,503,000
d: 750 mil KWH

Arizona:
a: 8 leases
b: 17,000 acres
c: $7,000
d: none

New Mexico
a: 90 leases
b: 131,000 acres
c: $113,000
d: none

Alaska
none

a: Number of leases
b: Acres under lease
c: Revenues to states
d: Production

Total for Region:

a: 1,380 leases
b: 2,548,000 acres
c: $8,559,000
d: 750 mil KWH

115

Department of Energy) to inventory resources, facilitate technological development, and guarantee loans for geothermal developers. One of the initial tasks of the Department of Energy was to aid in marketing geothermal energy, but this role receded after federal funding was withdrawn in 1982. It was hoped that states would fill the gap, but none have pushed programs to commercialize geothermal energy. The DOE program was later reduced to loan guarantees. Declining interest in geothermal energy may lead to further curtailment of the program. Coordination between DOE and DOI activities is limited.

The 1970 Act divides the pertinent lands into KGRAs (known geothermal resource area) and PGRAs (potential). Unlike the case of oil and gas, the threshold for knowing a "known" area is quite low. The Secretary of the Interior is authorized to conclude that any area in which there is "competitive interest" that is the focus of more than one application for a lease is known and therefore to be offered by competitive bids. This process supplements BLM's land planning process, which is to identify potential geothermal areas based on geologic surveys and USGS data. This definition may avoid the problems encountered in the oil and gas program [195], but it may do so at the cost of discouraging investment in exploration. A firm may obtain permission to explore an area from the pertinent land-managing agency and invest in exploration. However, if any other operator learns about an application for a lease and files one also, the area must be leased competitively. The explorer has no protection for investment in exploration and is subject to being outbid by competitors. [196] Although some overlapping noncompetitive applications were observed in the early 1970s, suggesting that this was a serious problem, the rate has been low since 1975.

In recent years the Reagan administration has pushed to reassess KGRA designation. The original round of KGRA identification in the early 1970s--totalling 2 million acres--was made hastily on the basis of U.S. Geological Survey data and has been little modified since. In an effort to limit KGRAs to areas which are both economically and geologically promising, the BLM intends to scale down KGRAs to 400,000-600,000 acres. In 1982, the administration offered all unleased KGRAs that were not environmentally sensitive and netted 200,000 leased acres.

Noncompetitive leasing is done at the discretion of the Secretary of the Interior. A potential lessee applies for a lease in a specific area. If the land is available and appropriate for leasing, the secretary may grant a lease to the first qualified applicant. Competitive leasing is done with a bonus bid system. According to regulations, the bid must be accompanied by a check for one-half of the amount of the bonus. Upon issuance of the lease, the bidder must pay the other half of the bonus and the first year's rent. [197] The royalty system is tightly designed to encourage diligent development of leases <u>and</u> to encourage investment in the industry. Royalties are set at not less than 10 or more than 15 percent of the value of steam or other heat sold or used by the developer. The BLM treats 10 percent as standard; the royalty on the California Geysers area was set at 12.5 percent. Reflecting the uncertainties of the industry, Congress also provided a minimum royalty of not less than two dollars per acre per year. Moreover, because the by-products of geothermal production (water, minerals carried in the water and deposited in pipes or settling basins, or gas) may be valuable, Congress also provided for royalties on them—5 percent of the value of the by-product unless it is a leasable under the MLA, in which case the normal MLA royalty rate applies.

Rents are sculpted to encourage both diligent development and investment. For the first one to five years of a lease, rent is one dollar per acre per year. However, the secretary is authorized in the sixth year and thereafter to charge the previous year's rent plus one dollar per acre until the lease is in commercial production. Moreover, starting in the sixth year of the lease, development operations each year must cost more than double the value the amount of the rent required that year. Exploration monies spent during the first five years and those development investments that exceed the minimum required in the sixth and succeeding years can be credited against the required development expenses and against required rental payments. In other words, development costs can be credited against rentals as an incentive for development. If there is no commercially producing well on a leased site, failure to pay the rent by the due date automatically terminates the lease. However, the secretary is also authorized to waive some or all of the rental if that seems necessary to make production economically feasible. [198]

Lease rents and royalties are renegotiated at twenty-year intervals beginning thirty-five years after production. This period was intended to give developers a sufficient term at fixed rates to establish markets for the energy without foreclosing government participation in anticipated increases in the value of the resource. However, the estimated life of a geothermal property is approximately forty years, so its impact is not clear. Royalties can be raised 50 percent in renegotiation, and another 50 percent after twenty years more, but may never exceed 22.5 percent of revenues.

Who Should Develop the Resource

Congress is on record as wanting to encourage development of geothermal resources. However, at this phase of evolution in the industry, risks are high, as are research and development expenses. The market for government geothermal leases is "open," but participation has been limited. Perhaps it is only a temporary phenomenon, but early sales have been dominated by large domestic petroleum firms.   This may be in part due to similarity in skills and equipment necessary for exploration and development in both fields, but it is, nevertheless, a reality. [199] A limit of 20,480 acres on the amount a company can lease nationwide is designed to encourage competition, but industry is advocating an upward revision of that figure.

Which Lands Should Be Developed

The federal government has instituted no formal program for identifying geothermal lease tracts or leasing targets. Many of the known deposits, especially in Oregon, are in wilderness areas. Subject to land availability and the land-use planning process, lands can be selected for noncompetitive leasing at the request of a firm. The government sets competitive leasing offers. In 1982, 41 percent of the new leases were competitive, but this figure is unusually high. Competitive leasing has been concentrated in California, where 148 competitive leases issued in 1982 produced over $23 million in revenues (see Table 11 for further detail). The secretary has absolute discretion to refuse to lease an area. For both competitive and noncompetitive leases, the acreage is limited to 2,560 acres, and an individual or firm is only allowed to hold 20,480 acres nationwide. The intent behind such restrictions has been to encourage competition in the industry, but at the time the Geothermal Steam Act was passed, the industry had not taken clear form. Because it was not known what effect the provisions would have, the secretary was given fifteen years to reconsider the 20,480 acre maximum and raise it to 51,200 acres if appropriate. A BLM proposal made in April 1986 to do just that has elicited no negative comments. [200]

Timing of Development

As noted above, Congress sought to force diligent development of geothermal leases without adding undue risk to leaseholding, and it did so with little knowledge of the future of geothermal energy. Therefore, the timing requirements in the act are less onerous than in the subsequent Coal Leasing Amendments (FCLAA). The length of leases are the same for competitive and noncompetitive leases. The primary term of the lease is ten years. If the lease is being diligently developed but is not producing at the end of its first term, the secretary can extend the lease for five more years in order to produce commercial quantities. If the lease is producing in commercial quantities at the end of the primary term, it may be automatically extended as long as it continues to produce in commercial quantities, but not longer than forty years. If the lessee has already had the five-year extension after the primary term, the next extension is limited to thirty-five years. Either way, if the lease is still

TABLE 11. Geothermal Receipts and State Shares (1976-1984)

	1976		1978		1980		1982		1984	
	Total Collections (a)	State Allocation	Total Collections	State Allocation	Total Collections	State Allocation	Total Collections	State Allocation	Total Collections	Payment to State
Alaska	0	0	0	0	0	0	0	0	0	0
Arizona	0	0	7,149	3,574	28,054	14,027	15,735	7,868	14,737	7,369
California	0	0	56,500	28,250	867,334	433,667	6,107,115	3,053,558	15,187,236	7,502,710
Colorado	0	0	36,248	18,124	27,719	13,860	16,959	8,480	0	0
Idaho	0	0	378,852	189,426	140,537	70,268	261,080	130,540	63,614	31,807
Montana	0	0	10,689	5,344	0	0	0	0	0	0
Nevada	0	0	1,197,508	598,754	1,287,468	643,734	1,888,610	944,305	863,229	431,615
New Mexico	0	0	731,357	365,678	415,937	207,968	0	0	225,679	112,839
North Dakota	0	0	0	0	0	0	0	0	0	0
Oregon	0	0	315,063	157,532	543,852	271,926	394,942	197,471	714,420	357,210
Utah	0	0	1,168,204	584,102	576,900	288,450	476,219	238,110	198,122	99,060
Washington	0	0	0	0	5,120	2,560	5,120	2,560	32,170	16,085
Wyoming	0	0	7,449	3,724	7,449	3,724	9,288	4,644	0	0
Regional Total	0	0	$3,909,019	$1,954,508	$3,900,370	$1,950,184	$9,175,068	$4,587,534	$17,299,207	$8,558,695
National Total			$3,909,019		$3,900,370		$9,175,068		$17,299,207	

Source: Public Land Statistics: 1976-Table 112; 1978-Table 117; 1980-Table 108; 1982-Table 105; 1984 - Table 104 for collections; payment data from Minerals Management Service. (See note for Table 3.)

(a) Geothermal revenues did not fall under the Mineral Leasing Act until 1977.

119

producing after fifty years, and if the secretary decides that the land is not needed for anything else, the lease may be extended for another forty years, but no longer.

Because many geothermal developers were encountering unexpected costs and uncertainty over future energy prices, Congress acted in 1985 to give lessees an emergency two-year extension on their ten-year primary period of their leases. In Spring 1986, Congress was considering lengthening the emergency extension to three five-year extensions. [201]

Intensity of Development

Geothermal development is subject to the standard environmental assessment and land-use planning programs. It is not the subject of special legislation beyond the basic 1970 statute already mentioned. Because of the potential for many extraction techniques to contaminate ground water, the provisions of the Safe Drinking Water Act have special salience for geothermal developers. Moreover, if Congress and the Environmental Protection Agency continue to emphasize ground-water quality, both state and federal legislation and regulation affecting geothermal energy could increase dramatically in the future.

Participation

As a resource on BLM or Forest Service land, geothermal energy is subject to the usual NEPA and multiple use planning processes. State regulation in licensing power plants, setting utility rates, and approving transmission lines plays an indirect but crucial role in facilitating—or blocking—geothermal development.

Distribution of the Revenues

Originally, the Geothermal Steam Act provided that on public domain lands the revenues were to be distributed in the same manner as monies received from the sale of public lands—that is, 5 percent net to the states. Monies received under the 1970 statute from other lands (for example, acquired Forest Service lands) were to be disposed of in the same manner as other receipts for such lands. In 1976, the statute was amended to adopt the standard MLA 50-40-10 pattern.

CHAPTER SEVEN

Surface Resources and Miscellaneous Revenue Producing Programs

Many people believe that compared to the energy minerals revenues, the receipts from surface resources—timber, grazing, recreation, and land sales—are small. Yet, federal timber receipts are typically between $500 million and $1 billion annually, which is considerably more than coal receipts, and comparable to onshore oil and gas leasing. [202] The Forest Service and the BLM manage 39 percent of the total forest area in the country [203], and revenue sharing provides many counties with a major proportion of their annual budgets. Although the recent depression in the timber industry demonstrates that the forest products industry still has potential for a boom-and-bust cycle, surface resource revenues are usually considered less socially and environmentally disruptive than minerals booms, busts, and other impacts.

Grazing receipts are far smaller than timber revenues. For example, in 1984, BLM grazing receipts were $15 million while timber revenues were $167 million. Even eliminating the O & C (Oregon and California Railroad Revested) lands and Coos Bay revenues, BLM timber sales alone generated $17 million. However, grazing receipts may be critical to some localities, in terms of contributions to the local budgets or in terms of their role in maintaining economically productive resources upon which families, communities, and regions depend. Over half (54 percent) of all rangeland in the United States is federally owned. [204]

The surface resources—grazing, recreation, and timber—are the traditional focus of agency attention. Surface resource management programs were the prime concern when agency traditions and social structures evolved. By contrast, the federal land managers have only recently been obliged to turn their attention to subsurface resources [205], and minerals generally do not fit comfortably into the planning processes or agency cultures. Agency-specific differences in the handling of surface resource management programs make it appropriate to discuss them agency by agency rather than resource by resource.

The conventional wisdom that the Forest Service manages the trees and the BLM manages the grass is absolutely incorrect. The

BLM manages some of the most productive public timber lands in the western United States--the O & C lands in western Oregon--and the Forest Service has, since its inception, been intimately involved in the politics and management of western livestock.

The distribution of lands and resources between the Forest Service and the BLM cannot be presumed stable. Ever since Gifford Pinchot succeeded in having the National Forests transferred from the Department of the Interior to the Department of Agriculture, interior secretaries have wanted them back. Harold Ickes, Franklin D. Roosevelt's Interior Secretary, succeeded in "recapturing" about 15 million Forest Service acres for inclusion in National Parks. However, the more general approach, recommended by the PLLRC and considered or proposed by almost every president since FDR, has been to "reorganize" the Forest Service back into Interior and combine it with the BLM. Forest Service partisans have successfully campaigned against this hardy perennial.

Currently, however, the Forest Service and the BLM are jointly pursuing a massive land interchange involving 15 million acres. This is the first time a land swap of such magnitude has been attempted, although smaller boundary adjustments occur quite commonly. This is also the first major reorganization proposal since the 1976 passage of FLPMA. The prospects for its success are significantly reduced by the fact that BLM lands are now covered by specific statutory mandates that conflict with Forest Service requirements in many particulars. The agencys' efforts to consummate the swap administratively have been abruptly halted, and intense congressional and public interest have put the whole matter in limbo. The current proposal involves less than half of the 34.8 million acre exchange originally discussed.

The goals of the swap--to reduce management costs and personnel levels and to eliminate situations in which the BLM and the Forest Service both have offices in the same small town—are difficult to criticize. However, localities are concerned about changes in revenue production and distribution that might result from changed management. The assertion that Forest Service employees will implement BLM programs on former BLM lands and vice versa (the "two hat" concept) has not mollified many interchange critics. The Office of Management and Budget (OMB) does not appear to support the BLM/Forest Service contention that revenue sharing will be unchanged.

Although the prognosis for the overall proposal is murky, parts of it are intriguing. Especially noteworthy is the idea that the Forest Service would be granted full authority to plan for and manage minerals resources on the national forests. Also intriguing is the unwanted attention currently focused on O & C's generous revenue sharing and timber-dominated management statute (see section on O & C Lands later in this chapter). The following discussion is based on the assumption that the proposed massive land exchanges between BLM and the Forest Service will not happen.

U.S. FOREST SERVICE SURFACE MANAGEMENT PROGRAMS

Timber

The Resource. Of the 737 million acres of forest land in the United States, 140 million acres (19 percent) is owned and managed by the Forest Service. [206]   National Forest acreage in the western states is shown in Figure 9. Most National Forests were reserved from the public domain by executive order between 1892 and 1907, so most of them are in the western states. The western National Forests and related landholdings are shown in Appendix Figure 11. However, in 1911 Congress authorized the purchase of cut-over mountain lands in specified areas of the East which contain most of the "acquired" National Forest lands.

Management of a major part of western timber, particularly in the Great Basin states, is impeded by inaccessibility (typically "inaccessible" means that the area does not have usable roads) and low site quality. Nevertheless, the pattern of regional differences in forest land and forest inventories is striking. Nationwide, 72 percent of the commercially productive forest land is privately owned. However, more than half the softwood timber inventory (51 percent) is on National Forests lands, and this inventory is concentrated in the western states. [207]   Almost all the Forest Service's commercial timber lands (68 of 89 million acres) and softwood timber inventory (967 of 1,008 billion board feet) are in the western states. By contrast, western forest industry lands include 15 percent of the western region's commercial timber lands and only 12.8 percent of the inventory. [208]   However, annual harvest from industry and Forest Service lands are about equal, 37.8 and 38 percent of the regional total, respectively. [209]

Pricing of Forest Service Timber. Because of these regional differences in market position and inventory, Forest Service timber sale programs are not uniform nationally.   Two major differences between the West and the rest of the country give rise to differences in policy. Outside the West (1) timber purchasers have greater alternative sources of supply and (2) timber sales are less likely to include inaccessible or difficult-to-work harvest sites.

The following discussion emphasizes the approach taken in the western states. Because the sales price of timber, its relationship to the appraised value of the timber, and its relationship to the

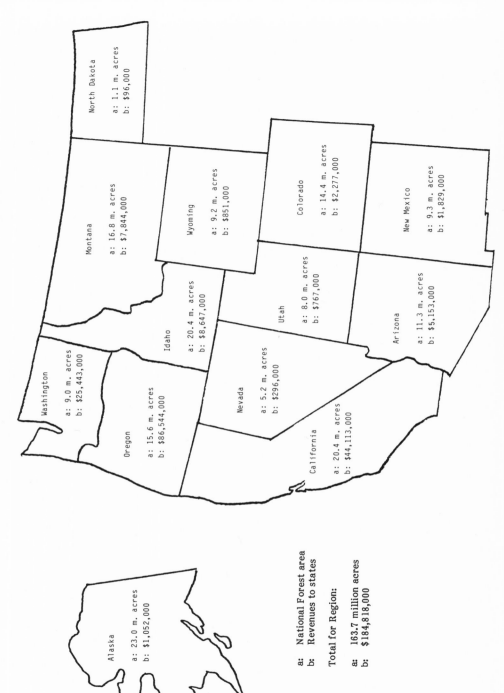

Alaska
a: 23.0 m. acres
b: $1,052,000

Washington
a: 9.0 m. acres
b: $25,443,000

Oregon
a: 15.6 m. acres
b: $86,544,000

California
a: 20.4 m. acres
b: $44,113,000

Nevada
a: 5.2 m. acres
b: $296,000

Idaho
a: 20.4 m. acres
b: $8,647,000

Utah
a: 8.0 m. acres
b: $767,000

Arizona
a: 11.3 m. acres
b: $5,153,000

Montana
a: 16.8 m. acres
b: $7,844,000

Wyoming
a: 9.2 m. acres
b: $851,000

Colorado
a: 14.4 m. acres
b: $2,277,000

New Mexico
a: 9.3 m. acres
b: $1,829,000

North Dakota
a: 1.1 m. acres
b: $96,000

a: National Forest area
b: Revenues to states

Total for Region:

a: 163.7 million acres
b: $184,818,000

FIGURE 8.   National Forest Area and Revenues from National Forest Lands (1981)

management and sales expenses have become intensely controversial, it will highlight sources of confusion in the pricing system.

Appraisals. Timber sales start with an "advertised price" based
on the appraised value of the timber. Actual bids are often more
than the appraised value. In California, Oregon, and Washington bids
ranged up to four times the appraised price during the years 1979-
1981. Faced with declining timber demand in the early 1980s, purchasers were unable to pay the contract price. Congressional action
averted widespread default, but reevaluation of the pricing mechan-
isms for federal timber continues.

In the West, the Forest Service has used a residual value
appraisal method for more than eighty years. The Forest Service
"cruises" the timber to estimate the amount and quality of each
species of timber in the sale area. "Mill case studies" are used to
estimate the cost of a typical mix of products that can be made
from the timber by an "operator of average efficiency." The sale
value of the products is estimated on the basis of a "price index"
calculated for different products from each species in each region.
From these data the Forest Service arrives at the appraised value by
simple addition and subtraction. It takes the total product sales
price, subtracts estimated costs for harvest, transportation, and
milling, and adds in an amount to cover a reasonable profit for the
firm and an estimate of the risk incurred. [210]   The result is the
appraised price of the timber.

Elsewhere the process is completely different. In the South,
forest products firms have never permitted the Forest Service such
intimate access to their books and internal operations as is required
to determine operating costs and selling prices in the West. Where
the residual value method is not used, Forest Service appraisals are
based on transaction evidence, data from comparable sales in each
region.

Sales. Outside the West, sealed bids are used, and the bid price
is the amount paid for the opportunity to harvest timber in a designated area. Thus, the purchaser pays a "lump sum" for the timber.
The cost to the purchaser does not depend on the quality or amount
cut. Western National Forest timber is bid and sold per thousand
board feet. The cut is "scaled" or measured at the harvest site, and
the purchaser pays the price bid per thousand for the amount of each
species of timber that is cut and removed.

Skewed Bidding. In multispecies sales, which are the norm in the
West, the Forest Service estimates how much of the total sales
volume will be contributed by each species. The high bid is determined by multiplying the offered price for each species by its estimated percentage of the total sale volume. Volume estimates can
be manipulated to the purchaser's advantage. A bidder can inflate

his or her total offer by bidding a relatively high price for a species that the Forest Service has apparently overestimated in the sale. If the bidder is correct in his or her assessment, the result could be that the government receives less than unsuccessful bidders offered for the species that are actually harvested. [211] Of course, bidders competitively skew their bids, and either the Forest Service or a bidder may err in the government's favor. Nevertheless, the relationship between the appraised price and the bid price is distorted. Modifications of the system that would curtail skewed bidding are presently being debated. [212]

Base Price and Road Costs. In all regions, the Forest Service identifies a "base price," a minimum amount that must be received in cash. The base price, not to be confused with the appraised value, assures that the agency will have enough cash from each sale to set aside in the mandatory "K-V" fund. In 1930, the Knutson Vandenberg Act authorized the Secretary of Agriculture to establish nurseries and to require purchasers of National Forest timber to make a deposit in a fund, which would be used to reforest the harvested area. The funds are used for general stand improvements, including habitat manipulation.

The minimum cash receipt is made necessary by the current policy regarding road building. The absence of roads makes western National Forest timber sales distinctive. Western timber is appraised and sold as if the harvest area were accessible; in most cases, it is not. Typically the purchaser builds the road and credits the road costs against the bid price of the timber. A key element in the sale offering is the Forest Service estimate of the cost (stated in per thousand board feet of timber) of building the roads to Forest Service specifications. If the road costs are underestimated, the timber sale is less attractive to potential purchasers. Conversely, a timber harvester can also profit from an erroneously high estimate. This further confuses the relationship between timber value and bid price. Although the system of allowing the Forest Service, in effect, to trade timber for roads is authorized in specific statutes, it is controversial. Particularly in the intermountain area where road costs are high and timber values are commonly low, it can result in timber sales where the road costs exceed the appraised value of the timber. This has raised questions about the appropriateness of harvesting in such areas.

Purchaser Road Credits. Sorting out that issue is confused by the system of "purchaser road credits." [213] Forest Service contracts permit purchasers whose road costs exceed the appraised value of the timber to apply their road costs as a credit to a sale in another area. This system works to the advantage of the counties because since 1976 returns to the counties have been based on gross rather than net receipts. Therefore, because the price of the road and the

K-V fund deposit are included in the bid price of the timber, the counties get a 25 percent share even though they represent costs, not revenues.

Below-Cost Sales. Although they financially benefit the counties, such sales have become quite controversial lately: environmental groups and diverse economists have argued that the government is losing money on "below-cost sales." A below-cost sale is one in which the receipts from a sale are insufficient to cover the costs of administering it, that is, cruising the timber, designing the sale and the roads, and the mitigation and environmental protection measures. Because of the Forest Service's accounting methods, data available to define "below cost" reflect only a short-term cash flow assessment of both costs and benefits. Other long-term costs and benefits figure in the discussion, but not in the identification of below-cost sales.

The argument of environmental groups, such as the Natural Resources Defense Council, is that the Forest Service is giving away marginal timber to subsidize road construction and the timber industry. Its position is that every individual sale, not the timber program in the aggregate, ought to be profitable for the government. Accompanying that concern is a long-term effort to protect "roadless areas," in part by keeping them roadless.

The Forest Service counters that its multiple use mandate requires it to achieve goals other than short-term profit maximization. Below-cost sales may be financially beneficial to the government if more comprehensive definitions of "benefit," such as "total value added" or "present net worth," are used. [214] Moreover, benefits other than cash receipts must be evaluated. The Forest Service argues that such harvests are the most cost-effective tool for achieving multiple use benefits: They contribute to community stability and employment, implement habitat management programs, pest control and fire protection efforts, and result in roads needed for administration, recreation, and fire control. [215] Management costs should therefore be allocated to all programs, not just the timber program.

The timber industry makes similar arguments. Industry agrees that the benefits of timber management are numerous but emphasizes that the costs incurred in achieving long-term, diverse, multiple use benefits should not be charged against timber management. Less than the Forest Service, perhaps, the timber industry is likely to believe that money appropriated for timber management should be used to manage timber on the most productive sites. Industry also argues that hidden in harvest costs, restrictions, and road standards are subsidies paid by the timber operator to multiple use beneficiaries, such as water users and recreationists, who generally pay little or nothing for their use of the national forests. Finally, industry objects to being forced, by Forest Service sale design and packaging, to harvest low-quality timber from difficult to access sites in order to obtain high-quality timber offered in the same sale. With these "punishment units" the Forest Service is able to remove low-quality or pest-infected timber and establish management programs.

Economists tend to share the environmentalists' dismay at below-cost sales and perhaps their doubts about the alleged multiple use benefits of timber harvests. They are also likely to share industry's emphasis on concentrating effort and investment on high-quality sites. However, some economists contend that the agency should charge for the currently unpriced benefits of national forest management (such as recreation). Some also argue more sweepingly that the costs of federal management or federal holding of the land outweigh the benefits. Rather than merely oppose below-cost sales, these economists are likely to advocate wholesale or partial divestment of the lands.

Forest Service cost accounting and economic analyses have long been considered inadequate. Moreover, the agency's effort to practice timber management on every acre regardless of cost has been a focus of controversy for decades. The below-cost sale issue will be an important one in the future. Public attention to the below-cost sale issue appears to express continuing opposition to timber harvest and roading generally. Nevertheless, the economic sense of federal timber harvesting deserves scrutiny both in its own right and as a means of understanding the real costs of nonrevenue producing National Forest goods and services. [216]

Proposed Improvements. The overbidding situation in the Pacific Northwest has led the Forest Service and the forest products industry to explore improvements in timber sale procedures that might prevent a similar crisis from occurring in the future. For example, the agency is making more sales, where roads permit, for shorter terms. This practice frees both buyer and seller from the need to forecast the timber market for as much as five years in the future. [217] The agency is also requiring a 5 percent cash down payment at the time of the sale, and the acceptable performance bond has been increased from $200,000 to $500,000 for all purchasers. The agency is broadening its use of "stumpage rate adjustment" (SRA) sales, in which the price per thousand fluctuates with the market price, thereby preventing the purchaser from speculating on rising prices. If the market price for lumber goes up, the sales price of the federal timber will rise accordingly. This is not a new concept, but it is being more widely applied in the West since the timber contract crisis. The agency is also offering premiums for early removal of timber. Finally, the Forest Service is experimenting with the "transaction evidence" appraisal method in the West.

These efforts may not solve the problem. One reason for the apparent overbidding on Pacific Northwest timber is anxiety about the continued availability of National Forest timber. Firms calcu-

late that it is better to risk going broke overbidding than to simply
shut down because of lack of raw materials. [218] Instability in the
Forest Service planning process and twenty years of reductions in
the commercial timber base have combined with the worst depression in the lumber industry in history (including the years of the
Great Depression) to cause bidding problems, which may not be
entirely alleviated by tinkering with the sales systems.

Access: Who Should Develop the Resource.   In the wake of the
Northwest timber contract problem, there has been some discussion
of limiting Forest Service sales to "bona fide operators" who have a
genuine interest in harvesting the sale.   However, it is not certain
that speculators create a problem by pushing prices up, or, if they
are pushing prices up, whether steps can be designed to eliminate
them without causing other more serious difficulties.   In contrast to
federal mineral lease auctions, Forest Service timber sales appear to
provide relatively small firms or individuals an opportunity to participate in and profit from public resource management and there is
some reluctance to regulate access in a way that would curtail this
opportunity. [219]

Access is a critical issue for the timber products industry. Small
firms dependent upon federal timber argue that they cannot afford
to transport materials very far away from their mills. In terms of
the standard fair market value definition, they argue that they are
frequently compelled to deal, and to outbid, larger firms with
greater flexibility in their range of operations, in order to have
access to timber near their mills. This mobility limitation on small
firms is exacerbated by reductions in the "general forest" (harvest-
able) zone on the National Forests and instability in Forest Service
planning and sales programs. The Forest Service spends about seven
years to "put up a sale." The area must be designated in a land-use
or other plan, the roads designed, the harvest restrictions identified
and written into the contract, and the costs estimated. None of that
can happen without adequate personnel and budget. Because the
planning program is site-specific and budgeting is primarily a congressional function, the relationship between the plans and implementation activities is not well established. Congress has generally
tended to fund a higher percentage of timber program requests than
wildlife or other "amenity" programs, but it is difficult for an investor to have much confidence that an operable amount of timber
will be available in a given area over the life of a mill. Some argue
that these supply uncertainties are at least partially responsible for
the western states' declining contribution to national timber production and consumption and to the migration of the forest products
industry to the Southeast. [220]

Which Lands Should Be Developed.   Areas for timber harvest are
identified through land-use planning. The same instability in the
planning process and reductions in the general forest zone that have

raised questions about access have also raised more general concern about which lands should be developed. The debate encompasses all actors and issues in public forest management. However, the inter-play between two concepts, "roadless areas" and "suitable lands," will be the focus of much of the conflict in the near term.

Wilderness area designations have been the most visible compo-nent of the "which lands" question for fifteen years. Roadless areas appear to be the next phase in the controversy. They consist of those areas identified as roadless during the RARE I and RARE II roadless area review and evaluation efforts undertaken by the Forest Service in the 1970s. When Congress has completed action on the state wilderness bills, roadless areas will either be in the wilderness system or "released" to multiple use management until the next planning cycle. The wilderness legislation collapses the three-tier system of the RARE I and II exercises, "in" the system, "out," or "further study"; the "out" and "further study" categories are now eliminated. Nonwilderness "released" lands are now termed "road-less," and they are generally the focus of the below-cost timber sales debate because it is basically the road costs that push the short-term cash flow into the negative. The post-RARE II status of wilderness lands as of summer 1986 is shown in Table 12.

TABLE 12.   Post-RARE II Wilderness Land Status as of Summer 1986

	Pre-RARE II Wilderness	RARE II Acres Inventoried	Wilderness Established Post-RARE II	Acreage Released	Acres Unresolved	Total NF Wilderness
Arizona	552,756	1,955,000	767,390	1,120,000	232,930	1,320,146
California	2,141,657	6,022,500	1,778,432	2,750,000	1,792,622	3,920,089
Colorado	1,191,187	6,493,200	1,393,045	4,519,000	661,510	2,584,232
Idaho	1,490,205	7,685,500	2,334,811	None	6,530,962	3,825,016
Montana	3,087,342	5,050,700	273,119(a)	135,642	4,660,868	3,360,394
Nevada	64,667	2,060,000	None	None	2,060,000	64,667
New Mexico	800,203	1,907,400	609,080	1,490,000	117,530	1,409,283
North Dakota	0	194,700	None	None	194,700	-0-
Oregon	1,214,208	2,976,400	853,312	2,013,000	24,000	2,067,520
South Dakota	0	61,800	9,824	None	51,976	9,824
Utah	30,088	3,002,400	749,550	2,576,000	None	779,638
Washington	1,501,212	2,520,100	1,021,933	1,402,000	96,357	2,522,345
Wyoming	2,200,918	3,794,500	883,359	2,941,000	209,340	3,084,277

Source: Chart based on National Forest Products Association files.

(a)   Wilderness areas added in Montana were not RARE II study lands. There has been no RARE II bill for Montana.

In three western states, no post-RARE II wilderness legislation has passed, so all RARE II study lands are still tied up (Montana, 4.7 million acres; Nevada, 2 million acres; North Dakota, .19 million acres). Seven states have wilderness bills, but significant acreage is yet to be released in Idaho (6.5 million acres) and Washington (.97 million acres). In addition, California and Colorado (after two bills) still have lands in the "further study" category (1.8 million acres in California and .66 million acres in Colorado).

The "which lands" question is also tied to the designation "suitable lands," the NFMA's analog to "areas unsuitable" in the coal program. During land-use planning, the secretary must identify lands that are "not suitable" for timber production, and, except for salvage or other sales necessary to protect other multiple use values, preclude timber harvest in nonsuitable lands. Unfortunately, a biologically marginal site may be economically quite desirable because of its location and vice versa. The law allows ample room for economic considerations in the definition of marginality. However, the FORPLAN linear program system used in the forest planning process does not treat specific areas as unsuitable or put unsuitable lands in a separate or inviolable category. It places all lands into categories defined by site characteristics according to stated criteria and then goes as far down in the ranking as is necessary to achieve management targets and goals. What is untouched under the various alternatives is defined, almost by default, as "unsuitable." Conflict over this approach seems inevitable.

Timing of Development. Theoretically, the Forest Service's national planning process under the Resources Planning Act (RPA) identifies a national production potential that is disaggregated into regional and forest harvest goals for ten- and fifty-year periods, more or less, given available budget work force and demand.

In reality, issues regarding the timing of development are closely related to "which area" questions. The timing issues have centered on questions of the appropriate "rotation age" and the definition of "sustained yield" management. "Nondeclining even flow (NDEF)" and "departures" from NDEF are key concepts. In the Pacific Northwest, these concerns are tied to bitter conflict about the "old growth."

Sustained Yield. The basic idea of renewable resource management in the United States, sustained yield, holds that one should harvest no more than one grows. In forestry terms this means, roughly, cut equals growth. In 1960, when the Multiple Use Sustained Yield Act was passed, this concept was defined as "the achievement and maintenance in perpetuity of a high level or regular periodic output of the various renewable resources of the national forests without impairment of the productivity of the land."

For the manager, sustained yield is based on a "regulated forest," one planned to provide the right amount of trees in every age class so that when one stand reaches its "rotation age" and is cut, another stand is planted.

Rotation Age. The apparently simple sustained yield model leads to serious conflict. It starts with defining the appropriate "rotation age" for a stand of trees: Is it (1) when it reaches the point of "senescence," that is, losing volume to decay and pests; (2) when it stops growing or adding volume annually; (3) when its period of maximum annual growth is over; or (4) when the economic value of its annual growth is surpassed by the costs of keeping the tree for another year? The National Forest Management Act seems to support definition (3): National Forest timber should be cut at the "culmination of mean annual increment." Depending on the measures used, however, that allows for enormous variation in actual rotation age. [221] Due to these "technical questions" the economically optimal harvest point is not therefore forbidden, but the agency is not encouraged to pursue it.

Nondeclining Even Flow. The timing of harvest is further defined by the NFMA's apparent endorsement of nondeclining even flow (NDEF), an extremely conservative formulation of the sustained yield concept. It allows for almost no upward flexibility in harvest output. Because cut can never fluctuate downward, this formulation allows little room for adjusting harvest to meet market conditions or anticipated increases in future forest productivity.

The NDEF issue is closely tied to the debate over whether or not (or how fast) to utilize the old growth in the Pacific Northwest. The sustainable yield from well-managed, well-stocked, rapidly growing trees (frequently called "thrifty" stands by foresters) is probably greater than the sustainable yield from an unmanaged forest. The NDEF constraint is particularly problematic in old growth regions because the old growth cut cannot exceed the growth of the next stand on the site. Because of the nature of old growth volumes, that severely restricts harvests. The timber industry and economists generally believe that the NDEF standard leads to enormous waste of public resources. More public timber rots every year in the National Forests than is harvested. Others see the harvest constraint as a means to protect old growth and related scenic, watershed, and recreation values.

The Forest Service has traditionally embraced this NDEF concept for three reasons. First, it is very aware of the boom-and-bust cycle in early American timber exploitation and believes that NDEF will fulfill part of its alleged mandate to provide a stable economic base for timber-dependent communities. [222] The Forest Service seems to ignore the fact that if National Forest output is constant while output from other landholdings varies, the goals of even flow of timber and community stability are not achieved. The second and third reasons are related to the "old growth" issue in the Pacific Northwest.

Old Growth. Old growth is controversial because it is basically an alternative view of the majority of the nation's standing softwood timber inventory, which is located in the Pacific Northwest. This timber has never been cut primarily because the areas have not been accessible. [223] The NDEF constraint permits the Forest Service to harvest the old growth timber at a very slow rate. Critics point out that this has two advantages for the agency. First, this slowest conceivable "conversion period" to a "regulated forest" has enabled the agency to deflect some criticism from environmental groups, which strongly oppose harvest of the old growth for aesthetic and ecological reasons. Second, this slow method of harvesting improves the apparent returns on investment. When the relatively inconsequential per acre reforestation expenses are compared to the value per acre of harvested old growth Douglas fir, the investments look very attractive. Although this is not a standard approach to evaluating investment opportunities [224], some observers argue that the Forest Service needs reserves of old growth for that purpose. [225]

Summary. Congress did not seriously attempt to unravel this tangle of issues. Instead, over the forest product industry's strenuous objections Congress embraced without specifically mandating NDEF. The secretary must limit sales from each National Forest to a "quantity equal to or less than a quantity which can be removed from such forest annually in perpetuity." This constraint is qualified by the fact that it can be achieved by averaging the total cut per decade, rather than annually. Salvage and sanitation cuts to deal with pest infestations and the like are also exempted from such calculations. Moreover, "departures" from the NDEF constraint are permitted if the plan demonstrates that they are necessary to meet "other multiple use objectives." Both Presidents Carter and Reagan have advocated "departures" in order to achieve further economic efficiency in National Forest management. However, environmental groups have promised to litigate any forest plan including a proposed departure.

Intensity of Development. The intensity issues have until recently been focused on debates over specific management tools--pesticides, fertilizers, monocultures, clear cutting, and the like. Current discussion of management intensity is likely to emphasize, in addition, the application of economic efficiency criteria to Forest Service management costs and timber investments. All of these issues were touched upon during debate over the National Forest Management Act of 1976 and will be debated anew forest-by-forest in the continuing forest planning saga.

Even on National Forest commercial timber lands, the trend is toward less intense management techniques. When the Wilderness Act passed in 1964, the stated agreement was that management would be intensified on the remaining lands to offset reduction in the commercial timber base. That has not occurred. As the environmental costs of management tools utilized by industry to increase fiber yields have been explored, numerous practices have become controversial—clear cutting, use of pesticides, genetic improvements, monocultures—and are restricted or prohibited on National Forest lands. The National Forest Management Act expresses growing national concensus that stands should be managed intensively only after lengthy analysis and public debate.

Economists take a different approach to intensity. As a group, they have long observed that timber management investments are being made "in regions, on forests, and on sites where timber values are so low that the areas should be abandoned for timber growing purposes." [226] Economists are apt to encourage intense investment on high-quality sites. Although the timber industry supports efficient timber investments, it does not always embrace the economists' position. Many forest products firms are dependent on management and harvest of economically suboptimal timber.

Nevertheless, industry and economists generally share concern over the fact that the timber production of the western National Forests is significantly lower than on equivalent industry lands. Typically, growth on national forest lands is about one-third of productive capacity, as compared to about 50 percent of capacity achieved on forest industry lands. Forest Service production costs and overhead are also significantly higher than industry. In part this difference is attributable to the extremely conservative NDEF harvest policy for federal timber, and the fact that the Forest Service invests less per acre than industry. It is also true, however, that the agency allocates those timber investments in ways that do not "maximize productivity gain." [227] For example, a significant portion of the agency's defense in the below-cost sales controversy is built on the idea that timber management expenses support other multiple use objectives. Although everyone agrees that National Forests exist for purposes other than profit maximization and timber production, there is ample data to support the argument that the public timber on National Forests is not being efficiently managed.

Participation. The Forest Service land-use planning programs have been characterized by some of the most elaborate public involvement efforts in government. States and localities probably have less impact in the process than they do in the BLM programs, however, because the Forest Service is more insulated by a variety of factors from local political pressures. For example, the Forest Service mandate includes no "consistency" provisions; moreover, the agency is a nationwide rather than a western institution and its middle level is organized regionally rather than by state. These factors are generally believed to make the Forest Service less susceptible to pressure from state governors and congressional delegations than are BLM officials.

Distribution of Revenues. Twenty-five percent of gross revenues from all Forest Service lands are distributed to the states for expenditure on roads and schools in the counties producing the revenues. There are four relatively minor exceptions to this general rule: (1) minerals on public domain lands; (2) revenues arising from the Forest Service's portion of the O & C revested lands; (3) revenues from salvage sales, which under the NFMA are retained in toto by the agency to fund such operations; and (4) National Grasslands. [228] In addition, an amount equal to an additional 10 percent of the revenues is available to the Forest Service for expenditure in the state for roads and trails. As noted above, the basis for calculating the returns was shifted from net to gross revenues in 1976. This removed pressure on the Forest Service from counties to minimize reforestation work and road standards; however, the Advisory Commission for Intergovernmental Relations has recently demonstrated that the charge did not achieve the stated objective of more equitable distribution of the revenues. Indeed, it had the opposite effect of concentrating new receipts in previously advantaged counties. [229] Recent distributions to the western states appear in Table 13.

Two modifications in the Forest Service distribution formula have recently been discussed. Some representatives have proposed "untying" the revenues, and permitting the counties to spend their share for purposes other than roads and schools, at their discretion. This proposal has frequently been made in connection with recommendations to raise the percentage of revenues shared with the states to 50 percent. More recently, Reagan appointees in the Department of Agriculture have proposed replacing the revenue-sharing program with a tax equivalence based payment. That concept was aired fully in the Public Land Law Review Commission Report [230] and rejected because of difficulties assessing the federal lands for tax purposes (among other reasons). Nevertheless, the proposal has perennially come up in debates and probably will again. The general argument in favor of tax equivalence payments is equity. In theory, in counties where National Forests produce substantial revenues, tax equivalence would reduce the take. In areas where national forest acreage is large but cash returns small, the proposal would increase the payments. However, no proposal that would reduce existing payments is likely to gain acceptance.

BUREAU OF LAND MANAGEMENT SURFACE RESOURCES MANAGEMENT PROGRAMS [231]

Management of Rangelands

The Resource. BLM controls private livestock operators' access to public rangeland and invests modest amounts in range improvements,

TABLE 13. National Forest Receipts and State Revenue Shares (a)

	1976 Total Collections(b)	1976 State Allocation	1978 Total Collections	1978 State Allocation	1980 Total Collections	1980 State Allocation	1982 Total Collections	1982 State Allocation	1984 Total Collections	1984 State Allocation
Alaska	n.a.	$308,651	n.a.	$3,110,320	$26,112,320	$6,528,080	$21,721,488	$5,430,372	$4,028,383	$1,052,096
Arizona	n.a.	2,624,810	n.a.	5,244,825	16,937,433	4,395,379	8,895,208	2,239,423	20,612,437	5,153,109
California	n.a.	23,429,806	n.a.	49,613,260	150,204,067	37,551,017	75,722,595	18,930,649	176,453,983	44,113,496
Colorado	n.a.	1,017,293	n.a.	1,336,442	7,831,708	1,957,927	6,900,472	1,725,118	9,109,155	2,277,289
Idaho	n.a.	4,415,282	n.a.	11,807,165	41,258,241	10,314,554	19,733,955	4,933,489	34,589,555	8,647,389
Montana	n.a.	2,642,354	n.a.	8,258,492	30,339,307	7,584,827	18,265,133	4,566,283	31,377,788	7,844,447
Nevada	n.a.	145,372	n.a.	227,736	1,242,182	310,546	1,115,969	278,992	1,184,414	296,103
New Mexico	n.a.	1,132,488	n.a.	2,357,098	9,715,500	2,428,875	4,313,442	1,078,361	7,314,659	1,828,665
North Dakota	n.a.	—	n.a.	—	332	83	272	68	382	96
Oregon	n.a.	47,376,203	n.a.	101,552,765	395,553,461	98,888,365	187,405,980	46,851,495	346,175,369	86,543,842
Utah	n.a.	446,889	n.a.	884,847	4,431,746	1,107,936	2,704,456	676,114	3,069,628	767,407
Washington	n.a.	12,777,082	n.a.	31,190,534	130,834,160	32,708,540	72,433,720	18,108,430	101,771,938	25,442,985
Wyoming	n.a.	463,372	n.a.	1,116,441	5,588,493	1,397,123	2,638,458	659,614	3,405,862	851,466
Regional Total		$96,779,602		$216,699,925	$820,048,950	$205,173,252	$421,851,148	$105,478,408	$739,093,553	$184,818,390
National Total		$109,929,231		$239,335,459	$934,491,843	$234,495,611	$530,402,712	$133,327,325	$899,746,557	$225,652,655

Source: U.S. Department of Agriculture, Forest Service, Accounting.

(a) Receipts include timber, grazing, salable minerals, minerals leased on acquired lands, recreation, power, and land use. Payments to the states are made under the Act of May 23, 1908 and Act of June 20, 1910 (Arizona and New Mexico).

(b) Net receipts are defined as gross receipts less adjustments for special acts.

revegetation, water developments, and fencing. There are fifty-four grazing districts in ten Western states that were organized under Section 3 of the Taylor Grazing Act of 1934. They include about 155 million acres of federal lands.   Another 17.5 million acres outside the grazing districts are leased under special provisions in Section 15 of the act and so are known as "Section 15" lands. Finally, about .75 million acres in Alaska are leased by the BLM for grazing purposes. The number and acreage of grazing leases and permits by state is shown in Figure 10.   The grazing lands in the lower forty-eight states are in some sense "residuals"--frequently scattered areas so arid or otherwise untenable that they have remained unreserved and unpatented during 150 years of land disposition. However, although the lands were not patented under legislation designed to encourage small family farms rather than ranches, they have been neither unoccupied nor unclaimed. Historic users of the public range have long considered the land to be their own. Although they have never been successful in having title or rights to the land recognized by the federal government, ranchers have enjoyed considerable success in having federal policy tailored to meet their needs and to protect their access.

The Taylor Grazing Act sought to conserve the public range by halting competitive overuse and range degradation by stabilizing the range livestock industry. Following passage of the act, President Roosevelt withdrew 143 million acres of land from entry. The land was divided into "grazing districts," and in a process known as "range adjudication" it was allocated to historic range users. Because priority was given to ranchers who owned "base property" near the public allotments, large cattle operations dominated the process. Forty-two years later, the FLPMA imposed multiple use criteria on the management of the public range, but it explicitly did not repeal the older statute or its use orientation. The cattle-grazing use still dominates the BLM range program.

Despite this persistent theme, in many critical aspects BLM's grazing program is characterized by variability. The average allotment size in acres varies from 68,583 acres in Nevada to 2,217 in Montana. Nevada also has the fewest animal unit months (AUMs) per allotment and per acre. The program varies because the forage resource varies considerably from year to year and place to place. Water availability (amount, intensity, periodicity, and retention of precipitation) is a key factor in determining where, when, and to what extent rangelands will support herbivores, including but not limited to domestic livestock. Areas where snowmelt provides most of the water have less variability in forage yield than those dependent upon annual rainfall. In some areas of the Southwest, ephemeral grasses contribute a large percentage of the annual forage.

Grazing Permits and Leases. [232] Grazing leases and permits run for ten years or less. Duration is supposedly determined by the

138

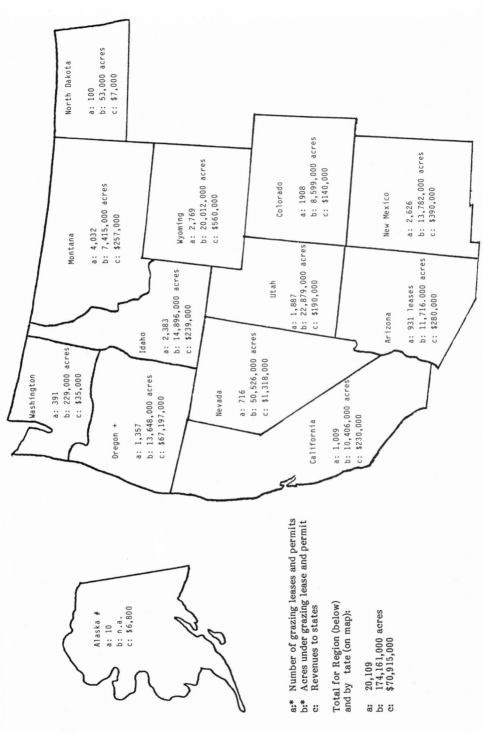

FIGURE 10. Grazing, Timber, and Land Sales Receipts from BLM Lands (1984).

North Dakota

a: 100
b: 53,000 acres
c: $7,000

Montana

a: 4,032
b: 7,415,000 acres
c: $257,000

Wyoming

a: 2,769
b: 20,012,000 acres
c: $560,000

Colorado

a: 1908
b: 8,599,000 acres
c: $140,000

New Mexico

a: 2,626
b: 13,782,000 acres
c: $390,000

Utah

a: 1,887
b: 22,879,000 acres
c: $190,000

Idaho

a: 2,383
b: 14,896,000 acres
c: $239,000

Washington

a: 391
b: 229,000 acres
c: $35,000

Oregon +

a: 1,357
b: 13,648,000 acres
c: $67,197,000

Nevada

a: 716
b: 50,526,000 acres
c: $1,318,000

Arizona

a: 931 leases
b: 11,716,000 acres
c: $280,000

California

a: 1,009
b: 10,406,000 acres
c: $230,000

Alaska #

a: 10
b: n.a.
c: $6,800

a:* Number of grazing leases and permits
b:* Acres under grazing lease and permit
c: Revenues to states

Total for Region (below)
and by tate (on map):

a: 20,109
b: 174,161,000 acres
c: $70,915,000

BLM, but in reality the agency rarely modifies the lease period or terminates a lease. Permittees are granted the privilege to graze a stated number of animals in a designated area for specified periods. The number of animals actually grazed in a given year may vary, given resource availability and market conditions. However, because the value of the base property is tied to the permitted number of AUMs, the BLM will allow actual use to fluctuate without altering the permit. The phenomenon known as "permitted nonuse" facilitates this process. One animal grazing for one month is called an "animal unit month" (AUM), but the figures are adjusted to provide for differences in animal size.

Because the federal grazing fees are less than the full market value of the grazing access, the grazing permit represents considerable value--known as "permit value"--to the holder. Obtaining a permit was a windfall to the original permittee. However, that value has been capitalized into the value of the base property and has been paid for by subsequent purchasers. Although permits are nominally nontransferable, permits typically are sold with the base property. The purchaser pays the "permit value" to the seller rather than the government because BLM does not officially recognize that any permit title exists or that the concept of permit value is valid. Nevertheless, IRS charges inheritance taxes on the permit value when the ranch operation is inherited. Similarly, when base properties including the permit value are used as collateral for a bank loan, the BLM is prohibited by law from altering or terminating the permits. [233]

Therefore, altering the number of permitted AUMs has significant financial impacts on the permittee quite beyond any lost income from reduced herd size. The agency has devised a number of devices that permit reduction of actual grazing use without eroding permit value. Taking "permitted nonuse" allows a rancher to graze fewer animals due to resource or economic considerations without losing "permit value." These same considerations explain the intensity with which the livestock industry and, most particularly, its supporters in the Senate, have fought permit reductions and fee increases, either of which would reduce the permit value.

Grazing Fees. Fees are established by a formula established in the Public Rangelands Improvement Act (PRIA). The formula, to be used on a trial basis for seven years, defines "fair market value" as a base price ($1.23 established for the year 1966) adjusted by three measures: (1) prices paid in production, (2) forage value, and (3) the average annual price for beef cattle. Using this formula, the annual fees per AUM rose from $1.51 in 1978 to a peak in 1980, although the calculated 1980 fee of $2.77 per AUM was reduced to $2.36 per AUM through a 25 percent cap on fee increases in any given year. Due to higher production costs and lower livestock prices the fee declined to $1.86 per AUM in 1982, and $1.37 in 1984.

Critics of BLM programs have long argued that BLM grazing should remain underpriced and have ample support for their position. Recent fees on private grazing lands have not declined since 1980 in the manner that BLM fees have under the PRIA formula. For instance, between 1980 and 1981 private fee rates rose from $7.88 to $8.83 per AUM (adjusted for inflation), while BLM receipts dropped from $2.36 to $2.31 per AUM. [234]   The recent BLM/Forest Service grazing fee study reports evidence of ranchers subleasing their permit areas for as much as eight times the BLM grazing fee. [235]

The struggle over BLM grazing fees has a long and politically bitter history, and it is beyond the scope of this book to renew the debate.   However, Congress has never consistently indicated that capture of "fair market value" is the priority in fee setting.   Use of market appraisals or bidding systems might be employed to approximate market price for public lands forage, but "equitable considerations" (for example, the interests of existing users, anticipated impacts on the local economy) have been overriding.

An all-competitive grazing system has been proposed from time to time [236], but whether ranchers could be induced to pay more under a more competitive system is not certain.   Numerous studies of average ranch budgets have demonstrated that most livestock operators either lose money or would do better putting their money into a passbook savings account.   Moreover, ranchers argue that it may be misleading to directly compare BLM-administered range with those other lands or even to assume that a "competitive" fair market value for public grazing land is an easily applicable standard.   Multiple use management may take precedence over maximizing use of the forage resource for livestock production on the federal lands; therefore, access to public acres may not be equal in value to access to private acres.   It is also arguable that uncertainties in tenure and permissible intensity of grazing introduced by the political and administrative dimensions of public land management reduce the value of access to the forage from the ranchers' perspective.   Finally, the location and character of a tract of land may limit the number of potential users.   Under these circumstances, pricing by competitive bidding or by comparison values with like tracts is difficult.

The current fee structure was, by statute, to run through 1985. Before it expired, a report prepared jointly by the Forest Service and the BLM recommended a fee schedule for subsequent years. Despite the report, as of this writing, changes in the fee schedule do not appear imminent.   On Valentine's Day 1986, President Reagan froze the 1986 grazing fee at the 1985 level, $1.35 per AUM. [237]

Supplementary range improvement funding is authorized under PRIA, which amended FLPMA.   However, no money has been appropriated under this provision since 1981 when $9.4 million was made available.   (See Appendix Table 15a.)   Rather than adjust fees or seek such supplementary funding, the administration appears to be looking for arrangements whereby management and improvement responsibilities are shared with permittees. For instance, in using the Experimental Stewardship Program authorized through PRIA, the bureau may grant permittees up to 50 percent credit (deducted from annual grazing fees) for making improvements. Depending on when the state share is calculated, implementation of such measures would directly reduce revenues distributed to the counties. However, it might also increase range improvement investments.

Who Should Develop the Resource. Congress has been consistent in its effort to protect established range users. Historic range users with a "base property" who survived the early years of the Great Depression were given absolute preference in the original allocation of permits. Present permittees also have preference when leases come up for renewal. The BLM is authorized to review transfers, but they rarely occur. Moreover, although the secretary has nominal authority to cancel or not renew permits, political pressure and statutory restriction make that very difficult. Congress may, however, make it illegal for permit holders to sublease them at a profit.

Which Lands Should Be Developed. Nothing in FLPMA directly undoes the land allocation inherent in the appellation "Grazing District." The Taylor Grazing Act is neither repealed nor, to be precise, amended. The lands were allocated at the time the grazing districts were established. Moreover, because livestock grazing is generally a permitted use in wilderness, those land withdrawals of the past twenty years have had relatively little impact on the extent of lands available for grazing. The planning process required under FLPMA has formalized efforts to reduce excessive allotments begun following NEPA litigation in the early 1970s. Efforts to allocate the forage and range resources to multiple users have already occasioned permit reductions. However, Congress has consistently acted to "phase in" and otherwise delay implementation of those decisions. The possibility of major land reallocation therefore seems slight.

Intensity of Use. When the range was adjudicated in the 1930s following passage of the Taylor Grazing Act, livestock use was the only consideration and the range was still grossly overallocated. [238] In the decades following World War II, the BLM attempted, with slight success, to reduce the number of livestock grazed on each allotment. Since the passage of FLPMA, the bureau has attempted to reallocate range resources to make room for nonlivestock uses. Wildlife habitat, wild and free roaming horses and burros, riparian zone protection, natural vegetation preservation, and recreation constitute new demands on the resource base. Permittees have experienced some reductions in the number of AUMs they are permitted and restrictions as to the season and location of use. They argue that these constitute federal regulation of their private ranch management practices. As noted above, Congress has reacted to planned allotment cuts by requiring the BLM to phase in or limit reductions. Control over and reduction in the intensity of use of the public range lands have therefore been difficult to achieve. Understandably, public expectations of reduced intensity of use by domestic livestock have been broadly established. Current emphasis on cooperative management and reductions in the BLM budget may significantly delay implementation. Ongoing efforts in Congress to compromise on the fee issue by adding concepts borrowed from the coal program about designation of areas "unsuitable for grazing" do not appear headed for success in the near future. [239]

Participation. Although the BLM planning is subject to an unusually broad set of public involvement requirements, participation in grazing allocation decisions is difficult to achieve. BLM is required by statute and budget realities to work with and through individual ranchers to achieve its conservation goals. [240] Moreover, the BLM's predecessor, the Grazing Service, did not take charge of unencumbered lands. From its inception, the service confronted established users of an overallocated resource to which most Americans paid very little attention.

The present planning situation reflects these historic realities. Environmentalists and multiple-use advocates are generally removed from the scene and are unfamiliar with the fine points of ranch management and range science jargon. Therefore, they favor fixed rules and criteria for allocations and statistically valid scientific data that will provide regular benchmarks against which they can assess the progress of BLM programs from a distance. Ranchers are intimately familiar with what they view as "their" allotments, and they are usually able to demonstrate why general rules are suboptimal guides to management of a diverse, frequently ephemeral resource, such as "their" particular grass. They have different criteria for successful management than either the BLM or the academic range science community and prefer to negotiate flexible zones for self-regulation of an otherwise firm commitment to graze livestock on the public range. Despite a decade of litigating, writing, and rewriting grazing EISs, and of drafting and redrafting planning regulations, "outsiders" continue to have difficulties in monitoring public range management decisions.

In April 1983, the BLM introduced a cost-cutting program known as a "Cooperative Management Agreement" (CMA), which compounded these participation problems. Under a CMA, livestock operators or associations with good records of stewardship define range management objectives to be met on an allotment. In return for secure tenure, the rancher assumes responsibility for all capital investments on the allotment and broad discretion in achieving allotment goals. [241] BLM evaluates the agreement at five-year intervals with full power to alter or terminate it. Environmental groups, most notably the Natural Resources Defense Council (NRDC), argue that they are unfairly excluded from these two-party negotiations. They successfully argued in court that the CMA program is an illegal delegation of authority that subverts the open FLPMA planning process. They also alleged that multiple-use values will suffer under reduced bureau control. Though the NRDC litigation was successful, livestock operators were unenthusiastic about the program anyway, and it will not have much impact as a result. [242]

Distribution of Revenues. Revenue sharing has two dimensions in the BLM grazing program: direct payments to counties under the Taylor Grazing Fund, and a "Range Improvement Fund" provided for in FLPMA. The Taylor Grazing Act provides for revenue sharing with counties at rates that differ for Section 3 and Section 15 lands. Although there seems to be little reason for the difference, 12.5 percent of revenues collected from grazing within districts (Section 3 lands) and 50 percent of revenues collected outside districts (Section 15 lands) are shared. In addition, 50 percent of revenue collections is directed to a Range Improvement Fund, which is spent exclusively in the western grazing states. The revenue generated is modest, due in part to a fee structure that historically has underpriced the forage resource. In 1982, grazing fees netted $20.8 million of which $3.5 million were distributed to the states (see Table 14). Direct payments to the states, which are passed on, unearmarked, to the grazing counties, do not describe the full scope of benefits western states receive from grazing revenues, since 50 percent of fees is also channeled to the fund for range improvement. Both the current fee formula, prescribed through PRIA, and the 50 percent fee contributions to the range improvement fund apply both to BLM grazing lands and grazing land under the administration of the Forest Service in the western states.

Revision of the Taylor Grazing Act distribution formula, which provides for a Range Improvement Fund, came about in 1976 under FLPMA. In addition to grazing fees, some mineral leasing receipts under the Bankhead-Jones Farm Tenant Act go to this fund. The Range Improvement Fund is authorized for expenditures at a level of 50 percent of the annual fees, or $10 million, whichever is greater. One-half of the monies must be made available for use in the district, region, or National Forest from which they were derived, and the remaining money may be distributed at the discretion of the administering agency. Funds are targeted to on-the-ground range rehabilitation, protection, and improvements. The 1981 authorization level was $13 million. (See Appendix Table 15b.)

TABLE 14. BLM Grazing Receipts and State Revenue Shares

	1976		1978		1980		1982		1984	
	Total Collections	State Allocation	Total Collections	State Allocation	Total Collections	State Allocation	Total Collections	State Allocation	Total Collections	State Allocation
Alaska (a)	0	0	0	0	0	0	0	0	0	0
Arizona	$826,369	$132,274	$989,657	$209,588	$1,364,560	$303,353	$1,081,561	$231,546	$1,023,231	$249,845
California	347,970	99,524	440,210	151,304	658,408	217,746	534,676	171,815	334,953	109,107
Colorado	815,896	86,065	674,986	117,481	1,107,520	186,999	998,429	157,722	645,741	104,601
Idaho	1,691,279	137,491	1,565,223	219,876	2,595,656	360,200	2,341,978	309,078	1,581,060	215,476
Montana (b)	1,943,145	183,309	2,052,111	271,458	3,039,621	393,326	2,503,761	338,568	1,757,049	236,696
Nevada	2,910,960	205,598	2,940,547	390,241	4,417,790	591,158	3,322,141	441,370	2,638,941	350,064
New Mexico (b)	2,510,924	317,851	2,501,801	454,873	3,559,701	649,214	3,176,551	559,308	2,035,687	366,494
North Dakota	14,572	7,286	12,198	6,099	20,206	10,103	18,303	9,152	13,000	6,500
Oregon	1,369,064	122,632	1,351,648	200,490	2,230,100	321,867	1,663,261	241,499	1,298,782	187,091
Utah	1,292,771	80,864	1,176,148	146,925	1,787,380	223,208	1,909,858	283,732	1,375,038	171,879
Washington	42,402	21,201	43,477	21,738	63,497	31,749	53,177	26,588	38,758	19,399
Wyoming	2,353,991	413,107	2,443,152	574,811	3,564,185	861,326	3,139,040	720,128	2,169,248	504,645
Regional Total	$16,119,343	$1,807,202	$16,191,158	$2,764,884	$24,408,624	$4,150,249	$20,742,736	$3,490,506	$14,911,488	$2,521,797
National Total	$16,240,734	$1,865,514	$16,317,237	$2,827,924	$24,601,500	$4,243,863	$20,878,691	$3,511,294	$15,015,371	$2,573,854

Source: Public Land Statistics: 1976–Tables 110 and 117; 1978–Tables 115 and 122; 1980–Tables 106 and 113; 1982–Tables 103 and 110. 1984 (publication August 1985)–Tables 101 and 108.

(a) Alaska is not included in the Taylor Grazing Act.
(b) Under Executive Order 10787 (November 6, 1958), two states receive additional grazing revenues:

	Montana	New Mexico
1976	73,165	5,065
1978	168,345	9,833
1980	251,818	13,175
1982	199,579	12,009
1984	134,798	7,846

144

Oregon and California Revested Lands
(O & C Lands)

The Resource. The O & C lands consist of 2.5 million acres of forested land in eighteen eastern Oregon counties. Eighty percent of the lands are managed by the BLM as successor agency to the General Land Office. Railroad lands that were within the boundaries of National Forests (about 20 percent of the O & C area) are known as "the controverted lands" and are managed by the Forest Service under the same terms and conditions as provided for in the 1937 legislation. Revenues from the National Forest portions of the O & C lands are distributed in accordance with the O & C, not the National Forest formula.

The O & C lands were originally granted to the Oregon and California Railroad for the purpose of supporting construction of a railroad from Portland to the California border. The railroad failed to comply with requirements of the grant—that the lands be sold to actual settlers for $1.25 per acre. In a complex series of judicial decisions and congressional enactments, the lands were returned to federal ownership and revested in the General Land Office as part of the public domain. The O & C Act of 1937 provides for management of the lands and distribution of the revenues.

Access. Two distinctive features characterize O & C land management. First, timber management and revenue sharing provisions of the 1937 statute are specifically protected from alteration by FLPMA. Thus, multiple use, wilderness, and all other FLPMA provisions apply on O & C lands only insofar as they do not conflict with timber management. The 1937 Act requires sustained yield timber management, watershed protection, and recreation, with the emphasis on timber management. BLM had interpreted this mandate to make room on the O & C lands for a variety of different uses, but they are nevertheless primarily timberlands.

The second distinctive feature about the O & C lands is the revenue sharing. Although the statute provides for sharing 75 percent of the revenues with the counties, the "O & C formula," reenacted annually during the appropriations process, provides that 50 percent of gross revenue goes without restriction to counties containing O & C revested land, prorated according to each county's proportion of the 1915 assessed value of the land, as adjusted in 1934 and 1955. The additional 25 percent of the revenue, known as the "plow back," is invested in roads and O & C land productivity. The remaining 25 percent of the revenues goes to the federal treasury. O & C lands are not entitlement lands under the PILT program.

The 25 percent now "reinvested" was originally set aside from revenues to reimburse the federal government for expenses incurred during reinvestment. When back taxes were paid and some equity interests compensated by the Treasury, the money was intended to go to the state school fund to total the 75 percent share. In 1952, that indebtedness was paid off. However, at that time the BLM budget was at or near zero as a result of conflict in Congress about grazing fees. [243] During that crisis a pattern developed of amending the 1937 Act annually in the appropriations process to "plow back" the 25 percent of revenues into intensive land management programs on the O & C lands. The pattern continues to this day. Predictably, the annual appropriation from the general fund for BLM management activities on the O & C lands dropped to near zero as the 25 percent of revenues grew to nearly $50 million in 1979. However, during the recent decline in revenues from timber sales, the BLM was pressured to invest other monies in O & C lands, and the appropriated funds exceeded the plow back.

The O & C formula, plus the enormous amounts of money involved, have long suggested to many observers that O & C revenues ought to be allocated at the same rate as National Forest revenues rather than at two to three times that rate. (It has also been suggested that the Forest Service percentage ought to be raised.) Although it is arguable that the "plow back" provisions were instituted primarily to deflect scrutiny away from the 75 percent state portion of extremely valuable resources, it is also true that the O & C lands may justify a higher return to counties. Unlike the public domain National Forests, they were on local tax rolls for some time before reinvestment. If there is any justification for treating acquired lands differently from the public domain lands in the context of alleged tax losses, then the O & C lands will require special thought despite the fact that they are combined with and indistinguishable from Forest Service lands that return only 25 percent to the counties. Moreover, though it might at first appear that equity would require the payout rate to be reduced, it would be worth comparing the O & C payout with the Forest Service payout adjusted to show agency investments in managing western Oregon National Forests. It could be that there is actually very little difference in the federal investment in heavily timbered Oregon counties.

Coos Bay Wagon Road Lands (CBWR)

Coos Bay Wagon Road (CBWR) lands are similar to the O & C lands in virtually every way except revenue payments. They are discussed separately here to underscore the fact that a pattern emerges in the apparently odd mix of revenue sharing programs when the original design of the programs is examined.

CBWR lands were originally granted to the Oregon and California Railroad. They include all odd-numbered sections in a six-mile wide swath between Coos Bay and Roseburg, Oregon. The grant, which was intended to finance construction of a military road between the two villages, was forfeited by the railroad for violating grant provisions identical to those that caused revestment of the O & C lands. After reinvestment, the CBWR lands were to be treated exactly like the O & C lands. However, Congress inadvertently omitted them from the section of the 1937 Act that dealt with revenue sharing and was therefore obliged to pass another act specifically pertaining to the CBWR lands. The statute, enacted in 1939, provides for payments to the counties based not on a percentage of revenues but on a tax-equivalence basis.

This odd quirk in the payout plan arises from the political history of the O & C lands. Prior to the passage of the O & C Act, the federal government had been making payments to the O & C counties based on the taxes previously paid on the lands. When the O & C Act was being debated in Congress, the revenues produced by the lands was small. Therefore, the Oregon delegation fought hard, but unsuccessfully, to retain the tax-equivalence basis for payment. Two years later, when the CBWR lands were up for renewed consideration, the Oregon delegation prevailed. It took only a decade for the revenue situation to reverse itself and demonstrate that the "defeat" in the O & C Act, which resulted in a revenue share rather than a tax-equivalence payment, was in reality a tremendous boon to the O & C counties. Revenues from O & C and Coos Bay timber appear in Table 15, along with state shares from other BLM-managed resources.

Sale of Land, Materials, and Timber (Bureau of Land Management)

The Resources. This discussion covers sales of land and materials, including the "common" varieties of minerals defined in the Common Varieties Act of 1955 and vegetation on the "public lands" administered by the BLM. These lands include both public domain and acquired acreage. With the exception of the O & C and Coos Bay timber lands, BLM timber sales follow a similar revenue distribution formula as other sales, but because the management and sales procedures are different timber sales have been taken up separately.

Pricing Land and Materials Sales. Under most circumstances, land and materials are to be sold at fair market value through competitive bidding. Bids may be sealed, oral, or a combination of the two, as determined by the bureau. Regulations for mineral materials disposal, under the Materials Act, provide that the materials be appraised and sold at no less than the appraised value, to be determined by a federal or independent appraiser.

Commercial timber sales are generally accomplished through competitive bidding, but the bureau also uses negotiated sales. In the latter case, timber is not to be sold at less than the appraised

TABLE 15. BLM Land and Timber Sales Receipts and State Revenue Shares

	1976		1978		1980		1982		1984	
	Total Collections	State Allocation	Total Collections	State Allocation	Total Collections	State Allocation	Total Collections	State Allocation	Total Collections	State Allocation
Alaska	$829,683	$33,187	$29,401	$1,176	($603,674)(a)	($24,147)(a)	$158,159	$6,326	$170,931	$6,837
Arizona	59,619	2,385	48,297	1,932	35,290	1,412	67,036	2,681	747,589	29,904
California	1,105,314	44,212	2,658,827	106,353	2,869,688	114,787	883,230	35,329	3,030,292	121,212
Colorado	161,377	6,455	256,388	10,256	384,661	15,386	739,985	29,599	895,303	35,812
Idaho	860,082	34,403	267,764	10,711	237,800	34,448	308,760	12,350	579,142	23,166
Montana	44,589	1,784	258,949	11,438	192,033	7,681	230,992	9,240	512,121	20,485
Nevada	1,886,418	75,457	210,843	8,434	6,617,465	264,699	769,866	11,902	6,970,670	968,074
New Mexico	740,825	29,633	145,405	5,816	203,904	8,130	309,068	12,363	577,040	23,082
North Dakota	0	0	0	0	0	0	0	0	14,217	569
Oregon (b)	129,775,461	60,617,783	192,472,655	88,437,735	212,364,921	98,543,741	86,179,213	40,071,005	150,653,844	67,010,333
Utah	536,207	21,448	49,657	1,986	205,662	8,226	366,806	14,672	454,719	18,189
Washington	437,341	17,494	338,336	13,533	52,994	2,120	334,927	13,397	398,342	15,934
Wyoming	164,349	6,574	229,981	9,199	665,470	26,619	604,498	24,180	1,383,331	55,333
Regional Total	$136,601,265	$60,890,815	$196,993,503	$88,618,569	$223,226,214	$99,003,102	$90,952,530	$40,243,046	$166,387,541	$68,328,930
National Total	$136,601,757(c)	$60,890,835	$197,002,757	$88,618,957	$223,865,781	$99,003,749	$90,999,326	$40,244,916	$166,688,006	$68,340,949

Source: Public Land Statistics: 1976—Tables 110 and 117; 1978—Tables 115 and 122; 1980—Tables 106 and 113; 1982—Tables 103 and 110. 1984 (to be published in August 1985) – Tables 101 and 108.

(a) Prior year adjustment.
(b) Includes O & C and Coos Bay lands. Figures for all other states apply to public lands only.
(c) Includes $2,604,884 from the sale of geothermal steam. From 1977 on, geothermal revenues have been shared with states according to the leased mineral formula (50 percent), rather than as a salable commodity (5 percent share).

fair market value. As with other materials disposal procedures, bidding may be by sealed, written, oral bids, or a combination of these methods.

Who Should Develop the Resources. Statutes and BLM policy protect two categories of potential purchasers: historic users of the public domain, and states and localities. With land sales, FLPMA and related regulations offer ample opportunity for modified competitive bidding "when . . . it is necessary to assure equitable distribution of land among purchasers or to recognize equitable consideration or public policies." Modifications include limitations on permitted bidders and a right of selected bidders to match the highest bid. [244] Noncompetitive sales of land may also be conducted (for example, to protect an existing, authorized use).

Noncompetitive, negotiated sales are allowed where competition is not feasible. Unless the materials are to be used for development of federal lands under a mineral lease, such sales may not exceed $5,000. Where a competitive market is expected, competitive sales are conducted. Free use of materials is allowed where the user is a government and the purpose is not-for-profit.

Which Resources Should Be Developed. Land and most other materials are offered for sale only after a land-use planning process. For land sales, it must be proven that a sale is "in the public interest," that is, that a tract is needed for community expansion or is "difficult and uneconomic" for the BLM to manage and not suited to management by another federal agency. At least two years' notice prior to disposal must be given any grazing permittee or lessee. Standard policy is to reserve mineral rights to the United States.

Participation. A sale of land or other material is, in theory, the result of a BLM planning process identifying suitability for sale. Because FLPMA requires state and local government as well as public involvement, all interested persons should have opportunities to influence contemplated sales at this stage. Moreover, local governments have a direct involvement in proposed land sales in that FLPMA requires that the bureau notify the land-use regulatory jurisdiction in which the proposed sale is located at least sixty days prior to sale. Under BLM planning regulations the BLM sales program must be consistent with land-use policy and zoning adopted by the community. A recent National Wildlife Federation lawsuit brought into question a whole series of real estate transactions, including land sales, which have gone forward since 1981. Any sales in areas that have had ramifications on withdrawals adjusted since that time are presently in limbo if the sale would have been barred by the pre-January 1981 land status. [245]

Distribution of the Revenues. Compared with mineral leasing, the direct state and local financial interest in these sales is miniscule. Only 5 percent of the revenues goes to the states; the other 95 percent goes to the Reclamation Fund. The 5 percent distribution is a relic of the original share that states received from domain land sales, usually set out in state admission acts. Since the advent of federal reclamation activities in 1902, the balance of land sales revenues have been sent to the Reclamation Fund.

Although receipts from land and materials sales were the mainstay of public land revenues prior to the development of leased minerals in the 1920s, they are now dwarfed by other revenue sources. In 1982, sales of land and materials from the lands administered by the Bureau of Land Management totaled only $3.6 million, $195,904 of which was distributed to the states. [246] Table 15 shows the states' shares of these sales.

Although FLPMA emphasizes fair market value in public land transactions, it also creates ample opportunity for discretionary BLM decisions to suspend or restrict market and price competition. Recent debates over proposed "privatization" of BLM lands illustrate the potential application of this authority. In part due to anticipated difficulties of purchasing lands at fair market value, most BLM constituency groups oppose sales unless "equitable considerations" are applied to favor established users. [247]

Furthermore, FLPMA left intact the Recreation and Public Purposes Act of 1926, a statute that authorizes donations of BLM land to states and localities for purposes suggested by the title of the statute. The states could lose revenues under this program, but they gain the lands.

BLM Leases and Rentals

The BLM issues leases, permits, and easements to use the public lands for a variety of purposes including residential, industrial, agricultural, and commercial uses. Permits are generally issued where little private investment or land improvements are involved, and they have a term of up to three years. More permanent uses require leases.

Commercial-purpose leases may be issued through competitive bidding if circumstances warrant. Negotiated, noncompetitive procedures are used where there is no competition or where "equity interests" are primary. In either case, no less than fair market value may be charged.

There is no special statutory provision for sharing lease and rental revenues with the states. The receipts are deposited in the U.S. General Fund.

CHAPTER EIGHT

Miscellaneous Funds

RECLAMATION FUND

Revenues generated by and allocated to reclamation projects are not distributed directly to western states or localities. This section summarizes the way in which substantial revenues generated by federal land use are channeled into reclamation projects. This constitutes a substantial investment in western resource development, in progress since the passage of the Reclamation Act in 1902. Through that act, a fund was established to provide federal advances to finance irrigation projects. The fund was to revolve so that the federal seed money was to be repaid in ten years through sales of irrigated lands and water. By 1910, additional funding was needed. At that time a $20 million Treasury "loan" began a long pattern of failure to sustain the revolving fund through project repayments and the resulting need for additional Treasury support and outside revenue sources.

In the Mineral Leasing Act, Congress allocated 52.5 percent (reduced to 40 percent in 1976) of mineral revenues to the Reclamation Fund. Other "accretions" to the fund, that is, revenues collected by agencies not associated with Bureau of Reclamation activities, come from sales of public lands and timber, rights-of-way, and various leases and permits on public lands. Total allocation of public land revenues to the fund in 1982 was $487.9 million (see Appendix Table 17). By 1980, leased minerals had contributed 36 percent of all fund revenues from 1903 to 1980 (Appendix Table 16), and the total cumulative contribution from public land revenues had been $2.6 billion--almost 43 percent of all Reclamation Fund monies (see Appendix Table 16). The Reclamation Fund receives revenues from the following sources:

(1) Forty percent (52.5 percent prior to 1977) of the revenues from minerals leased under the Mineral Lands Leasing Act and those leased minerals on acquired lands subject to the Mineral Leasing Act distribution formula go to the Reclamation Fund.

(2) All money received from sale and disposal of public lands in the reclamation states, except for 5 percent distributed to the

states for education and other purposes, goes to the Reclamation Fund to be used for projects in these states. (The 95-5 percent split is calculated on net proceeds.) In addition to these land sales revenues, various provisions direct to the fund all payments received in connection with a project (for example, sales of lands withdrawn in connection with a project and sales of hydroelectric power).

(3) Fifty percent of the revenues from licenses issued for hydroelectric projects using public lands and National Forests are distributed to the Reclamation Fund. The remainder are allocated as follows: 37.5 percent to the states (unearmarked) in which the lands are located and 12.5 percent to the Treasury. Originally under authority of the Bureau of Reclamation, these licenses are now administered by the Federal Energy Regulatory Commission (FERC).

Reclamation Fund expenditures require Congressional appropriations and are limited to the "reclamation states": Arizona, California, Colorado, Idaho, Kansas, Montana, Nebraska, Nevada, New Mexico, North Dakota, Oklahoma, Oregon, South Dakota, Washington, Wyoming, and Texas. Reclamation expenditures from the Reclamation Fund and all other sources (shown in Figure 11 and Appendix Table 18) have vastly outstripped collections in the Reclamation Fund.

Although it is in many ways a bookkeeping fiction, the Reclamation Fund has interesting distributional effects. The revenues (shown in Appendix Table 17) are not like shared minerals revenues, returned to the state of origin. Until 1910, reclamation law stipulated that "where practicable," reclamation funds should be spent in the state generating the revenues. This apparently proved unfeasible and was changed. Since the 1950s, Reclamation Fund monies have not even been accounted for separately in western water projects. Instead, the fund appropriations are combined with other sources—chiefly General Fund appropriations (see Appendix Table 16). For this reason it is not practical to treat Reclamation Fund expenditures as a discrete category. However, it is meaningful to point out that to date, the chief reclamation project beneficiaries have been states such as California and Arizona, while the mineral revenue-generating states, such as Wyoming and New Mexico, have benefitted less (see Appendix Table 18).

PAYMENTS IN LIEU OF TAXES

The PILTs program, established in 1976, provides for payments of up to seventy-five cents per acre for any federally owned "entitlement" lands (shown in Figure 12). The program sends $95 to 105 million per year in payments to localities. [248] Approximately two-thirds of this amount is distributed in the western states (see Appendix Table 15).

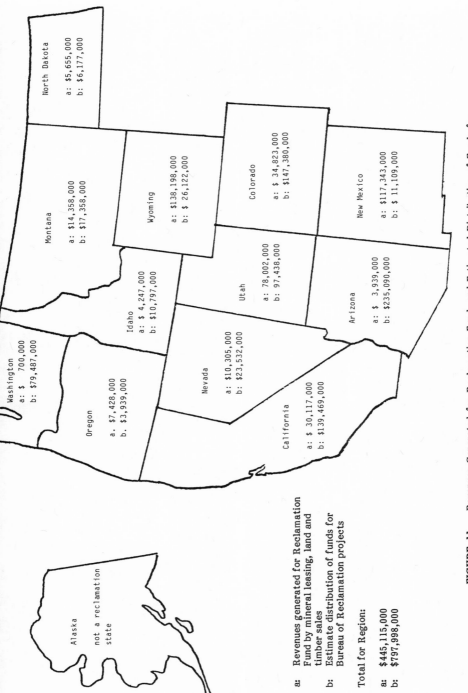

FIGURE 11. Revenues Generated for Reclamation Fund, and Estimated Distribution of Funds for Bureau of Reclamation Projects (1982).

North Dakota
a: $5,655,000
b: $6,177,000

Montana
a: $14,358,000
b: $17,358,000

Wyoming
a: $138,198,000
b: $ 26,122,000

Colorado
a: $ 34,823,000
b: $147,380,000

New Mexico
a: $117,343,000
b: $ 11,109,000

Idaho
a: $ 4,247,000
b: $10,797,000

Utah
a: 78,002,000
b: 97,438,000

Arizona
a: $ 3,939,000
b: $235,090,000

Washington
a: $ 700,000
b: $79,487,000

Oregon
a. $7,428,000
b. $3,939,000

Nevada
a: $10,305,000
b: $23,532,000

California
a: $ 30,117,000
b: $139,469,000

Alaska
not a reclamation
state

a: Revenues generated for Reclamation Fund by mineral leasing, land and timber sales

b: Estimate distribution of funds for Bureau of Reclamation projects

Total for Region:

a: $445,115,000
b: $797,998,000

Washington
a: 11.3 million acres
b: $3 million

Oregon
a: 29 million acres
b: $2.7 million

Montana
a: 27.1 million acres
b: $8.5 million

North Dakota
a: .5 million acres
b: .5 million

Idaho
a: 32.7 million acres
b: $7.6 million

Wyoming
a: 29.5 million acres
b: $7.7 million

Nevada
a: 56.9 million acres
b: $5.5 million

Utah
a: 32.9 million acres
b: $8.8 million

Colorado
a: 23.4 million acres
b. $7.6 million

California
a: 42.1 million acres
b: $11.7 million

Arizona
a: 30 million acres
b: $8.7 million

New Mexico
a: 22.3 million acres
b: $10.1 million

Alaska
a: 81.9 million acres
b: $3.2 million

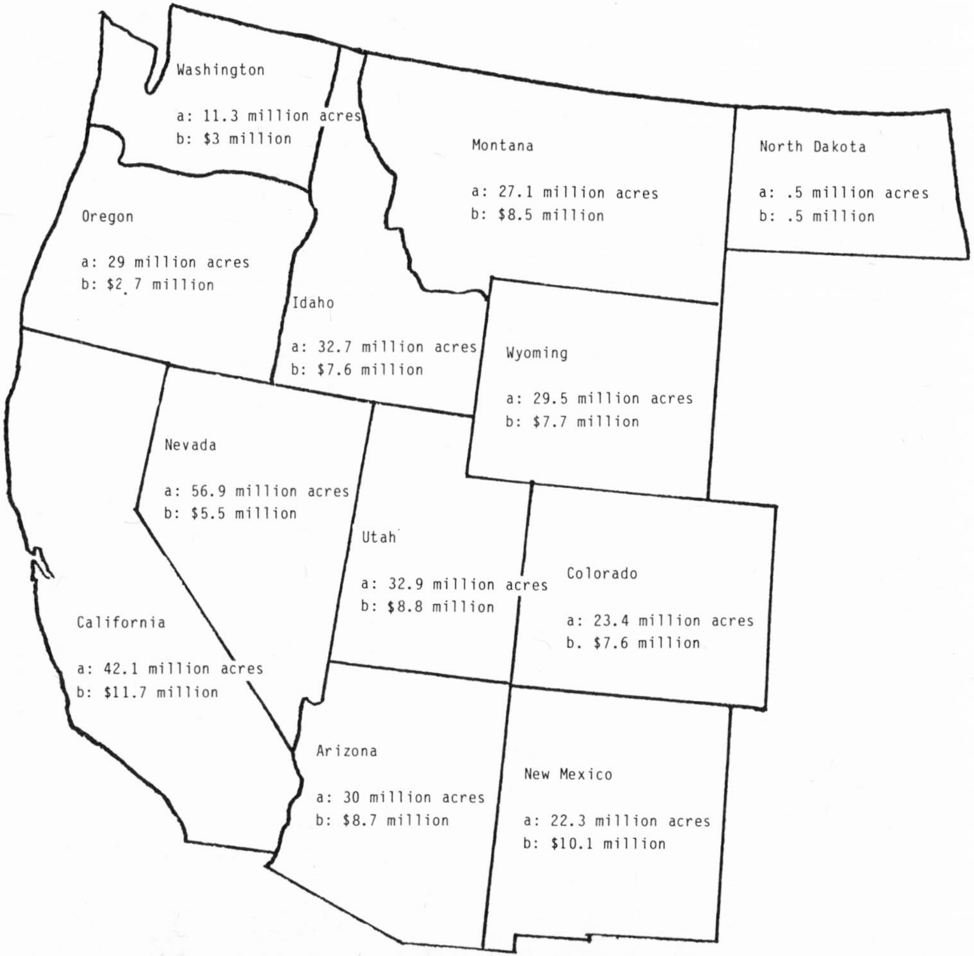

Total for Region:

a: Entitlement acres: 419.6 acres
b: Payments: $85.7 million

a: Entitlement Land Area and Payments Made in Lieu of Taxes (1984)

154

FIGURE 19.

PILT monies are paid to the principal level of government delivering services. The statute offers two formulas for determining the payment, and localities get whichever amount is greater: either ten cents per acre, or seventy-five cents per acre adjusted by a population-based formula and reduced by the amount received by the local government under any of six named revenue sharing programs. Revenue shares to be deducted include those under the MLA, the Taylor Grazing Act, the National Forest Revenues Act, the Bankhead Jones Farm Tenants Act, the Mineral Leasing on Acquired Lands Act, and the Material Disposal Act. Densely populated counties and those with limited revenue sharing income get the full seventy-five cents, whereas sparsely populated areas already receiving large amounts of resource revenues receive another ten cents an acre minimum under PILTS. However, the resource revenues shared with the states but not passed through to the counties are not deducted from the PILT payment. Thus, the program discourages the states from passing through shared revenues. In addition to the annual per acre payment, the PILT Act provides that 1 percent of the fair market value of any land acquired for park or wilderness purposes since December 31, 1970 must be paid to the locality for five years after the date of purchase. (The influence of the California delegation is apparent in the bending of that cutoff date. Redwoods National Park acquisitions are compensated beginning in November 2, 1968.) Total amounts paid to western states in recent years are shown in Table 16.

The general principles of the program were nominally defined by the Public Land Law Commission (PLLRC). In its 1970 Report, the PLLRC evaluated all of the inconsistencies, inequities, and confusion created by the complex of revenue sharing programs and recommended that the whole system be scrapped. However, the commission was explicit that states and localities ought to be compensated for the actual burdens created by tax-exempt and immune federal lands. It therefore recommended a PILTS program based on a tax-equivalence approach. The PLLRC argued that the federal government should pay an amount roughly equivalent to the taxes a private landholder would pay for the federal lands. The PLLRC also recommended that the PILT payment should be reduced to account for the benefits accruing to localities because of the federal lands, and to provide extraordinary compensation for any extraordinary burdens.

Congress embraced the PLLRC commitment to compensating counties for the burdens of federal land ownership but rejected its specific proposals. Any tax-equivalence based program for the public domain lands imposes vast problems in terms of assessing for tax purposes enormous areas never previously taxed. Moreover, the process of trying to identify and quantify benefits and burdens is complex and inconclusive. Indeed, the available data point almost without exception to the conclusion that the federal lands are not a

TABLE 16.   Payments in Lieu of Taxes to States (Thousands of Dollars)

State	FY 1978 (a)	FY 1980	FY 1982	FY 1984
Alaska	$ 4,594	$ 4,079	$ 3,475	$ 3,197
Arizona	7,707	7,613	8,173	8,708
California	7,959	12,760	10,861	11,720
Colorado	7,604	7,507	6,608	7,643
Idaho	7,558	6,707	6,868	7,596
Montana	6,455	8,078	7,214	8,504
Nevada	4,253	5,200	5,069	5,528
New Mexico	9,676	9,590	8,935	10,071
North Dakota	438	572	513	534
Oregon	3,884	2,831	2,532	2,728
Utah	6,436	8,147	7,930	8,750
Washington	3,321	1,455	1,595	3,001
Wyoming	7,327	6,551	6,974	7,706
Regional Total	$77,212	$81,090	$76,747	$85,686
National Total	$98,600 (est.)	$103,425	$95,482	$104,598

Source: U.S. Department of the Interior, Bureau of Land Management.

(a)   The Act was passed in 1976; payments began the following year.

burden on the localities. [249] Therefore, Congress bypassed the costly and potentially disruptive calculations and simply put another layer of payments over the existing revenue sharing scheme. In an obvious effort to attract eastern support for the measure, National Parks (which are an undeniable benefit to the localities) were also included, not merely as entitlement lands, but also for the "double dip" payments on acquired parks and wilderness lands.

An interesting and previously unnoted provision in the PILTs statute was revealed in May 1984, in the process of a BLM land exchange with South Dakota. The question was raised whether the lands that BLM acquires in trade from the state become entitlement lands for PILTs purposes. If the lands traded by the state were state-owned prior to the trade, and thus immune from local taxation, they do not become entitlement lands under the statute. [250]

Alterations of the program have consisted of occasionally successful efforts to expand or contract the entitlement categories. The original components of the category included lands managed by the Forest Service, the Park Service, and the BLM. Additions include the wildlife refuges (which were originally omitted due to a power struggle between congressional committees, not because they ought not to have been included) and inactive military lands.   Frequent candidates for inclusion include active military lands, and lands removed from the tax roles because they are used by international organizations or foreign embassies.

Attention to the PILTS program is reactivated annually during the budget process.   Although one ostensible goal of the program was to provide some stability in payments for local budget processes, this has not been achieved.   Generally, Congress supports the PILTs program, but the OMB and the President see it as wasteful. Annual funding is therefore a perennial cliffhanger.   PILTs payments are typically omitted from the executive budget, only to be rescued by Congress at the last minute in the process.   In the last several years, the White House and the OMB have taken up earlier proposals by congressional opponents of the program to fund PILTs and/or the Minerals Management Service out of gross revenues provided by the onshore leasing programs.   Counties and states have rallied their supporters in Congress, but the debate may become an annual feature of the deficit-era budget battle.   In addition, PILTs payments are frequently the target of less direct, "reallocation" efforts.   For example, facing a reduced budget the Animal and Plant Health Inspection Service (APHIS) proposed (unsuccessfully, it scarcely needs noting) diverting funds from PILT to pay for spraying grasshoppers on 3 million acres of heavily infested rangeland in Wyoming. [251]

LAND AND WATER CONSERVATION FUND

The Land and Water Conservation Fund (LWCF) is a matching grant program designed to assist states, counties, and cities plan, acquire, and develop public recreation, park, and open-space areas.   LWCF funds are appropriated annually and provided to the states on a 50 percent matching basis.   Western state allocations for 1984 are shown in Figure 13.   The same program also funds acquisitions by federal agencies for recreation purposes, wild and scenic rivers, and national scenic and recreation trails.

Forty percent of the state share is apportioned equally among all fifty states.   The remaining 60 percent is apportioned on the basis of eed.   Although the determination of need is supposedly discretionary and made by the Director of the National Park Service, a well-established formula based on factors such as population and the amount of federal property within state borders guides the decision making.

In order to be eligible for federal matching funds under the LWCF, states produce a comprehensive statewide outdoor recreation plan (SCORP), which must be updated every five years.   The plans and updates are reviewed by the regional offices of the National

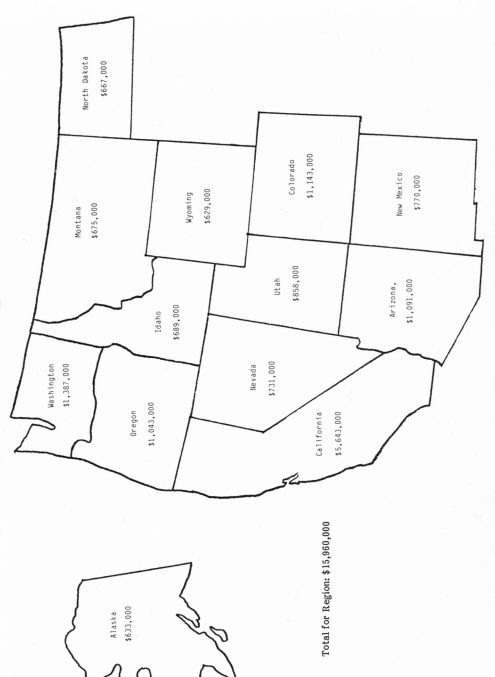

Total for Region: $15,960,000

FIGURE 13. Apportionment of Land and Water Conservation Fund (1984).

Park Service to make sure that the plans meet federal standards and that LWCF funding requests correspond to the priorities established in the plan.

Counties and municipalities participate through the state government by submitting project proposals to the state government where they are screened by a "state liaison officer." Each state is officially notified by letter from the Department of the Interior of the amount of funds it will receive that year. State, county, and city projects then compete for the available funds. Using federal criteria, the states establish their own priorities but final funding decisions are made by the Park Service.

Revenues for the fund are made up from the following sources: (1) motorboat fuels tax of fourteen cents per gallon originally earmarked for the Highway Trust fund and transferred to the LWCF; (2) receipts from the sale of surplus federal real property; (3) entrance and user fees at national recreation areas; and (4) revenues from leasing on the Outer Continental Shelf.

Originally, the user and entrance fees were supposed to supply the bulk of the fund. However, federal recreation agencies, particularly the National Park Service and the Army Corps of Engineers, were reluctant to charge for services that they promise "free" to the public, and Congress was reluctant to brook public hostility to even nominal entrance fees such as the annual "Golden Eagle Passport." As a result, the funding level was inadequate. In 1969, Congress amended the law to provide for a $200 million annual appropriation for the fund, part of which would come from the sale of offshore oil leases. Since then the level has been raised three times, and at present $900 million is supposed to be added annually to the fund. The OCS revenues are to make up the difference between revenues derived from other sources and the authorized funding level. Only once, in 1980, has the full $900 million been appropriated for the fund. (See Appendix Table 19.) More typically, the Land and Water Fund appropriation is rescued at the last minute from budget cutters in OMB and the White House.

Table 17 shows the apportionment of LWCF monies to the states during the period 1976 to 1984.

TABLE 17. Apportionment of Receipts to States from Land and Water Conservation Fund (1976-1984)

State	1976 (a) (5 quarters)	1978	1980	1982	1984
Alaska	$1,911,000	$2,471,385	$2,442,461	No	$ 633,453
Arizona	2,962,000	4,026,227	4,033,803	Funding	1,090,888
California	1,495,000	21,788,862	21,801,545	in	5,643,205
Colorado	3,234,000	4,430,013	4,401,518	1982	1,143,260
Idaho	2,044,000	2,664,674	2,632,116		689,464
Montana	2,044,000	2,665,458	2,629,685		675,096
Nevada	2,088,000	2,733,943	2,710,846		731,052
New Mexico	2,229,000	2,938,761	2,906,996		770,410
North Dakota	1,978,000	2,567,511	2,564,699		666,629
Oregon	2,921,000	3,963,376	3,935,246		1,043,247
Utah	2,439,000	3,252,691	3,228,346		857,704
Washington	3,698,000	5,114,884	5,101,344		1,386,574
Wyoming	1,866,000	2,403,359	2,367,522		628,852
Regional Total	$30,909,000	$60,756,127	$63,712,226		$15,959,834
National Total	$219,800,000	$306,070,000	$300,000,000		$72,919,000

Funds are distributed to the fifty states, Puerto Rico, Virgin Islands, Guam, American Samoa, and District of Columbia. In 1984, the Marianas were added.

Source: U.S. Department of the Interior, National Parks Service.

(a) 1976 figures are estimated to nearest $1,000.

Part Two Notes

1. Most uranium produced from federal lands is a locatable mineral, subject to the claim and patent system; accordingly, it produces no revenues for the states to share. Because of its strategic significance, however, uranium has a unique and interesting history. Until 1964, only the federal government could own nuclear materials, including uranium. Miners had to sell it to the government. The Atomic Energy Commission (AEC) aided prospectors and paid bonuses for high quality uranium. In 1964, amendments to the Atomic Energy Act gave the AEC additional authority to withdraw uranium lands from mineral entry and to establish a leasing system for uranium on special AEC reservations. However, due to slow development of the nuclear power industry, interest in uranium slowed throughout the 1960s, even after 1964 legislation permitted public and private utilities to purchase and own uranium. The Arab oil boycott led to resurgent interest in uranium and the Energy Research and Development Agency (ERDA), which replaced the AEC, granted forty-three uranium leases still in effect today. These leases are administered by the Department of Energy, successor to ERDA, and the lessees pay no revenues to the states. There are eleven leases on acquired public lands, in six states, only one of which--Wyoming--produces uranium. Wyoming therefore receives an annual share of royalties paid on that lease.

2. W. Marsh and D. Sherwood, "Metamorphosis in Mining Law: Federal Legislation and Regulatory Amendment and Supplementation of the General Mining Law Since 1955," 26 Rocky Mtn. Mineral L. Inst. (1980) 209.

3. U.S. v. Locke, 53 U.S.L.W. (1985) 4433.

4. See L. Masouredis and J. Barbieri, "State Environmental Regulation of Private Mining on Federal Lands" Winter WNRL Commentary 27 (1985). See also, Part Two notes 59, 60 and 61 and text accompanying them. The issue of what constitutes a discovery is technically the same when a prospector is claiming rights of pedis possessio (protection for claim from rival claimant) and when a miner is seeking to patent a claim. However, the courts typically use a more rigorous definition of discovery in the latter instance, when land may pass from federal ownership.

5. Regarding uranium, see note 1 above. Although the 1920 Act is considerably more restrictive than the 1872 Act that it partially replaced, it was viewed by many at the time as a way to make the minerals accessible to development. Many of those deposits had been withdrawn from entry during the administration of Theodore Roosevelt. In order to open them to development, both states and entrepreneurs were willing to accept constraints

insisted upon by the burgeoning conservation movement. For more detailed history see P. Gates, History of Public Land Law Development, Public Land Law Review Commission (1968), chapter 23, and E.L. Peffer, The Closing of the Public Domain (Palo Alto: Stanford University Press, 1951), 119, 148.

6. 30 U.S.C. Sections 187, 189, interpreted in Ventura County v. Gulf Oil Corp., 601 F.2d 1080 (9th Cir. 1979). See generally L. Macdonnel, "State and Local Regulation Affecting Public Lands Mineral Lease Activities: What are the Limits," paper presented at Public Lands Mineral Leasing: Issues and Directions Short Course, University of Colorado Law School, June 1985 (hereafter cited as Short Course).

7. See Part One notes 59, 60, and 61, and text accompanying them. See also, U.S. Public Land Law Review Commission, Energy Fuel Mineral Resources of the Public Lands, vol. III (Federal Competitive and Noncompetitive Oil & Gas Leasing Systems), report prepared by the Rocky Mountain Mineral Law Foundation (1970), at 590-597 (hereafter cited as RMMLF).

8. This 50-40-10 formula is a 1976 simplification and reordering of the original bargain, which allocated the nonfederal 90 percent, 52.5 percent to the Reclamation Fund and 37.5 percent to the states. There is no earmark or restriction on use of the states' 50 percent, although priority in allocation is ostensibly to be given to "those subdivisions of the state socially or economically affected by development of the minerals."

9. For a full discussion of this issue, see Chapter 8.

10. See Chapter 7 for a discussion of earlier Forest Service programs.

11. RMMLF, at 51.

12. It is not entirely clear that the MLA as originally written excluded the other categories of federal lands, but the Secretary of the Interior and the courts took consistently narrow approaches to the reach of the act and Congress obliged by enacting specific legislation to extend the MLA to more lands. For a more detailed discussion, see U.S. Public Land Law Review Commission, Energy Fuel Mineral Resources of the Public Lands, vol. I (Master Report), prepared by ABT Associates, Inc. (1970), pp. S-12-S-16 (hereafter cited as PLLRC, Master Report).

13. The Acquired Lands Leasing Act was amended in 1981 to provide that receipts from leasing on acquired military lands be distributed under the MLA formula.

14. All of these minerals management programs are treated separately in following chapters.

15. See, for example, S. K. Fairfax and B. Andrews, "Debate Within and Debate Without: NEPA and the Prudent Man Rule," 19 Nat. Res. J. (1979) 505 (hereafter cited as Fairfax and Andrews) discussing a policy by which the secretary redefined the criteria for determining when "commercial quantities" of coal had been discovered on a prospecting permit, which completely altered rights to a lease.

16. What is a "known reserve" of oil and gas? The classification system was devised by the U.S. Bureau of Mines and the U.S. Geological Survey. "Identi-

fied resources" include three kinds of reserve that can be specified as to location, quality, and quantity on the basis of geological evidence and, in some cases, engineering measurements. "Known reserves" are simply the part of the identified resource "from which a usable mineral or energy commodity can be economically and legally extracted at the time of determination." Office of Technology Assessment, Management of Fuel & Nonfuel Minerals in Federal Land (1979) 296 (hereafter cited as OTA, Management). "Subeconomic reserves" are the rest of the identified resources, which are not extractible under current legal and economic conditions. "Undiscovered reserves" are speculative, that is, "surmised to exist on the basis of broad geologic knowledge and theory." (Ibid., at 297, 314). Two-thirds of the known oil reserves and two-fifths of the known natural gas reserves are in five western regions, including Alaska. Offshore reserves are not covered by the Mineral Leasing Act. Separate legislation for offshore mineral resources has established a system similar to but independent of the onshore system. The present discussion applies only to onshore resources and programs.

17. RMMLF at 23. Most oil and gas leases are noncompetitive. In 1947 only 4.9 percent of domestic production came from federal lands. At its peak in 1972, the proportion was 17.6 percent. Gas production off federal lands rose from 5 percent in 1955 to 30 percent in 1980.

18. OTA, Management, at 314-315.

19. Only about 15 to 20 percent of all leases ever get to the point of exploratory drilling; the actual acreage devoted to production (8.6 million acres in 1982) is much less than the amount of land leased.

20. U.S., Senate Federal Oil and Gas Leasing Act of 1979, hearing on S.1637 before the Subcommittee on Energy Resources and Materials Production, ninety-sixth Congress, First session, (1980) 78 (hereafter cited as Senate Hearings, 1979).

21. Ibid., at 144.

22. See RMMLF, at 9, for interesting discussion of rules of capture as opposed to rules of ownership.

23. Some states require that overlying owners enter into unitizing agreements for pool development. Other states use a system of "correlative rights," whereby overlying owners receive a portion of proceeds, prorated according to the percentage of the pool they overlie. In fact, the secretary is authorized under the MLA to prescribe a cooperative development plan and require compliance, but the power has never been exercised. S. McDonald, The Leasing of Federal Lands for Fossil Fuels Production: Resources for the Future (1979), Baltimore: Johns Hopkins University Press, 125) (hereafter cited as McDonald).

24. The original provisions, which relied on prospecting permits similar to the pre-1976 coal program, were eliminated in 1930.

25. U.S. General Accounting Office, Opportunity to Increase Oil and Gas Exploration and Lease Rental Income, GAO/RCED-83-77 (1983) at 2.

26. See RMMLF, at 268-270 for a discussion of KGS definitions.

27. Arkla Exp. Co. v. Texas Oil & Gas Corp., 734 F.2d 347 (8th Cir. 1984), cert. denied January 14, 1985.

28. See Public Lands News, March 15, 1984, at 1-2; September 19, 1984, at 2.

29. Senate Hearings, 1979, at 79.

30. Special provisions have been made for leasing in the National Petroleum Reserves in Alaska. First made available for leasing through the Interior Appropriations Act in 1981, tracts in this area are leased through competitive, sealed bids.

31. Senate Hearings, 1979, at 61. See also K. Sheldon, "Environmental Considerations in Public Lands Mineral Leasing and Development, I" in Short Course.

32. See Conner v. Burford, No. CV-82-42 BU (D. Mont. March 8, 1985); Sierra Club v. Peterson, 17 ERC (D.D.C. 1982), rev'd in part, 717 F.2d 1409 (D.C. Cir. 1983) cited in Sheldon, Ibid. See also Part One note 57 and text accompanying it.

33. U.S. Department of the Interior, Bureau of Land Management, Public Land Statistics 1982, Tables 64, 65. For comparison, note that 445 leases were issued competitively.

34. Public Land News, February 16, 1984, at 2.

35. Senate Hearings, 1979, at 48.

36. There has been discussion of reducing that acreage to a 2,560 maximum. Industry is divided on the issue. Public Land News, November 8, 1984, at 7.

37. Department of the Interior, Bureau of Land Management, U.S. News Release, March 15, 1984.

38. Ibid.

39. PLLRC, Master Report, at 149-150.

40. Ibid, at 150.

41. Ibid, at 100.

42. McDonald, at 122.

43. Ibid., at 123.

44. The key cases are Sierra Club v. Peterson and Conner v. Burford, (see Part Two note 32), see also Public Land News, February 3, 1983, at 6; September 29, 1983.

45. See K. Sheldon and J. Muys, "Environmental Considerations in Public Lands Mineral Leasing and Development, II" in Short Course.

46. See Public Land News, January 23, 1986, at 1.

47. FLPMA also authorized the Secretary of the Interior to "make loans to

states and their political subdivisions in order to relieve social or economic impacts occasioned by the development of minerals leased in such states." 43 U.S.C. 1747 (1976). The amount of the loans received by a state cannot exceed federal mineral revenues anticipated during a ten-year revenue period and must be repaid from future mineral revenue payments to the states. When neither President Ford nor President Carter would budget money for loans at the statutory 3 percent rate, Congress amended the statute to allow for a higher rate, thereby making the program less attractive to needy communities. The program continues to be bogged down in budget cutting and a dispute between states and counties over which should receive the money; thus far, neither has.

48. See L. Macdonnel, "State and Local Regulation Affecting Public Lands Mineral Lease Activities: What Are the Limits," in Short Course. For an older but still accurate perspective, see RMMLF; at 5-53.

49. R. Boldt, "Royalty Management I: Current Status" in Short Course.

50. U.S. Report of the Commission, Fiscal Accountability of the Nation's Energy Resources, January 1982 (hereafter cited as Linowes I. The commission's major recommendations included: (1) to place more of the accounting burden on industry, assuming design of effective accounting and verification systems; (2) to enhance federal enforcement powers; (3) to require industry, with IRS oversight, to calculate the windfall profits; and (4) to establish an emergency audit fund to reimburse states for expenses.

51. See 48 Fed. Reg. 8983 (March 2, 1983). In December 1982, the department transferred collection and accounting functions from the Conservation Division of the U.S. Geological Survey to the Minerals Management Service, at the same time consolidating nonfinancial onshore functions in the Bureau of Land Management. The BLM handles multiple use and resource evaluation, permits for drilling, and production plans, inspection of operations, and enforcement; the MMS has assumed the controversial financial functions.

52. J.C. Harvey, "Federal Royalty Management on Federal Onshore and Indian Lands: Industry Concerns," in Short Course.

53. Industry has strongly opposed the department's "single payor" approach (one person or company responsible for the royalty payments on each lease) because (1) it would create administrative problems that would have a chilling effect on joint undertakings and (2) it could force companies to share confidential data with competitors. 49 Fed. Reg. 47624 (December 6, 1984). See Harvey, Ibid., at 30-31.

54. Harvey, at 26-27.

55. Ibid., at 48-52 for a recounting of recent criticisms of MMS programs.

56. Ibid., at 28.

57. R. Boldt, passim, at 1.

58. These agreements are set up under Section 202 of FOGRMA.

59. U.S., House of Representatives, Report on H.R. 5, "Ocean and Coastal Resource Management and Development Block Grant Program," Ninety-eighth Congress, First Session, May 16, 1983, at 39.

60. Linowes I, at 33.

61. The cooperative audit program is, however, only one of a number of audit activities in which the federal government is involved. Others include look-back audits, routine lease audits, lease reconciliations, and special audits. U.S. Department of the Interior, Minerals Management Service, Annual Report, February 1983, at 13 (hereafter cited as "Minerals Management Service, Annual Report). Sorting this tangle of activities is difficult, but the net result was reported to be recovery of over $55 million by December 1982. States argue that they are being shortchanged by an Interior decision to ignore accounts with a balance of less than $100,000. The look-back audits are particularly controversial and are being conducted as a one-time special program under the Office of the Inspector General and MMS. Begun in 1982, the audits are to be of twenty-five large companies responsible for over 80 percent of all royalties. (Linowes I, at 70.) The MMS describes this effort as an overview of the companies' accounting and payment systems, not as a lease review to identify under- or overpayment. (Minerals Management Service, Annual Report, at 12.) States do not concur in that approach — they want all the money owed to them. The MMS cooperative audit rules are limited to that agency's audit-related functions. Therefore, states wishing to undertake inspection and enforcement activities must make separate agreement with BLM, which is responsible for those programs.

62. Jan Stevens, personal communication.

63. Ibid.

64. New Mexico v. Regan, Civ. No. 81-0452-M, (D.C.N.M. June 8, 1983; trans-ferred to Ct. of Claims, 745 F.2d 1318 (10th Cir., 1984); cert. denied, April 29, 1985.

65. Linowes I, at 64.

66. Marathon Oil Co. v. U.S., 604 F. Supp. 1375 (D. Alaska 1985) appeal docket-ed (9th Cir., April 22, 1985), cited in American Bar Association, Section of Natural Resources Law, Natural Resources Law (1985); The Year in Review (1986), at 236.

67. Harvey, in Short Course, at 4-7, 46.

68. Public Land News, February 20, 1986, at 1.

69. Memo from Dave Frohnmayer, chair, Conference of Western Attorneys General to Donald Hodel, Secretary of the Interior, February 20, 1986, at 4.

70. Public Land News, June 12, 1980, at 4.

71. U.S. Department of the Interior, Bureau of Land Management, Sunnyside Environmental Impact Statement, at 1-1.

72. Ibid., at 1-2.

73. Coal Commission, Fair Market Value for Federal Coal Leasing (February 1984) (hereafter cited as Coal Commission, Fair Market Value). Pages 12-15 summarize the coal utilization picture in this century. Before 1920, coal provided more than 80 percent of the total U.S. energy consumption. How-ever, enormous oil discoveries in California, Texas, and elsewhere led to increased reliance on that fuel, which is much "cleaner" to burn. By 1940,

coal supplied only 50 percent of U.S. energy consumption, and by 1973, it was at its low point of 18 percent. The coal market enjoyed a resurgence following the Arab boycotts when oil became too expensive to use for generation of electricity. In 1982, the utility industry obtained 53 percent of its energy from coal, up from 46 percent at coal's nadir year in 1973.

74. Some low-sulfur advantage of western coal is offset by the fact that it is also low-BTU, so it is necessary to burn more of it to get the same heat. Carolyn Johnson, personal communication.

75. See Coal Commission, Fair Market Value, at 19. Declining oil prices and a drop in consumption of electricity have weakened coal markets generally. Eastern markets for western coal suffered further from increasing rail rates (deregulated under the 1976 Railroad Revitalization and Regulatory Reform Act and the 1980 Staggers Rail Act) and changes in the Air Quality Act designed to offset western coal's "natural" advantage. Rail transport constitutes up to 70 percent of western coal prices. For a discussion of the relationship between rail prices and coal prices, see Ibid., at 330-337. However, demand for western coal may be increased by provisions in acid rain legislation. But the trend in the market is reflected in revised estimates of coal that will be needed for use in power plants by 1995. They fell from 1,039 million tons estimated in 1981 to 921 million tons projected in 1983. See Ibid., at 19.

76. Robert Nelson, personal communication. See also OTA, Management, at 298.

77. OTA, Management, at 301. "Qualified" is defined in 30 U.S.C. 1304(e), Section 714(e) and includes such requirements as the owner using the property as his or her principal residence or primary source of income, and owning it for three years prior to leasing. Protection for surface owners was being judicially developed prior to SMCRA's passage. See Acker v. Gwinn, 464 S.W.2d 346 (1971).

78. U.S. Department of the Interior, Bureau of Land Management, Public Land Statistics, Tables 64, 65, 67, and 71.

79. Adapted from U.S. General Accounting Office, Analysis of the Powder River Basin Federal Coal Lease Sale: Economic Valuation Improvements and Legislative Changes Needed (1983).

80. Prior to 1976 the Reclamation Fund received 52.5 percent of the funds and the states received 37.5 percent under the 1920 MLA formula. In 1976, the Federal Land Policy and Management Act established the current 50-40-10 formula. Therefore, data showing increased state coal revenues 1976-1982 partially reflect increases in the percentage shared with the states. The bonuses bid in 1982 are not reflected in the figures as they will be paid over a number of years.

81. OTA, Management, at 147.

82. The royalty issue is complex. Coal Commission, Fair Market Value, at 314 reported that Congress appears to have set the 12.5 percent royalty figure in FCLAA without much study or consideration. Not coincidentally, it is exactly the same as the long-standing minimum oil and gas royalty. It was, however, above the prevailing rate for coal royalties in the pre-FCLAA period. After the act passed, royalties in the West, where federal market power virtually dictates the price of coal, rapidly rose to 12.5 percent.

However, in the East where federal coal has no market influence, the federal government has not been able to sell coal and is suggesting to potential bidders that they should seek royalty reductions after the lease sale. For a fuller report on the impacts of federal royalty minimums see summaries in Ibid., at 313-16. M. Kite, "Readjustment of Federal Coal Leases," in Short Course, argues that unevenness in readjustments and the dramatic difference between pre- and post-1976 royalty rates has put holders of new or adjusted leases at a competitive disadvantage. Needless to say, the matter is being litigated. See Rosebud Coal Sales Co. v. Andrus, 667 F.2d 949 (10th Cir. 1982); FMC v. Watt, 587 F.Supp. 1545 (D.C. Wyo. 1984).

83. See U.S. Office of Technology Assessment, An Assessment of Development and Production Potential of Federal Coal Leases (December 1981).

84. Coal Commission, Fair Market Value, at 106. This is, however, less than 90 percent of the net present value.

85. Given the concern with nonproducing coal leases it is interesting to compare coal with oil and gas. In 1982, 102 of 569, or 18 percent of western coal leases were producing. Of 115,910 oil and gas leases, 13,849 or less than 12 percent were producing. Stated in acres, 178,353 of 916,479 leased coal acres were producing while only 8,654,023 of 151,497,974 leased oil and gas leases were producing.

86. To do so, the government changed the rules for the sale midstream, which intensified the controversy considerably. See Part One note 41 and text accompanying it.

87. U.S. Office of Technology Assessment, Environmental Protection in the Federal Coal Leasing Program (1984) at 49 (hereafter cited as "OTA Protection").

88. See Fairfax and Andrews.

89. See M. Kite, "Readjustment of Federal Coal Leases," in Short Course.

90. OTA, Protection, at 90-91.

91. For example, special federal lands such as National Parks or Wildlife Refuges (Criterion no. 1), wilderness study areas (no. 4), and lands within rights-of-way (no. 2).

92. For example, outstanding scenic areas (no. 5).

93. OTA, Protection, at 40-42, 80-84.

94. Ibid., at 88-89.

95. Immediately after the passage of FCLAA, the Department of Energy set coal production goals. The Department of the Interior then estimated how much coal would be produced in each major coal-producing region in the absence of federal leasing and set target leasing to make up the shortfall, if any. Regional Coal Teams were established to negotiate political differences and recommend lease targets to the secretary. The Department of Energy's role has been eliminated, and the Interior Secretary, still in consultation with the RCTs, sets the targets.

96. R. Burford, "BLM's Role in Mineral Leasing on the Public Lands," paper presented at the Public Land Law Conference, Missoula, Montana (May 1984).

97. Coal Commission, Fair Market Value, at 74. Environmentalists counter that the same companies holding nonproducing leases are simply leasing more under the new theory and therefore competition is not increased. Carolyn Johnson, personal communication.

98. One of the lease level options typically analyzed in this debate is a "minimum leasing" option. It suggests some of the differences that create conflict in this difficult area. The minimum program is typically defined as one that would maintain existing operations by providing for "bypass," and "maintenance," or "reasonable expansion" tracts. Bypass tracts are those that are in the path of an ongoing operation but are not available for development. If they are not made available before all of the coal around them is extracted, it is argued that it would not be worth anybody's time and effort to return at a later time to mine the area; hence, they would be bypassed. Maintenance tracts are federal reserves adjacent to an operating mine that would allow the mine to stay in production or to expand its output "reasonably." Those emphasizing minimum social and environmental disruption, especially state governors in recent years, have supported reasonable expansion and bypass leasing as the major focus of the federal program, for obvious reasons. So have those who want to keep the federal coal program moving. This does, however, risk developing suboptimal deposits and clearly restricts the market to established firms. These antitrust implications are part of the reason that the federal government has tended to favor more leasing than the states. Coal Commission, Fair Market Value, at 72, 122.

99. See OTA, Management, at 136.

100. In spite of the fact that Congress did agree, both the premises underlying the FCLAA requirements and the specific means for achieving "diligence" are debatable. Because of the ten to fifteen years required to get a potential sale identified, consented to by qualified surface owners, planned for, leased, issued, declared suitable for mining, integrated into a developable tract, permitted for production, and a market for the coal identified, it may be beneficial to allow some reserves. It may also be wise to allow the firms some flexibility regarding where and when to develop. Some argue that diligence requirements will force production on leases that were granted without much analysis up to fifty years ago. Developing them now could impose unnecessary environmental and economic costs. The Coal Commission on Fair Market Value was emphatic that diligence requirements substantially lower the bid price for federal leases. See Coal Commission, Fair Market Value, at 103. Thus, there may be more public benefit to "speculative" holding of leases than the unflattering term suggests. Even granting the virtues of diligence, the FCLAA provisions may be an inappropriate means for achieving them. An alternative would be to assess diligence in terms of progress toward development (planning, permit procurement, mitigation programs, or other investments) rather than solely in terms of production of commercial quantities. Or, there may be advantages to providing financial incentives for development, perhaps in the form of escalating rentals on nonproducing leases.

101. Any production counts toward the calculation of commercial quantities. Hence, a development involving federal coal but including state or private coal as well can use production from the nonfederal segments to meet the

federal diligence requirements. There is no intent that the reserves of the LMU should be exhausted within forty years. The lease continues as long as the mine is producing. The requirement is a planning exercise.

102. For an excellent guide to the complex diligence issue, see G. Wurtzler, "Special Issues 1: Diligence Requirements" in Short Course.

103. See Public Land News, October 17, 1985, at 2-3; November 14, 1985, at 1-2.

104. See Public Land News, October 17, 1985, at 3.

105. See Public Land News, January 9, 1986, at 7.

106. Nevertheless, the OTA has produced a volume that suggests that even taking into account these factors, the amount of developable coal under lease is not difficult to approximate and is adequate. See Part Two note 93.

107. Although there is arguably not too much leased in every coal region. For example, little coal has been leased in the San Juan Region. Robert Nelson, personal communication. See also U.S. Office of Technology Assessment, An Assessment of Development and Production Potential of Federal Coal Leases (December 1981).

108. The key enactments are the FCLAA of 1976 and the SMCRA of 1977.

109. OTA, Protection, at 35-39.

110. The Forest Service is shifting from "unit planning" to forest "land management planning" under the FMNA, and BLM is casting its old MFPs (management framework plans) to become new RMPs (resource management plans), which comply with FLPMA.

111. Budget constraints, delays in promulgation and revision of regulations, and legal challenges have delayed completion of the mandated plans in both agencies.

112. The agencies' continuing to do business under the old, presumably less comprehensive plans is controversial in coal activity planning. See OTA, Protection, at 43-45.

113. The OTA has argued that in the rush, coal planning has gone forward without adequate data. OTA, Protection, at 65-75.

114. A supplemental draft EIS on the most recent coal program modifications was issued in February 1985 and met with criticism from both industry and environmental groups. Public Land News was found (May 16, 1985), at 7. The classic case in which an earlier coal programatic EIS was found inadequate is NRDC v. Hughes 437 F.Supp. 981 (D.D.C. 1977), modified 454 F.Supp. 148 (D.D.C. 1978).

115. More or less, depending on with whom one is speaking.

116. OTA, Protection, at 19, 57, 91-110.

117. Absolutely or pending improvements in technology or the data base. See OTA, Protection, at 104.

118. See R. Cowart, L. Wilson, and S. Fairfax, "State Sovereignty and Federal Lands: Strategies Beyond Sagebrush," paper, Western Conference of State Governments (1984) on the local and state activities in the planning and permitting process and the basic types of "conditions" and "exactions" that may emerge from the interaction (hereafter cited as Cowart, et al.).

119. U.S. General Accounting Office, Possible Ways to Streamline Existing Federal Energy Mineral Leasing Rules (1981) (hereafter cited as GAO, Streamlining).

120. OTA, Protection, at 115-116, argues that opportunities for general participation have been curtailed and ought to be expanded.

121. Cowart, et al.

122. See Part One notes 58-62 and text accompanying.

123. Cowart, et al.

124. See Public Land News, October 3, 1985, at 7.

125. For a lengthy history of oil shale exploitation see U.S. Public Land Law Review Commission, Energy Fuel Mineral Resources of the Public Lands Vol. V: Legal Study of Oil Shale on Public Lands, prepared by University of Denver College of Law (1970) at 31-46.

126. U.S. Department of the Interior, Bureau of Land Management, Draft Environmental Impact Statement, Oil Shale Management Program, at 1-4-1-9 (1983) (hereafter cited as BLM, Oil Shale DEIS). However, there are extensive unpatented mining claims to about 800,000 acres that, if validated, would substantially reduce federal holdings in Colorado. They have been tied up in court since the 1930s. DeWitt John, personal communication.

127. BLM, Oil Shale DEIS, at 1-4-1-9.

128. T.F. Cope, "Leases for Other Minerals: Recent Developments," in Short Course, at 9.

129. Public Land News, January 9, 1986, at 7.

130. Public Land News, April 17, 1986, at 7.

131. Public Land News, May 15, 1986, at 8-9.

132. Union's project (including the industry's first commercial scale module) was completed in September 1983 but never got out of the start-up mode. DeWitt John, personal communication.

133. See BLM, Oil Shale DEIS, Appendix 5.

134. M.J. Due, "Oil Shale Problems and Issues" in Johnston and Emerson, eds., Public Lands and the U.S. Economy (Boulder, Colorado: Westview Press, 1984), at 286-287.

135. Public Land News, January 6, 1983, at 9.

136. DeWitt John, personal communication.

137. Sulfur on the public domain lands is a "locatable" under the 1872 General Mining Act.

138. The authority for leasing these minerals comes through Reorganization Plan No. 3 (1946). See OTA, Management, at 104.

139. T.F. Cope, in Short Course, at 3. See also Fairfax and Andrews, for a discussion of marketability, valuable deposits, and coal leasing. The amended regulations are in 49 Fed. Reg. 17,892-17,902, codified at 43 C.F.R. Section 3500.0-5(j) (1984).

140. Cope, in Short Course, at 3-4.

141. See Cope, in Short Course, and 50 Fed. Reg. 14,512 (February 1, 1985).

142. 51 Fed. Reg. 15,204 (April 22, 1986).

143. OTA, Management, at 104.

144. The Land and Water Conservation Fund and implementation of the Historic Preservation Act; see Chapter 8.

145. Distribution of receipts under Section 8(g) of the OCS Leasing Act Amendments of 1978 may constitute an exception and will be discussed in the context of the Land and Water Conservation Fund in Chapter 8.

146. See, Part Two note 185 and text accompanying it.

147. The standard cite is to Pollard's Lessee v. Hagan, 44 U.S. (3 How.) 212 (1845).

148. D.S. Miller, "Offshore Federalism: Evolving Federal State Relations in Offshore Oil and Gas Development, 11 Ecology Law Quarterly (1984) 401 provides the basis for the next several paragraphs and will be cited as Miller hereafter.

149. A twelve-mile limit is recognized off the coasts of Florida, Puerto Rico, and Louisiana.

150. See Miller.

151. Ibid., at 407.

152. 332 U.S. (1947) 19.

153. Miller, at 409.

154. Ibid., at 411. Rights to offshore minerals may also be obtained under the Deep Seabed Hard Resources Act of 1980, which Congress adopted in connection with negotiations surrounding the Law of the Sea Treaty. Because the U.S. did not sign the treaty, the OCSLA is the preferred vehicle for OCS minerals exploitation. See Cope, at 10-11.

155. W.M. Christopher, "The Outer Continental Shelf Lands Act—Key to a New Frontier," 6 Stanford Law Rev. (1953) 23, at 30 note 22. See also Miller, at 411.

156. Miller, Ibid., at 410-414.

157. Ibid., at 414.

158. Ibid., at 427.

159. See note 171 and text accompanying for more detail on this litigation. See also Shapiro, "Status of Energy Leasing Activities Offshore California," Western Natural Resource Litigation Digest Commentary, Winter 1984, at 12-18 (hereafter cited as Shapiro, Status). See also discussion of the Granite Rock case, Part Two note 62 and text accompanying it.

160. Shapiro, States, at 1. This case is different from the OCS consistency case discussed in Part Two note 181, and was ultimately dismissed.

161. See Part Two note 170.

162. Jan Stevens, personal communication.

163. U.S. Department of the Interior, Bureau of Land Management, Final Supplement to the Final Environmental Statement: Proposed Five-Year OCS Oil and Gas Lease Sale Schedule January 1982-December 1986, vol. II, Appendix 2, at 6 (hereafter cited as Final Supplement).

164. 43 U.S.C. 1337(a)(i).

165. Seven alternative bidding forms were listed in the OCSLAA statute, of which three have been tried: a fixed, nominal bonus with royalty bidding; cash bonus bidding with fixed net profit-sharing; and a cash bonus bid with sliding scale royalty depending on the value of production. See generally U.S. General Accounting Office, Congress Should Extend Mandate to Experiment with Alternative Bidding Systems in Leasing Offshore Lands, GAO/RCED-83-139 (May 27, 1983). In addition, the department modified the royalties in some bonus sales, offering tracts at low (12.5 percent) and high (33.5 percent) rates.

166. R. Stroup, "Private Use of the Public Lands," paper presented at Fifth Annual Summer Program, Fleming Law Building, Boulder, Colorado, June 1984, Summary, at 2 (hereafter cited as Stroup).

167. The State, Columbia, S.C., "Interior Department's Sales Netting Less of Oil, Gas Leases," at 13-A, October 9, 1983.

168. California v. Watt, 712 F.2d 584 DCC, July 5, 1983, cited in Stroup, Ibid., at 2.

169. Heather Ross, personal communication.

170. Land Letter, March 1, 1986, at 7.

171. Under the previous system one of the first steps was to issue a "call for nominations" of tracts within a planning area.

172. U.S. Department of the Interior, Minerals Management Service "Outer Continental Shelf Lease Offering Statistics Gulf of Mexico Region," prepared by E. Swiler, February 13, 1984, at 1.

173. Ibid., Table 1.

174. U.S. General Accounting Office, Congress Should Extend Mandate to Experiment with Alternative Bidding Systems in Leasing Offshore Lands, GAO/RCED-83-139 (May 27, 1983), at 41 (hereafter cited as GAO, Congress Should Extend Mandate).

175. Ibid., at 42.

176. BLM, Final Supplement, vol. 1, at 7.

177. There are others, of course; the National Environmental Policy Act, the Endangered Species Act, the Marine Mammal Protection Act, and the Fishery Conservation and Management Act are among the most germane. This discussion will focus on the two most critical statutes.

178. 43 U.S.C. 1345(c) Supp 1980.

179. 43 U.S.C. 1332(4)(b) and (5) Supp. 1980.

180. California v. Watt, 668 F.2d 1290 (D.C. Cir. 1981).

181. California v. Watt, 520 F.Supp. 1359 (C.D. Cal.), aff'd 683 F.2d 1253 (9th Cir. 1982); Clark v. California, 464 U.S. 1304 (1983). Discussed in Miller, at 444-446.

182. Shapiro, Status, at 84.

183. See Miller, at 448.

184. See Chapter 8.

185. HR 3128. Congressional Record, March 20, 1986, H1519, ff. Immediate payments to states as follows (in millions): Louisiana, $572; Texas, $382; California, $338; Alabama, $68; Arkansas, $51; Missouri, $14; Florida, $103. The remaining $600 million will be divided as follows over the next fifteen years (in millions): Louisiana, $84; Texas, $134; California, $289; Alabama, $7; Arkansas, $134; Missouri, $2.

186. 50 Fed.Reg. 2,264 (1985). This paragraph is based entirely on Cope, in Short Course, at 10-12.

187. Futures Group, A Technology Assessment of Geothermal Energy Resource Development, prepared for National Sciences Foundation (April 15, 1975), at 1 (hereafter cited as Futures Group, Technology Assessment).

188. California Department of Conservation, Division of Oil and Gas, Geothermal Hotline, 15 (July 1985), at 8.

189. Futures group, Technology Assessment, at 4.

190. Oil & Gas Journal, April 16, 1983, at 39.

191. Futures Group, Technology Assessment, at 1.

192. Ibid., at 4.

193. OTA, Management, at 360.

194. P.L. 91-581, December 24, 1970; 84 Stat. 1566.

195. The secretary is frequently accused of virtually giving away promising oil and gas areas because of the definition of the KGS turns on the certainty of a producing well within one mile. (See notes 27-28 and text accompanying.)

196. Futures Group, Technology Assessment, at 1, 22, 76.

197. Ibid., at 77.

198. Statutory language refers to "exploration operations" but has been interpreted to embrace all phases of exploration and development leading up to production.

199. See Futures Group, Technology Assessment, at 49, 77.

200. Public Land News, June 25, 1986, at 8.

201. Ibid.

202. Robert Nelson, personal communication.

203. U.S. Department of Agriculture, Forest Service, An Assessment of the Forest and Rangeland Situation in the United States, January 1980, at xii (hereafter cited as Forest Service, Assessment).

204. Ibid.

205. Since the Grazing Service was merged with the General Land Office to form the BLM in 1946, BLM has had major responsibility for administering mineral leasing programs on all federal lands. However, no effort has been made to integrate minerals and land management until quite recently.

206. Another 146 million acres of federal forests are managed by other federal agencies. Forest Service, Assessment, at xiii.

207. U.S. Department of Agriculture Forest Service, An Analysis of the Timber Situation in the United States 1952-2000, Forest Resources Report No. 23, December 1982, at 27.

208. Adapted and quoted from data presented in Dowdle and Hanke, "Public Timber and the Wood-Products Industry," in Deacon and Johnson, eds. Forestlands: Public and Private (1985), at 78-81. Hereafter cited as Dowdle and Hanke. The authors argue that in part these figures explain the migration of the timber industry from the Northwest to the Southeast since investors are reluctant to develop wood conversion facilities dependent on federal timber.

209. M. Levy, "An Economic Alternative to Current Public Forest Policy." Federal Reserve Bank of San Francisco, 1978 Economic Review 20 (Winter) at 22 (hereafter cited as Levy).

210. All of the figures involved are averages and estimates. There is ample room for an operator of above-average efficiency, whose equipment allows greater "product recovery" from the timber, whose costs are lower, or whose market opportunities or financial position require it, to find a particular sale more valuable than the average operator.

211. For an example of how this works readers are directed to 49 Fed. Reg. no. 137, at 28743 (July 16, 1984).

212. Ibid.

213. See Western Timber Association, Mimeo 3 11066, File 2.633 (August 2, 1983).

214. Based on reevaluation of the cases examined in U.S. General Accounting Office, Congress Needs Better Information on Forest Service's Below Cost Timber Sales, GAO/RCED-84-96 (June 28, 1984). Mark Rey, personal communication.

215. Forest Service, "The Role of Below-Cost Timber Sales in National Forest Management," mimeo (July 25, 1984).

216. See Society of American Foresters, Fiscal and Social Responsibility in National Forest Management: The Report of the Below Cost Timber Sales Task Force (1986).

217. Note, however, that it also reduces the purchaser's flexibility to time harvests to meet market conditions. In this context, short-term sales act similarly to diligence requirements in minerals programs. Robert Nelson, personal communication.

218. Willingness to overbid is related to the inflationary economy of the late-1970s and a general correct perception (as recently demonstrated by legislation adjusting timber sale contracts) that the federal government could not and would not bankrupt the timber industry.

219. George Craig, personal communication.

220. Dowdle and Hanke, at 78.

221. See J. Zivnuska, "Timber Harvesting and Land-Use Planning Under the National Forest Management Act of 1976," unpublished presentation, cited in S.T. Dana and S. K. Fairfax. Forest and Range Policy: Its Development in the United States (New York: McGraw-Hill Book Company (1980), at 330-331.

222. It is not, of course, clear that the Forest Service has a mandate to (as opposed to a traditional commitment to) maintaining economic stability in "timber-dependent" communities. Moreover, extensive efforts to locate timber dependent communities according to the agency's traditional view of them have generally been failures. See generally F.W. Obermiller and L. Wear, "National Economic Efficiency versus Local Community Stability Goals in Public Land Management: A Review of Relevant Literature," mimeo (1982). Nevertheless, the notion persists.

223. Because "inaccessible" typically means "not roaded," this controversy is closely related to the "roadless areas" controversy mentioned above.

224. The more normal method is to evaluate anticipated future gains from the investment.

225. See Popvitch, "Harvest Schedules: Parts I and II" 74 J. Forestry 634 (September 1976) and 695 (October 1976) cited in Dana and Fairfax, at 333.

226. See M. Clawson, "The National Forests," 191 Science 765 (February 20, 1976).

227. See Levy.

228. National Grasslands return 25 percent of revenues to the counties, but the basis for calculation may create confusion. First, the National Grasslands were <u>not</u> shifted to calculations as a percentage of gross revenues in 1976; so they pay 25 percent of net receipts. Second, the grazing "fee" is not the same as for BLM or other national forest lands. Grasslands are administered by the Grassland Association. The charge made for grazing use of national grasslands is calculated similarly to the normal BLM and Forest Service grazing fee, but it uses different indexes appropriate to the Midwest, where the grasslands are located. It is called a "grazing value," not a fee. Typically, it is a dollar or more higher than the standard fee. In 1985, the grazing "value" was $2.50 per AUM, as opposed to a grazing fee of $1.35 per AUM. More significant, the Grassland Association subtracts from the "value" receipts administrative overhead and money for "conservation practices" (CPs) before forwarding the proceeds to the Treasury. The association spends as much as 90 percent of the receipts. The money sent forward is, in grasslands parlance, called the "fee." Counties receive 25 percent of the fee. Adela Backiel, personal communication.

229. Advisory Commission on Intergovernmental Relations, <u>The Adequacy of Federal Compensation to Local Governments for Tax Exempt Federal Lands,</u> Washington, D.C. A-68 (1978).

230. U.S. Public Land Law Review Commission. <u>One Third of the Nation's Land: A Report to the President and the Congress</u> (1970). See Part Three, Section VI.

231. See Appendix Table 5 for a count of BLM lands by state.

232. Technically, "permits" are associated with Section 3 (Grazing District) lands and "leases" are granted on Section 15 lands. However, BLM uses the term "permit" for year-to-year authorization and "leases" for multiyear arrangements. Johanna Wald, personal communication.

233. BLM has, in some cases, found ways to get around this provision. Gail L. Ackerman, personal communication.

234. U.S. General Accounting Office, <u>Public Rangeland Improvements -- A Slow, Costly Process in Need of Alternate Funding,</u> October 14, 1982, at 36. Johanna Wald, personal communication.

235. U.S. BLM and Forest Service, 1985 <u>Grazing Fee Review and Evaluation.</u>

236. <u>Public Land News,</u> April 18, 1985, at 7.

237. <u>Public Land News,</u> February 20, 1986, at 3.

238. A recent and exhaustive inquiry into range management under the National Academy of Science auspices frequently noted that data regarding range trend and condition were sparse at best. Nevertheless, the assertion that the range was grossly overallocated is accepted without dissent. See National Research Council/National Academy of Sciences, <u>Developing Strategies for Rangeland Management: A Report Prepared by the Committee on Developing Strategies for Rangeland Management</u> (Boulder, Colorado: Westview Press, 1984) (hereafter cited as "NRC/NAS <u>Strategies</u>").

239. Public Land News, June 13, 1985, at 1-2.

240. S.K. Fairfax, "Coming of Age in the BLM: Range Management in Search of a Gospel," in NRC/NAS, Strategies.

241. In conjunction with the BLM's new policy on water rights, however, the CMA program appears to facilitate a significant loss of federal control over federal lands. BLM will no longer file for water rights on an allotment, but will encourage the permittee to do so, even if the water was developed with federal funds. If the water rights are privately held, BLM's authority to terminate, transfer, or control the allotment would be significantly impaired. See NRC/NAS, Strategies at 26-28 and 6 Pub. Lands Inst. News. (May 1983) at 1-3.

242. N.R.D.C. v. Hodel, 618 F. Supp. 848 (E.D. Cal. 1985). U.S. Congress House "A Report to the Committee on Appropriations ... on the BLM Grazing and Rangeland Improvement Program," mimeo, August 20, 1984, at 29-30.

243. The Senate wanted fees lowered; the House wanted them raised. The only thing that both houses could agree on was to cut BLM's budget. See P. Foss, Politics and Grass, (Seattle: University of Washington Press, 1960), chapter 8.

244. Federal Land Policy and Management Act, P.L. 94-579, Sec. 203(f).

245. NWF v. Burford, see Part Two note 20 and text accompanying it.

246. U.S. Bureau of Land Management, Public Land Statistics (1982) Table 109.

247. See J.D. Leshy, "Sharing Federal Multiple Use Lands — Historic Lessons and Speculations for the Future," in Sterling Brubaker, ed., Rethinking the Federal Lands. Resources for the Future. (Baltimore: Johns Hopkins University Press, 1984.)

248. Questions regarding which local government is the appropriate recipient were raised in litigation: the courts held that the smallest level of government delivering services should get the payments. Congress rapidly reinstated its interpretation of the statute: the appropriate recipient is the principal level of government (not the smallest) delivering services.

249. See S.K. Fairfax, "PILTs — A Study of the Conceptual Basis, Legal Background and Management Implications of the PILT Program," paper, Western Legislative Conference (1983).

250. Memo to Director, Bureau of Land Management from Associate Solicitor, Energy and Reserves, Lawrence J. Jensen, n.d. (BLM BL 0062).

251. Public Land News, April 18, 1985, at 10.

APPENDICES

Key Abbreviations

ACECs: Areas of critical environmental concern.

ACIR: Advisory Commission on Intergovernmental Relations.

AEC: Atomic Energy Commission.

AFS: Auditing and Financial System, an accounting system used by the MMS (oil and gas).

APD: Application for Permit to Drill (oil and gas).

AUM: Animal unit month.

BLM: Bureau of Land Management.

CBWR: Coos Bay Wagon Roads Lands (BLM).

CEIP: Coastal Energy Impact Program.

CFR: Code of Federal Regulations. This is the rulebook for federal agencies. The CFR title that pertains to public lands managed by the Department of the Interior is Title 43. The subchapter dealing with minerals management is 6000; the specific group that deals with coal management is 3400. This citation appears as 43 CFR 3400.

CMA: Cooperative Management Agreement (grazing).

CRS: Contingent right stipulations. Allows the government to grant leases prior to the environmental analysis, contingent upon subsequently identified restrictions (oil and gas).

CZMA: Coastal Zone Management Act of 1972.

DEIS: Draft Environmental Impact Statement.

DOE: Department of Energy.

DOI: Department of the Interior.

EIS: Environmental Impact Statement.

ERDA: Energy Research and Development Agency (now FERC).

ESA: Endangered Species Act of 1973.

FCLAA: Federal Coal Leasing Amendments Act of 1976.

FEIS: Final Environmental Impact Statement.

FERC: Federal Energy Regulatory Commission.

FMV: Fair market value.

FOGRMA: Federal Oil and Gas Royalty Management Act of 1982.

FORPLAN: A linear program used by the Forest Service for forest planning. The output of multiple use resources can be evaluated subject to various constraints.

GAO: General Accounting Office.

GLO: General Land Office.

IRS: Internal Revenue Service.

KGRA: Known Geothermal Resource Area (see also PGRA).

KGS: Known geological structures (oil and gas).

KRCRA: Known recoverable coal resource area.

LMU: Logical mining unit. An area of not more than 25,000 acres in which the coal resources can be developed. It can include one or more federal leaseholds and/or nonfederal coal but the holdings must all be under the effective control of one operation.

LUP: Land use plan.

LWCF: Land and Water Conservation Fund. Established by the Land and Water Conservation Fund Act of 1965.

MFP: Management framework plan. A BLM land-use plan; replaced RMPs.

MLA: Mineral Leasing Act of 1920.

MMS: Minerals Management Service.

NDEF: Nondeclining even flow. The federal policy of not harvesting more timber on a national forest than it is growing at a given point in time.

NEPA: National Environmental Policy Act of 1969.

NFMA: National Forest Management Act of 1976.

NFRA: National Forest Revenues Act of 1908.

NOAA: National Oceanic Atmospheric Administration (Department of Commerce).

NSO: No surface occupancy, a provision to expedite lease processing in the event that no surface occupancy is required. Less complicated environmental analysis is then allowed (oil and gas).

OCS: Outer Continental Shelf.

OCSLA: Outer Continental Shelf Lands Act of 1953.

OCSLAA: Outer Continental Shelf Lands Act Amendments of 1978.

O & C Lands: Oregon and California Revested Lands (BLM).

OMB: Office of Management and Budget.

OSM: Office of Surface Mining.

OTA: Office of Technology Assessment (Congress).

PGRA: Potential Geothermal Resource Area.

PILT: Payment in lieu of taxes.

PLLRC: Public Land Law Review Commission.

PRIA: Public Rangelands Improvement Act of 1978.

PRLA: Preference right lease application. Prior to the adoption of the current federal coal program, a company could obtain a permit to explore an unknown area for coal and, if successful, apply for a so-called "preference right lease." Some of these applications were pending at the time the moratorium was imposed on federal coal leasing in the 1970s, and some leases are still pending.

RARE I & II: Roadless area review and evaluation, conducted by the Forest Service to determine which roadless areas should be included in the wilderness system.

RAS: Royalty Accounting Service is an earlier accounting system used by the MMS and has been replaced by the AFS (oil and gas).

RCT: Regional Coal Team. A team is made up of federal and state government representatives.

RMP: Resource Management Plan. A BLM land-use plan.

ROST: Regional Oil Shale Team. Similar to the RCT.

RPA: Forest and Rangeland Renewable Resources Act of 1974.

RPP: Recreation and Public Purposes Act of 1926.

SCORP: Statewide Comprehensive Outdoor Recreation Plan.

SIMO: Simultaneous filing system to reallocate terminated or expired leases. Applicants submit a filing fee of $75 and the lease is awarded in a lottery to avoid confusion over who first applied for the lease (oil and gas).

SMCRA: Surface Mine Control and Reclamation Act (coal).

SOG: Same as SIMO.

SRA: Stumpage rate adjustment. Some U.S. Forest Service timber sale contracts allow the price paid for timber in a given sale to fluctuate to adjust for changes in the market price of the manufactured lumber.

STSA: Special Tar Sands Areas.

TPR: Tract profile report. An environmental assessment of a coal tract.

USGS: United States Geological Survey.

Appendix Figures

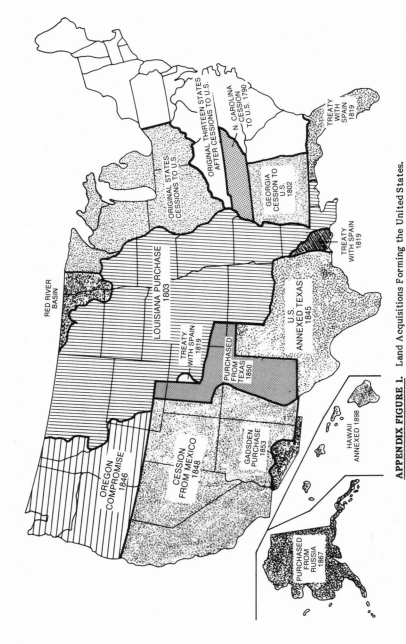

APPENDIX FIGURE 1. Land Acquisitions Forming the United States. (Reproduced from Paul Gates, Public Land Law Development. Source: Bureau of Land Management. Washington, D.C.: Government Printing Office, 1968, p. 76.)

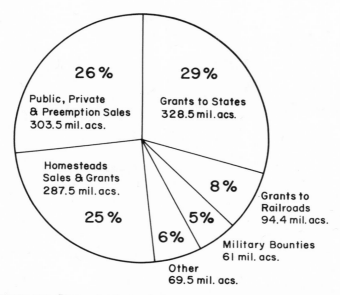

APPENDIX FIGURE 2.   Public Land Disposals under the Public Land Laws (as of 1983).

Source: Adapted from Bureau of Land Management, Public Land Statistics, Table 3, 1983.

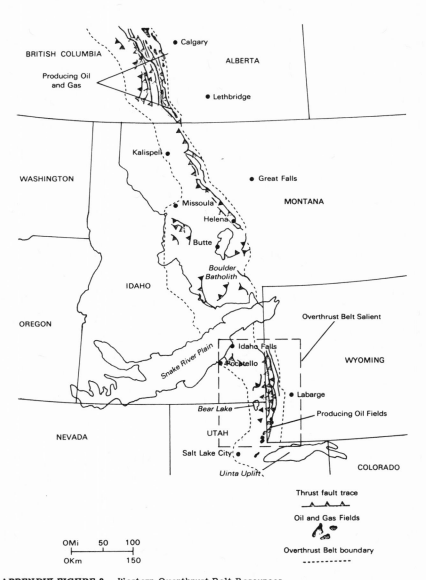

APPENDIX FIGURE 3.   Western Overthrust Belt Resources.

Source: U.S. Bureau of Mines, Federal Land Status in the Overthrust Belt of Idaho, Utah, Montana, and Wyoming, 1979. A Special Report (1980).

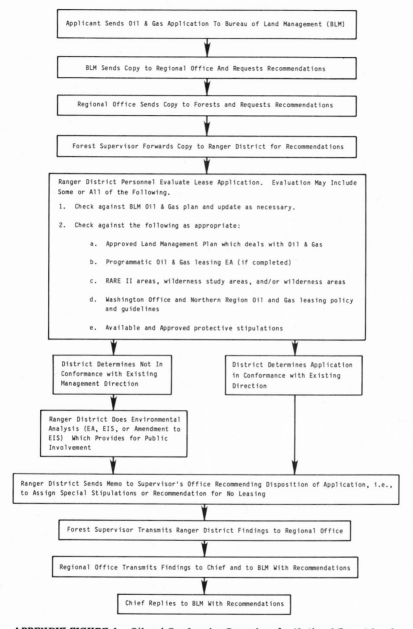

APPENDIX FIGURE 4.   Oil and Gas Leasing Procedure for National Forest Lands.

<u>Source:</u>   Oil and Gas Lease Applications of the Los Padres National Forest, Draft Environmental Analysis, USDA/USFS Pacific Southwest Region, Los Padres National Forest, July 1981.

Stage	Federal Requirements
Preliminary Investigation:	
Geophysical Analysis	No approvals needed if no surface impact involved
Seismic Testing	Special Use Prospecting Permit required from USFS District Ranger
Exploratory Drilling	Lease to the area must first be acquired from the BLM subject to USFS Regional Forester's review and recommendation
	Permit to drill must be acquired from the Minerals Management Service (MMS) subject to USFS Regional Forester's review and recommendation
Development and Production	License from MMS subject to USFS Regional Forester review and recommendation
Abandonment	Bond released if USFS and MMS conditions satisfied upon agency review.

APPENDIX FIGURE 5. Four Stages of Oil and Gas Exploration and Development in the National Forest System and Required Federal Approvals at Each Stage.

<u>Source:</u>   Julia M. Wondolleck, "Oil and Gas and the Public Lands," Ph.D. dissertation, Massachusetts Institute of Technology, 1983, p. 65.

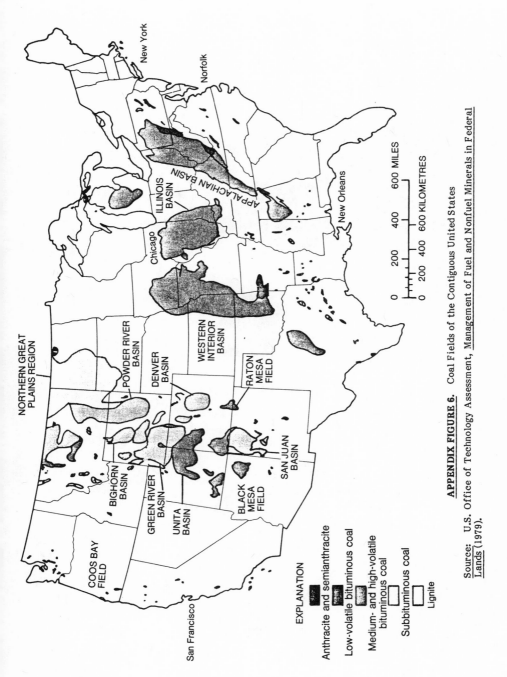

APPENDIX FIGURE 6. Coal Fields of the Contiguous United States

Source: U.S. Office of Technology Assessment, Management of Fuel and Nonfuel Minerals in Federal Lands (1979).

189

APPENDIX FIGURE 7. Oil Shale Resources of the United States.

Source: U.S. Department of the Interior, Bureau of Land Management Draft Environmental Impact

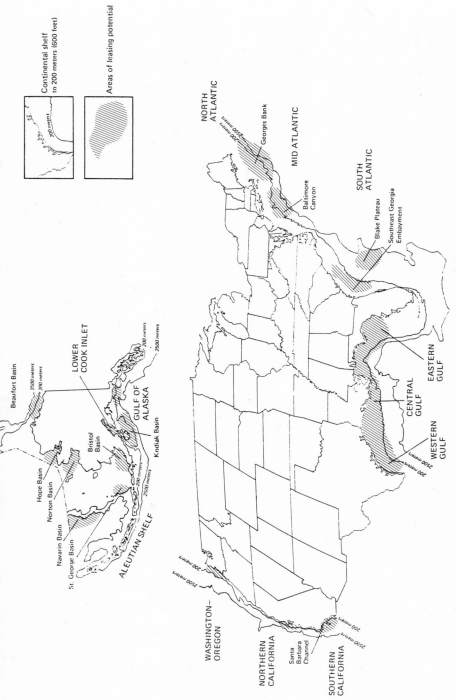

APPENDIX FIGURE 8. Outer Continental Shelf Petroleum and Natural Gas Resource Areas.

Source: U.S. Geological Survey Yearbook (Fiscal Year 1979).

191

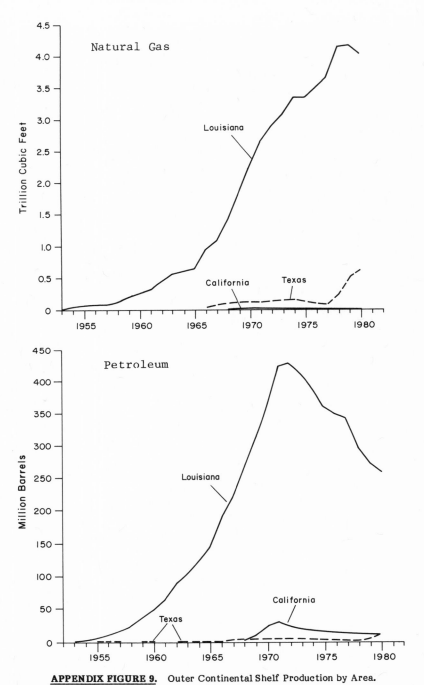

APPENDIX FIGURE 9. Outer Continental Shelf Production by Area.

Source: Department of Interior and Energy, Energy Resources on Federally Administered Lands (November 1981).

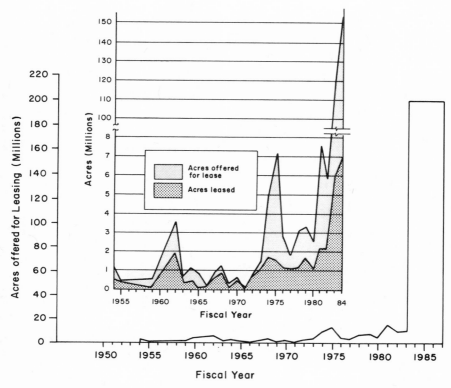

APPENDIX FIGURE 10.   Outer Continental Shelf Acres Offered for Lease, and Acres Leased (1954-1984).

Source: Adapted from Department of Interior and Energy, Energy Resources on Federally Administered Land (November 1981).

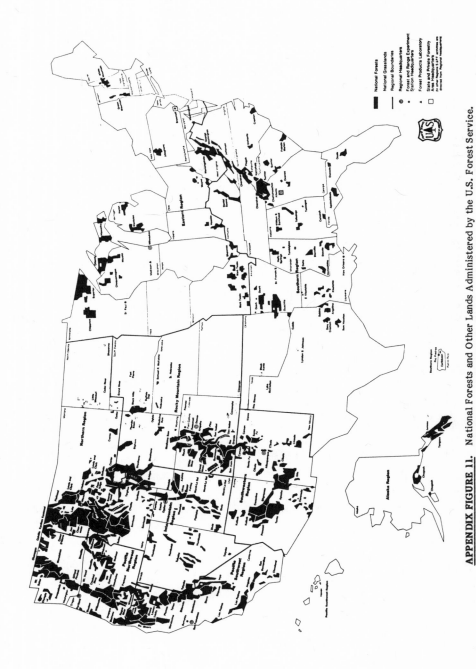

APPENDIX FIGURE 11. National Forests and Other Lands Administered by the U.S. Forest Service.

Source: U.S. Forest Service.

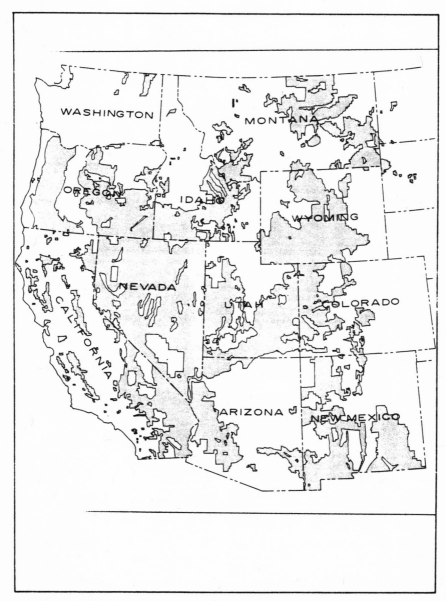

APPENDIX FIGURE 12.   BLM Public Lands in the western United States.
Source: United States Department of the Interior, Bureau of Land Management.

Appendix Tables

APPENDIX TABLE 1. Total Federal Payments to States from Federal Natural Resource Revenues (as Percent of Total State and Local Revenues)

	1970	1975	1980
Alaska	0.7%	1.0%	0.3%
Arizona	0.1	0.2	0.3
California	0.1	0.1	0.2
Colorado	0.3	1.3	0.6
Idaho	1.1	1.0	1.8
Montana	1.5	1.1	1.9
Nevada	0.1	0.1	0.9
New Mexico	1.8	2.0	4.7
North Dakota	0	0.1	0.4
Oregon	4.3	3.4	4.4
Utah	0.5	0.5	1.2
Washington	0.5	0.4	0.6
Wyoming	6.6	6.6	9.7
All 13 States	0.5	0.6	0.9

Source: Robert H. Nelson, "An Analysis of 1978 Revenues and Costs of Public Land Management by the Interior Department in 13 Western States," Office of Policy Analysis, Department of the Interior, December 1979.

APPENDIX TABLE 2. Acquisition of Original Public Domain

Origin	Year	Land Area Million Acres	Total Cost Million Dollars	Average Cost Cents Per Acre	Percent of Total Public Domain	Percent of Total U.S. Land
State Cessions	1781–1802	233	6.2(a)	2.7	13	10
Louisiana Purchase	1803	523	23.2	4.4	29	23
Red River Basin (b)	—	29	—	—	2	1
Florida Purchase	1819	43	6.7	15.6	2	2
Oregon Compromise	1846	181	—	—	10	8
Mexican Cession	1848	334	16.3	4.9	18	15
Texas Purchase	1850	79	15.5	19.6	4	3
Gadsden Purchase	1853	19	10.0	52.6	1	1
Alaska Purchase	1867	365(c)	7.2	2.0	20	16
Total Public Domain		1,806(c)	85.1		100	79

Source: U.S. Department of the Interior, Bureau of Land Management, Public Land Statistics, 1983, Table 2.

(a) Payment to Georgia.
(b) Drainage basin of the Red River of the north, south of the forty–ninth parallel. Authorities differ about the method and date of its acquisition. Some hold it was a part of the Louisiana Purchase; others, that it was acquired from Great Britain.
(c) Inland waters comprise an additional area of 20 million acres in the continental United States and 10 million acres in Alaska.

APPENDIX TABLE 3. Federal Land Disposition (1781–1983)

Type of Disposition	Acres
Grants to states	328,480,000
Public, private, and preemption sales, mineral entries, and other	303,500,000
Homestead sales and grants	287,500,000
Railroad grants	94,400,000
Military bounties to veterans	61,000,000
Other private land claims, sales, and grants (a)	69,500,000
Total	1,144,380,000

Source: Public Land Statistics, 1983, Table 3.

(a) Includes Timber and Stone Law and Desert Land Law sales; Timber Culture Law grants and sales; and land claims recognized as valid grants by foreign governments prior to acquisition of the territory by the United States.

APPENDIX TABLE 4. Land Grants to States (in Acres) (1803–Fiscal Year 1982)

State (Date of Admission)	Common Schools Section(s)	Common Schools Acres	Other Schools	Other Institutions, Railroads, or Wagon Roads	Other Purposes	Total
California (1850)	16, 36	5,534,293	196,080	320	3,094,964(c)	8,825,657
Oregon (1859)	16, 36	3,399,360	136,165	2,583,890(b)	913,432	7,032,847
Nevada (1864)	16, 36	2,061,967(a)	136,080	12,800	514,379	2,725,226
Colorado (1876)	16, 36	3,685,618	138,040	32,000	500,000	4,471,604
North Dakota (1889)	16, 36	2,495,396	336,080	250,000	82,076	3,163,552
Montana (1889)	16, 36	5,198,258	388,721	100,000	276,359	5,963,338
Washington (1889)	16, 36	2,376,391	336,080	200,000	132,000	3,044,471
Idaho (1890)	16, 36	2,963,698	386,686	250,000	654,064	4,254,448
Wyoming (1890)	16, 36	3,472,872	136,080	420,000	316,431	4,342,520
Utah (1890)	2, 16, 32, 36	5,844,196	556,141	500,160	601,240	7,501,737
New Mexico (1912)	2, 16, 32, 36	8,711,324	1,346,546	850,000	1,886,848	12,794,718
Arizona (1912)	2, 16, 32, 36	8,093,156	849,197	500,000	1,101,400	10,543,753
Alaska (1960)	—	106,000	112,064	1,000,000	103,351,187	104,569,251
Regional Total		53,942,529	5,053,960	6,474,170	113,424,380	179,233,122
National Total		77,629,220	16,707,787	51,840,063	182,505,615	328,426,685

Source: Public Land Statistics, 1982; Table 4.

(a) Nevada was permitted in 1880 to exchange section grants for 2 million acres, selected by the state, which appeared most valuable.
(b) 2,583,890 acres for wagon roads.
(c) Includes 2,194,196 for swamp reclamation.

APPENDIX TABLE 5.   Federal Lands in Western States (in Thousands of Acres)

	Total State Area	Total Federally Owned	BLM	Forest Service	Other Federal Lands	Federal as Percent of Total State
Alaska	365,482	327,029	166,985	23,120	136,924	89%
Arizona	72,688	29,195	11,882	11,881	5,432	40%
California	100,207	47,526	18,002	20,414	9,110	47%
Colorado	66,486	23,950	8,346	14,419	1,185	36%
Idaho	52,933	34,282	11,907	21,244	1,131	65%
Montana	93,271	27,468	8,125	16,765	2,578	29%
Nevada	70,264	57,384	48,282	5,150	3,952	82%
New Mexico	77,766	25,862	12,719	9,348	3,795	33%
North Dakota	44,452	2,246	68	1,106	1,072	5%
Oregon	61,599	30,103	13,573	15,616	914	49%
Utah	52,697	32,167	22,076	8,046	2,045	61%
Washington	42,694	12,104	311	8,902	2,891	28%
Wyoming	62,343	30,610	18,416	9,254	2,940	49%
Regional Total	1,162,882	679,926	340,692	165,265	173,969	58%
Balance U.S.	1,108,461	49,895	367	26,810	22,718	4%
U.S. Total	2,271,343	729,821	341,059	192,075	196,687	32%

Source: Public Land Statistics, 1983, Tables 7, 9.

APPENDIX TABLE 6. Acreage Limitations Applied to Leaseable Minerals and Lessees

	Competitive Oil & Gas	Noncompetitive Oil & Gas	Coal	Oil Shale	Tar Sands	Geothermal	Sulfur	Phosphate	Sodium	Potash	Hardrock Minerals (a)
Acreage limitations per lease, permit, or mining unit	640	2,560	no limitation on lease size per se, but 25,000 combined acreage per logical mining unit	5,120	5,120	2,560	640	2,560	2,560	2,560	2,560
Acreage limitations per lessee:										25,600 in leases	
Per state	246,060(b)	246,080(b)	46,080		7,680	20,480(c)			5,120	51,200 in permits	20,480(d)
Per total U.S.			100,000					20,480			
Other				no more than one lease nationwide			no more than three permits or leases per state				

Source: U.S. Office of Technology Assessment, Management of Fuel and Nonfuel Minerals in Federal Land (1979).

(a) Hardrock, or solid, minerals that are leaseable on acquired lands only. On public domain lands, hardrock minerals are locatable and subject to the claim and patent system.
(b) In all states except Alaska, where the limitation is 300,000 acres.
(c) After December 24, 1985, DOI can raise geothermal leases to 51,200 acres per lessee per state.
(d) No more than 10,240 acres can be held under lease (rather than permit), except under special conditions.

APPENDIX TABLE 7. Lease Tenure: Lease Period and Adjustability of Lease Provisions

Mineral Leased	Initial Lease Period (Primary)	Extension of Initial Lease Period	Preferential Right to Renew Lease	Adjustment of Lease Provisions
Phosphate or potassium	Indeterminate (20 yrs. and so long thereafter as terms complied with)	—	—	May be adjusted every 20 years.
Coal leased before 8/4/76	Indeterminate	—	—	Every 20 years
After 8/3/76	20 yrs., but terminates after 10 yrs. if no production	So long as coal produced annually in commercial quantities	—	End of primary term every 10 yrs. thereafter
Oil Shale	Can be indeterminate, but 20 yrs. for prototype leases	Prototype leases so long as production in commercial quantities	—	Prototype leases every 20 years
Oil or Gas	Initial 5 years for competitive or 10 years for noncompetitive, plus 2 years if then drilling	So long as producing or capable of producing in paying quantities or reworking or redrilling	—	—
Geothermal Steam	Initial 10 years, plus 5 years if drilling at end of initial 10 years	Up to 40 years after initial 10, so long as producing or utilizing in commercial quantities	For another 40 years	Every 10 years (20 for rentals, royalties) beginning 10 years (35 for rentals, royalties) after steam produced
Sulfur	None mentioned in law, but 20 years under regulations	—	For successive 20-year periods	Every 20 years
Sodium	20 years	—	For successive 20-year period	Upon each renewal
Hardrock Minerals	Maximum of 20 yrs under regulations	Unconditioned right to renew for successive 10-yr. period	—	Upon each renewal

Source: U.S. Office of Technology Assessment, Management of Fuel and Nonfuel Minerals in Federal Land (1979) p. 135.

APPENDIX TABLE 8.   Geographic Distribution of Identified Onshore Oil and Gas Resources (a)

Region	Percent of Total Identified Onshore Resources in the U.S.
CRUDE OIL	
Alaska	28.8%
West Texas and Eastern New Mexico	19.1
Pacific Coast	7.3
Northern Rockies	5.2
Western Rockies	2.2
Total West	62.6%
NATURAL GAS	
West Texas and Eastern New Mexico	14.3%
Alaska	13.8
Western Rockies	3.6
Eastern Rockies	3.6
Pacific Coast	2.6
Total West	37.9%

Source: Adapted from U.S. Office of Technology Assessment, Management of Fuel and Nonfuel Minerals in Federal Lands (1979).

(a)   Identified resources are "specific bodies of mineral-bearing material, the location, quality, and quantity of which are known from geologic evidence."

APPENDIX TABLE 9. Proposed Cost Recovery for Oil and Gas Management (in Thousands of Dollars)

	FY 1983 Outlays	FY 1984 Gross Payments with No Cost Recovery	Cost Recovery	FY 1984 Estimated Net Payments
Alabama	$ 379	$ 536	$ 10	$ 526
Alaska	48,170	27,197	490	26,707
Arizona	4,295	6,076	109	5,967
Arkansas	579	819	15	804
California	35,829	50,688	913	49,775
Colorado	33,649	47,604	857	46,747
Florida	47	67	1	66
Idaho	4,346	6,148	111	6,037
Kansas	1,010	1,429	26	1,403
Louisiana	709	1,003	18	985
Michigan	70	99	2	97
Mississippi	7,419	10,496	189	10,307
Montana	18,489	26,157	471	25,686
Nebraska	259	367	7	360
Nevada	12,185	17,238	310	16,928
New Mexico	131,241	185,669	3,344	182,325
North Dakota	9,177	12,983	234	12,749
Oklahoma	2,025	2,865	52	2,813
Oregon	5,105	7,222	130	7,092
South Dakota	1,526	2,159	39	2,120
Utah	36,162	51,159	921	50,238
Washington	823	1,164	21	1,143
Wyoming	180,720	255,667	4,604	251,063
	$534,214	$714,812	$12,874	$701,938

Source: Department of the Interior answers to U.S. Congress' House Committee on Interior and Insular Affairs questions during Clark Confirmation Hearings.

APPENDIX TABLE 10. Severed Mineral Title and Federal Coal Ownership (a)

Region	Fed. Surface (b) Fed. Coal (Acres)	(%)	Nonfed. Surface/Fed. Coal (Acres)	(%)	Nonfed. or Fed. Surface/Nonfed. Coal (Acres)	(%)	Total Acreage
Fort Union							
North Dakota		.2		32		68	2,512,370
Montana		2.5		42		56	1,238,100
Subtotal	34,370	.9	1,311,640	35	2,404,460	64	3,750,470
Powder River							
Montana		28		47		25	2,256,180
Wyoming		11		72		17	3,985,338
Subtotal	1,074,832	17	3,928,697	63	1,237,989	20	6,241,518
Green River/Hams Fork							
Wyoming		52		3.5		45	2,172,374
Colorado		11		56		33	513,880
Subtotal	1,181,960	44	366,235	13.6	1,138,059	42.4	2,686,254
Uinta-SW Utah							
Utah		74		11		15	1,116,100
Colorado		57		33		10	565,170
Subtotal	1,149,900	68	305,410	18	225,960	13	1,681,270
San Juan River							
New Mexico		53		31		16	2,246,780
Colorado		33		25		42	274,060
Subtotal	1,282,420	51	747,791	30	490,569	19	2,520,840
GRAND TOTAL	4,723,482	28	6,659,773	39	5,497,037	33	16,880,352
Percentage of Federal Only		42		58			

Source: U.S. Department of Interior, Final Environmental Impact Statement, Federal Coal Management Program (April 1979). Percentages expressed are as proportion of total acreage (federal plus nonfederal). Commission on Fair Market Value for Federal Coal Leasing, David F. Linowes, Chairman. Report. Washington, D.C., February 1984, p. 158.

(a) Includes known recoverable coal resource areas defined as of March 1978.
(b) Includes public domain (BLM) and Forest Service-administered surface.

APPENDIX TABLE 11. Numbers, Acreage, and Coal Reserves in Preference
Right Right Lease Applications (by State)

State	Number of PRLAs	Acreage	Recoverable Coal Reserves (in billions of tons)
Colorado	37	82,923	1.0
Montana	4	14,673	0.3(a)
New Mexico	28	77,600	1.5
Oklahoma	4	5,956	(a)
Utah	25	75,598	0.4
Wyoming	74	139,210	2.5
Alaska	4	7,840	0.1
Total	176	403,800	5.8

Source: U.S. Office of Technology Assessment, An Assessment of Development and
Production Potential of Federal Coal Leases (1981).

(a) Figures for Montana and Oklahoma are combined.

APPENDIX TABLE 12. Monies Received by States under Coastal Zone
Management Act

Program	Period	Average Annual Amount Nationwide
Coastal Zone Management Plans under Section 305	1977–1981	$6.6 million
Coastal Zone Management Plans under Section 306	1977–1981	$22.9 million
Coastal Energy Impact Program (CEIP) under Section 308		
a. Formula Grants	1977–1981	$18.1 million
b. CEIP Fund (includes monies through planning grants, OCS participation grants and loans)	1977–1981	$32.8 million
Sea Grant Program (Coastal Universities)	1977–1981	$35.0 million
TOTAL		$115.4 million

Source: Doug Larson, Executive Director, Western Interstate Energy Board,
Denver, Colorado.

APPENDIX TABLE 13. Five-Year Federal Offshore Oil and Gas Leasing Schedule

Offering Date	Location	No. Tracts Offered	No. Tracts Leased	Acres Offered	Acres Leased	Total Bonus Leased Tracts
08/05/82	Reoffering (RS2) Atl., CA, AK	554	36	1,320,819	204,955	$11,149,450
10/13/82	Diapir Field, AK (71)	338	121	1,825,770	662,861	$2,055,632,336
11/17/82	Gulf of Mexico LA, TX (69-1)	144	56	732,570	281,213	$609,178,233
03/08/83	Gulf of Mexico MS, AL, FL (69-2)	125	11	665,478	58,120	$37,570,900
03/15/83	Norton Basin, AK (57)	418	59	2,379,751	335,898	$317,873,372
03/29/83	N. Atlantic (52) (a)	—	—	—	—	—
04/12/83	St. George Basin, AK (70)	479	96(b)	2,688,787	546,546(b)	$426,458,830
04/26/83	Mid Atlantic (76)	4,050	37	22,670,685	210,641	$68,410,240
05/25/83	C. Gulf of Mexico (72)	7,050	623	37,867,762	3,089,872	$3,367,606,134
07/26/83	S. Atlantic (78)	3,582	11	20,392,985	62,625	$13,362,040
08/24/83	W. Gulf of Mexico (74)	5,848	406	32,620,248	2,246,005	$1,501,712,517
11/30/83	So. Calif. (73)	137	8	768,341	48,801	$16,022,336
01/05/84	E. Gulf of Mexico (79)	8,868	156	50,631,513	897,786	$310,586,261
04/17/84	Navarin Basin,AK (83) (c)	5,036	180	28,048,995	1,024,772	$624,491,332
04/24/84	C.Gulf of Mexico (81)	6,502	453	34,743,780	2,278,179	$1,323,036,649
07/18/84	W.Gulf of Mexico (84)	5,441	361	30,038,593	1,949,213	$884,850,488
08/22/84	Diapir Field,AK(87) (d)	1,475	227	7,773,447	1,230,486	$871,964,327
10/17/84	S. Calif. (80)	657	23	3,147,352	14,362	$62,121,252
05/22/85	C.Gulf of Mexico (98)	n.a.	n.a.	n.a.	n.a.	n.a.
	N. Atlantic (82)	—	—	—	—	—
	Gulf of AK/Cook Inlet (88)	--	—	—	—	—
	St. George Basin, AK (89)	—	—	—	—	—
	S. Atlantic (90)	—	—	—	—	—
	Barrow Arch, AK (85)	—	—	—	—	—
	N. Aleutian Basin, AK (92)	--	—	—	—	—
	Mid Atlantic (111)	—	—	—	—	—
	W. Gulf of Mexico (102)	—	—	—	—	—
(e)	C & N California (91) Norton Basin, AK (100) E. Gulf of Mexico	—	—	—	—	—
(e)	S. California (95)	—	—	—	—	—
(e)	N. Atlantic (96)	—	—	—	—	—
(e)	Navarin Basin, AK (107) C. Gulf of Mexico (104)	—	—	—	—	—
(e)	Diapir Field, AK (97)	—	—	—	—	—
(e)	W. Gulf of Mexico (105) Kodiak, AK (99)	—	—	—	—	—
(e)	St. George Basin, AK (101)	--	—	—	—	—
(e)	S. Atlantic (108)	—	—	—	—	—
(e)	Barrow Arch, AK (109)	—	—	—	—	—
(e)	C. Gulf of Mexico (110)	—	—	—	—	—
(e)	Shumagin, AK (86)	—	—	—	—	—
NON-ENERGY OFFERINGS						
Feb 84	Arctic Sand and Gravel (f)	--	—	—	—	—
Aug 84	Arctic Sand and Gravel	—	—	—	—	—
Aug 84	Polymetallic Sulfides	—	—	—	—	—

Source: U.S. Department of the Interior, Minerals Management Service.

(a) Sale canceled.
(b) Tentatively accepted pending resolution of litigation.
(c) Totals include 17 tracts ($108,174,000 bonus) involved in a boundary dispute with the U.S.S.R.
(d) Totals include 4 tracts ($5,104,000) involved in a boundary dispute with Canada.
(e) Proposed to be rescheduled for the mid-1986-1991 leasing program.
(f) Sale on hold.

APPENDIX TABLE 14.   Outer Continental Shelf Oil and Gas Leases and Acreage

	Total Leases and Acreage					Producing & Producible Leases (a) as of: 12/31/83
	FY 1976	FY 1978	FY 1980	FY 1982	FY 1983	
Number of Leases:						
Alaska	11	163	113	129	231	3
California	124	108	142	184	179	38
Other States Offshore (b)	1,743	1,839	1,920	2,359	3,362	1,352
OCS Total	1,878	2,110	2,175	2,672	3,772	1,393
Acreage Under Lease:						
Alaska	409,057	904,364	572,425	1,407,071	1,374,939	12,294
California	656,857	557,159	760,685	906,529(c)	941,118	194,776
Other States Offshore	7,756,018	8,610,130	9,013,855	10,427,893	16,231,296	6,110,353
OCS Total	8,821,932	10,071,653	10,346,965	12,801,493	18,547,353	6,317,423

Source: Bureau of Land Management, Public Land Statistics: 1976–Table 75; 1978–Table 77; 1980–Table 69; 1982–Table 70. 1983 – Minerals Management Service, Federal Offshore Statistics, September 1984, Table 5.

(a)   A producible lease is one where a well or wells have encountered hydrocarbons in paying quantities but where production has not occurred during the reporting period. (Minerals Management Service, Federal Offshore Statistics, September 1984, Table 5).
(b)   Offshore: Alabama, Florida, Louisiana, Mississippi, Texas, Atlantic states.
(c)   Pacific region as a whole; no leases current offshore Oregon or Washington.

APPENDIX TABLE 15(A). Supplemental Range Improvement Funds (PRIA)

Public Rangeland Improvement Act Funding:

1978	— 0 —
1979	— 0 —
1980	$5.6 million
1981	$9.4 million
1982	no appropriations
1983	no request for funds; no appropriation

Data 1978-80: U.S. Congress, House Subcommittee on Public Lands, 96th Congress, Serial No. 96-28, p. 83.

Data 1981-83: General Accounting Office, "Public Rangeland Improvement — A Slow, Costly Process in Need of Alternate Funding," 1982, p. 33.

APPENDIX TABLE 15(B). Range Improvement Fund (TGA)

Rangeland Improvement Funding: *

1979	$8.7 million	(a)
1980	$12.3 million (est.)	(b)
1981	$8.0 million	(a)
1982	$11.9 million	(c)
1983	$11.2 million (est.)	(c)
1984	$9.7 million (est.)	(c)

---

*   Source of Funds: (1) Public land grazing fees; (2) Graze fees and mineral leasing receipts from Bankhead-Jones Farm Tenant Act Land.

(a)   Source: U.S. Congress, House Subcommittee on Public Lands, 96th Congress, Serial No. 96-28, p. 83.

(b)   Source: U.S. General Accounting Office. Estimate based on 5% of grazing fee receipts.

(c)   Source: U.S. Office of Management & Budget, Budget of the U.S. 1984, Appendix, p. I-M5.

APPENDIX TABLE 16. Contributions to Reclamation Fund

	1903 – 1980 (cumulative)	
	Percent	**$ Million**
Accretions		
1. Revenues from public land resources:		
– Oil and gas royalties	35.8	2,216.3
– Sales of land, timber	4.7	289.7
– Potassium leases	1.2	74.4
2. Other (a)	.9	56.5
Subtotal	42.6%	$2,636.9
Direct Collections		
3. Construction repayments	6.8	419.7
4. Sales of water	6.0	369.4
5. Power revenues	39.2	2,429.3
6. Operation, maintenance, miscellaneous	3.2	202.3
Subtotal	55.2%	$3,420.7
Other (Reimbursements)	2.2	132.4
TOTAL	100.0%	$6,190.0

Source: Bureau of Reclamation, 1980 Annual Report, Appendix II.

(a)   Includes transfer from the Naval Oil Reserve, federal water power licenses, and other minor sources.

APPENDIX TABLE 17.   Public Land Receipts Allocated to Reclamation Fund

Source	FY 1976	FY 1978	FY 1980	FY 1982	FY 1984
Mineral leases and permits	$170,771,713	$149,980,455	$250,436,335	$480,846,444	$402,738,835(a)
Sale of public land	3,747,920	1,200,901	6,352,141	2,247,483	5,305,012
Sale of public timber	6,342,861	7,766,256	10,703,950	4,814,237	11,050,528
Rights of way	1,874	1,993	2,533	—	—
Misc. leases and permits	9,207	11,429	20,616	—	—
TOTAL	$183,873,575	$158,961,034	$267,515,575	$487,908,164	$419,094,375

Source: Public Land Statistics: 1976–Table 116; 1978–Table 121; 1980–Table 112; 1982–Table 109.
1984–Tables 106, 109 (provisional numbering, Public Land Statistics, published August 1985).

(a)   As of October 1, 1983, the Minerals Management Service assumed responsibility for the collection and distribution of most leased minerals receipts. MMS receipts allocated to the Reclamation Fund in FY 1984: $402,008,622 (est.) based on 40% of MMS onshore minerals receipts under the Mineral Leasing Act of 1920 (Table 106, Public Land Statistics, 1984, published in August 1985.)

APPENDIX TABLE 18. Reclamation Appropriations: Reclamation Fund and Other Funds (in Thousands of Dollars)

State	1976	1978	1980	1982	1984 est.
Reclamation Fund	$272,950	$323,657	$201,551	$374,362	$602,909
Colorado River Development and Dam Funds	3,994	5,427	7,948	9,455	17,501
Upper & Lower Colorado River Funds (Advances)	89,984	141,447	145,340	279,482	316,700
U.S. General Fund	294,335	237,702	282,629	101,687	354,470
Other Bureau of Reclamation Funding	65,517	48,605	65,590	74,221	30,000
TOTAL	$726,780	$756,838	$703,058	$839,207	$1,321,580

Sources: 1976–1982: Bureau of Reclamation, Annual Accomplishments. 1984: Office of Management & Budget, Budget of the U.S. 1984.

APPENDIX TABLE 19. Disbursement of Revenues from Outer Continental Shelf (in Millions of Dollars)

Fiscal Year	Bonus and Rental U.S.Treasury	Royalty to U.S.Treasury	Land & Water Conservation Fund	Historic Preservation Fund	Total
1976	1,385	1,001	277	—	2,662
Transition Quarter	1,090	179	42	—	1,311
1978	319	1,006	833	100	2,258
1980	1,361	1,840	901	—	4,101
1982	1,744	3,529	826	150	6,250
1983	6,579	2,948	815	150	10,491

Source: U.S. Department of the Interior, Minerals Management Service, Federal Offshore Statistics: Leasing, Exploration, Production, Revenue (December 1983), p. 79.

Data Collection Procedures and Problems

This volume was initiated primarily as an effort to gather an accurate, up-to-date record of state receipts from federal lands. Having defined what seemed to be straightforward questions, we found that the data were not available to answer them. There is no readily accessible source or set of data for public lands resources and revenues. Anyone accustomed to using Bureau of the Census documents would be frustrated by the lack of comprehensive public information on a subject presumably of substantial interest to both the federal government and the states.

The principal handicap is lack of a uniform reporting system across agencies and resources. Twenty years ago, former BLM director Marion Clawson complained that there was too much of an agency-by-agency "annual report" approach to public lands data, too little attention to gathering consistent data useful for planning and management.* This approach persists today, although some agencies, notably the Bureau of Land Management, have made commendable strides in establishing regular statistical publications. Unfortunately, advances in reporting public land mineral activities have been frustrated by the transfer to the Minerals Management Service of responsibilities for revenue collections and distribution.

We are still confronted by a diversity of agencies, each maintaining and occasionally publishing records with little coordination of reporting time periods, units of measurement, and land units for which data are kept. Even within individual agencies, skimpy documentation of record-keeping methods renders interpretation of available statistics difficult. Although many resource statistics are subject to caveats, interpretation of leased minerals is especially hazardous.

---

* Marion Clawson and Charles L. Stewart, Land Use Information: a Critical Survey of U.S. Statistics, Including Possibilities for Greater Uniformity. (Baltimore: Johns Hopkins University Press, 1965), p. 51.

The more data we have collected, the more sensitive we have become to its limitations and potential inaccuracies. As a result some disclaimers are in order. Whenever possible we have used published public records, supplemented by material provided by agency staff at the federal level. Records produced by regional, state, or field offices vary considerably over time and place and are not included. Most tables in this book are carried through fiscal 1984, the most recent year of record; idiosyncrasies for specific data are detailed in the table footnotes. General data limitations are discussed below, followed by a brief introduction to the major data sources used for this study.

CAVEATS

Reporting Period

Most agencies report data on an annual basis, either a fiscal or a calendar year. The preponderance of our data refer to the BLM's October 1 through September 30 fiscal year, as in the annual Public Land Statistics. Production data that was issued through the USGS Conservation Division and much of the published MMS production and revenue data, on the other hand, use a calendar year and thus cannot be readily linked with the BLM numbers. The MMS production accounting system is adaptable to various reporting periods, however: the MMS provides the mineral production tables in Public Land Statistics, following BLM's fiscal year.

Land Units for which Data Are Reported

In the normal course of events one can reasonably expect an agency such as the BLM or Forest Service to record and publish data on the various resources on lands which it manages. Thus, for example, the Forest Service accounts for revenues from timber, land use, grazing, power, recreation, and the like, on national forests and grasslands. With respect to subsurface minerals, however, matters are more complex.

In this book mineral revenues are counted, explicitly or implicitly, in several tables. Tables explicitly representing revenues from leased minerals (Tables 3, 5, 8, 9 and 11) cover only minerals on public domain lands (which never left federal ownership) and acquired military lands. These are collections and distributions under the Mineral Lands Leasing Act, as reported through 1984 by the BLM in Public Lands Statistics (see Chapter 4 for treatment of 1984 data). MLA coverage includes public domain in national forests.

Mineral revenue distributions made pursuant to the Acquired Lands Leasing Act by agencies other than the BLM are not covered in Public Lands Statistics. Notably, revenues from mineral leases on acquired lands in national forests and grasslands administered by the Forest Service are included in Table 12, "National Forest Receipts and State Revenue Shares."

These reporting divisions can be traced to agency responsibilities for administering mineral leasing laws. As a general rule, the BLM issues and manages leases under the MLA and other leasing laws, while the MMS collects most revenues from public domain and acquired land leases and also disburses revenues for public domain leases (that is, leases under the MLA). With acquired land leases, the MMS passes funds on to the surface management agency for distribution according to the appropriate sharing formula.

As with most rules, there are exceptions. For example, the BLM makes collections and distributions on oil and gas right-of-way rentals and certain nonenergy minerals; it also collects first-year rentals and bonuses, which are paid in advance in the leasing process, but sends the funds to MMS for distribution. On the other hand, the MMS receives royalty collections from the National Petroleum Reserve in Alaska, but disbursement of funds is carried out by the BLM. In interpreting statistical publications from the BLM or other agencies it is vital to know what components of the mineral revenues puzzle are included or excluded; unfortunately this information is rarely provided to guide users.

State Shares

Some "state shares" in the tables for this volume are reported as allocations from federal collections to states while others are actual payments to states during the time period reported. For example, LWCF and PILT figures for a given year report actual distributions. On the other hand, the revenue shares from leased minerals through fiscal year 1982 are based on estimated allocations to states, using data in BLM's Public Land Statistics. For 1984, the mineral tables identify actual payments to the states from federal mineral revenues collections, using MMS records. These MMS records were supplemented by a small amount of BLM revenue disbursements, again estimated from reported collections.

Because of potential inaccuracies introduced by our estimating methods, the leased mineral allocations through fiscal year 1982 only approximate the shares that states would expect to receive. Starting with figures from Public Land Statistics for total collections, by resource and state, the state share was calculated using the appropriate formula after deducting nondistributed revenues. Sources of error include applying the wrong formula, misrepresentation of the time when distributions to a state will actually be made, and inaccuracies regarding nondistributed revenues. As an example of the vagaries of formulas, public land Alaskan oil and gas revenues fall under a 90 percent state share, while National Petroleum Reserve production in Alaska is shared 50 percent; also, Utah oil shale bonus shares, stalled for years by litigation, fall under the pre-1976 formula (37.5 percent to the state) despite distribution in the 1980s.

This oil shale case also exemplifies the possibility of delayed distribution of revenues to the state.

Revenues from mineral production on certain acquired lands are not distributed to the states although they are counted among total collections in Public Land Statistics. A tabulation of nondistributed revenues is not available in Public Land Statistics but was provided by BLM staff in the Division of Finance, Washington, D.C. In deducting these nonshared revenues we made the assumption that only oil and gas collections were significantly affected; minor amounts of revenues from other leasables may not be shared with the states, but no adjustments have been made.

The 1984 calculation of state payments from leased mineral revenues deserves special comment. For past years we worked from a table in Public Land Statistics giving a state-by-state and resource-by-resource tally of revenue collections. Lacking a published 1984 Public Land Statistics, we drew on two sources: tables prepared by BLM and MMS staff for the upcoming Statistics and a special computation of mineral revenue disbursements provided by the MMS. Note that out of $1.1 billion onshore mineral revenue collections, $1.08 billion was received by the MMS. Because of the MMS disbursement data, it was not necessary to compute state allocations based on collections data; however, since these figures reflect actual payments rather than estimated allocations, they are not comparable to earlier years.

Inaccuracies in the fiscal 1984 calculation of state shares may be attributed to our methods of estimating disbursements made by the BLM and, for MMS payments, the classification of payments by resource. The aggregate revenue payments to states reported by the MMS should be accurate, but not necessarily the breakdown by resource. Notably, for California, Colorado, North Dakota, Montana, New Mexico, and Wyoming, "oil and gas" receipts include "other" payments, which, for simplicity, were assumed to be windfall profits tax reimbursements.

We should also emphasize that all revenue data in this report come from federal records: a systematic check with state records on revenue receipts was not attempted.

Administrative Changes

As of October 1, 1983 (the beginning of fiscal 1984), collection and distribution responsibilities for receipts under the Mineral Leasing Act were transferred to the MMS. This has repercussions for the reporting of minerals receipts and distributions in the BLM's Public Land Statistics. Staff from the bureau and MMS worked on a revised format to provide comprehensive revenue data in the 1984 Public Land Statistics, but the final product was not available in time for inclusion in this book. (Subsequent to completion of the tables and figures for this book, both the 1984 and 1985 Public Land Statistics have been released.)

Based on a review of preliminary tables provided by the bureau, there was reason to believe that some comparability with previous years may have been lost and that distinctions between BLM and MMS collections and disbursements may confuse readers. For example, in previous years a single table summarized "receipts from mineral leases, licenses, and permits on public lands and acquired military lands," whereas the preliminary tables list MMS and BLM data separately. This has proved to be the case. See, for example, Public Land Statistics, Tables 101 and 107, 1984. Mineral lease revenues allocated to the Reclamation Fund cover only BLM accounts, a minor amount compared with MMS collections. For the 1985 Public Land Statistics and publications in following years, the BLM has decided to omit altogether data from other agencies. Consequently, MMS minerals collections and disbursements -- the lion's share of leased mineral revenues -- will not appear in Public Land Statistics. Moreover, the MMS does not publish these data at a comparable level of detail and time period. For fiscal 1985 the MMS did prepare tables supplementing the BLM's reporting, and these are available upon request from the Information Section, MMS, Lakewood, Colorado.

The bureau, as the agency actually publishing Public Land Statistics, could take several measures to improve the usefulness of the data. One is to provide summary tables consolidating MMS and BLM data. At the same time readers should be provided with thorough explanations of the components of the tables, such as types of revenue charges and lands covered. Finally, collaboration with the MMS offers the opportunity to expand certain reporting: In the past, detailed revenue data by mineral type and state were only listed for collections, but it is clear that the MMS could also develop a detailed tabulation of state distributions.

Data for Leased Mineral Figures

Figures 3 through 8 rely on lease and production data from preliminary tables designed for the 1984 Public Land Statistics. Production data come from the MMS and follow a format established in earlier editions of Statistics. However, beginning in 1984 the continuing lease data for all states except Alaska come from the BLM's Automated Land and Minerals Record System (ALMRS). We include the lease data with some qualms regarding completeness and accuracy because of observed inconsistencies with earlier lease counts and with production and revenues reporting. (We worked from Table 78: "Continuing Mineral Leases, Licenses, Agreements, and Permits by State as of January 23, 1985.") Among our concerns: several states report modest coal rents or royalties (California, Oregon, Washington), but no continuing leases are listed. Comparing coal leases reported in 1985 with 1982 data, the number of leases as of 1985 for several states (Montana and Wyoming in particular) seems low. In general, the lease figures for all minerals should be scrutinized carefully.

Relationship between Production and Revenue Data

Production figures do not correspond reliably to revenues based on production, a problem cited in depth by the first Linowes Commission. (Linowes, Fiscal Accountability of the Nation's Energy Resources.) Historically this has been due both to inadequate accounting practices and to differences between reporting agency practices: the BLM, as statistical bookkeeper, has used a fiscal year, while the USGS (and now the MMS) has published data on a calendar-year basis. Consequently, for past years, the wealth of production data from the USGS cannot be readily integrated with BLM statistics. The MMS' Production Accounting and Auditing System (PAAS), if implemented, is intended to collect production data independently from production reported in calculating royalties through AFS.*

Audits

Although some effort has gone into identifying oil and gas revenues captured through audits, the variety of audit "programs" within the federal government and controversy over federal audits have made it impossible to produce credible numbers summarizing the combined results of the various routine and lookback audits enumerated in the MMS Annual Report (February 1983, pp. 11-12).

Exclusion of Indirect Benefits to States

This book does not count indirect benefits to the states, notably from the Reclamation Fund. Although it is possible to report gross revenues deposited to the fund from western public land resources

---

* Onshore use of PAAS has been tested for some leases; a decision to fully implement the system is scheduled for fall 1986.

and expenditures for western reclamation projects and to estimate expenditures by state (see Figure 11), the Bureau of Reclamation argues with considerable justification that a state-by-state break-down of benefits would be difficult and in many cases meaningless. The bureau accounts expenditures by project, not by state; expenditures on a project component, such as a dam, often benefit other states as well as the state in which it is located.

MAJOR STATISTICAL SOURCES

Bureau of Land Management

Public Land Statistics, issued annually by the BLM, has been unquestionably our most valuable source of revenue data. Published regularly since 1964, the publication includes increasingly thorough coverage of sharing formulas, changes in tables, and the like. Since 1978, data have been reported for fiscal years running from October 1 to September 30, with a five to six month lag before publication.

We have used Public Land Statistics as the primary source for all revenues generated from BLM-administered lands, but the leased minerals tables in this publication deserve special comment. Although most sections of Public Land Statistics are devoted to lands managed by the BLM, minerals coverage is broader because the bureau is responsible for administering leasing programs for federal minerals. This introduces a serious complication in interpreting the various lease and revenue tables: The "land bases" — public lands, National Forest, acquired lands, and so on — vary, making comparability between tables and calculation of the state share tricky. The publication would benefit from more detailed notes to the tables. With the publication of the 1985 Public Land Statistics, there is a marked decrease in coverage because of the exclusion of data from other agencies. Minerals reporting is especially truncated: Although preproduction activities (leasing, permitting, drilling) are listed for all federal lands, production data (a MMS responsibility) have been eliminated completely, and revenues pertain only to the minor programs administered by the BLM.

Reporting of revenues has always been complicated by an administrative split between preproduction and production revenues, the former collected by the BLM, the latter by the USGS and subsequently the MMS.* However, prior to 1984 the Bureau included

---

* This fact explains tables in Public Land Statistics prior to 1984 identifying "MMS receipts deposited to BLM accounts": these are royalty revenues.

USGS or MMS data. The shift to MMS has spanned several years, starting with collection of public domain and acquired land royalties. As of fiscal year 1984, the MMS assumed reporting of preproduction revenues as well -- with the exception of rental and bonus payments for the initial year of a lease.

Minerals Management Service

The MMS has onshore and offshore lease accounting responsibilities. Outer Continental Shelf records are kept by the MMS; management jurisdiction of the OCS was transferred to MMS in January 1983. Until 1983 some OCS data (oil and gas leases, bonuses, production) appeared in Public Land Statistics, but these tables have been discontinued. The slack has been taken up by MMS's Mineral Revenues, discussed below. In addition to the BLM and MMS publications, we have relied on excellent summaries of lease sales compiled by staff in various regional offices.

As successor to the USGS Conservation Division, the MMS's statistical publications show a gradual evolution from earlier, discontinued USGS issues. Detailed production data are available in the USGS's Federal and Indian Lands: oil and gas production, royalty income, and related statistics (last issued for calendar year 1980). To cover other leasables, the USGS also issued Federal and Indian Lands: coal, phosphate, potash, sodium, and other minerals production. Both have been superceded by Mineral Revenues, which, as the name suggests, includes rental and bonus as well as royalty data. (The first MMS annual, published in 1981, was titled Royalties.) For the OCS, the MMS's Federal Offshore Statistics is an excellent product whose chief limitation is slow publication. The most recent issue available, containing calendar year 1983 data, came out in September 1984.

Published annually, Mineral Revenues is based on a calendar year and is generally not available until late the following year. It has more the character of an agency accomplishments record and does not contain the detailed production tables of earlier USGS publications. Because of differences in time frame and "land base" these MMS data do not mesh with those in Public Land Statistics.

Forest Service

Unlike the BLM, the Forest Service does not issue a regular statistical compendium documenting activities and revenues nationwide; the revenue figures used in this book were provided by the national headquarters office upon request. The Report of the Chief has the flavor of an agency accomplishments document and does not offer summary revenue data for states. The most detailed revenue data are compiled and issued through the regional Forest Service offices. Although these data are not published formally, records broken down by county into various categories of revenue sources are typically available.

Bureau of Reclamation

The Bureau of Reclamation statistics are chiefly available in appendices to the Annual Report (the most recent being for fiscal year 1981) and reports on specific projects, such as the Colorado River Storage Project. That other data appear in the annual State Congressional Tabulation and the annual OMB budget document illustrates an emphasis on producing numbers to justify agency activities. Figures used in this study rely on the Annual Report, updated with the assistance of staff in the Statistics Office of the Bureau in Washington, D.C.

CONCLUSIONS

The effort to compile state revenue shares has resulted in an informal but revealing review of the condition of federal land statistics. Behind the lack of consistent, comprehensive, and reliable data lie several problems: diversity of purposes for which data are collected and reported; lack of statistical expertise within agencies; and failure to investigate and act upon user needs. Users have not, however, consistently defined and articulated their needs.

Historically, statistics have been collected principally to document agency accomplishments and to justify budget requests. Documentation of accomplishments and plans relate to the agencies' chief expertise. For example, the Forest Service has excellent data on timber conditions. Although these data are important, there is need to assess the broader potential of data applications, both within the agencies and outside, for policy analysis, fiscal planning, trend projections, and the like. The western states in particular are interested parties in reforming federal land statistics. The events surrounding oil and gas royalty accounting illustrate how a clarification of state interests and expectations can give impetus for change. Unfortunately, the rush to "upgrade" revenue accounting — and the focus on oil and gas lease accounts in particular — may be undermining development of a more comprehensive, integrated statistical base. To the degree that the states, as a major coalition of data users, can assess and articulate their broader needs — not only for monitoring federal activities but for their own planning — there will be greater incentive for improved federal record keeping.

Statutes and Regulations

GENERAL

Alaska National Interest Lands Conservation Act of 1980
16 U.S.C. Sec. 3101 et seq.
43 C.F.R. 3000, 3040, 3100, 3110, 5120

Antiquities Act of 1906
16 U.S.C. Sec. 431

Bankhead Jones Farm Tenants Act of 1937
7 U.S.C. Sec. 1010 et seq.

Coastal Zone Management Act of 1972
16 U.S.C. Sec. 1451 et seq.

Coordination and Cooperation	16 U.S.C. Sec. 1456; 30 C.F.R. 250
CEIP	16 U.S.C. Sec. 1456a

Endangered Species Act of 1973
16 U.S.C. Sec. 1531 et seq.

Listing	16 U.S.C. Sec. 1533; 50 C.F.R. 17
Federal/State Cooperation	16 U.S.C. Sec. 1535; 50 C.F.R. 81, 225
Interagency Cooperation	16 U.S.C. Sec. 1536; 50 C.F.R. 402

Federal Land Policy and Management Act of 1976
43 U.S.C. Sec. 1701 et seq.

Land-Use Plans	43 U.S.C. Sec. 1712; 43 C.F.R. 1600

Coordination with State and Local Governments	43 U.S.C. Sec. 1720; 43 C.F.R. 1600
Law Enforcement	43 U.S.C. Sec. 1733; 43 C.F.R. 9260
Grazing Fees	43 U.S.C. Sec. 1751; 43 C.F.R. 222
Minerals Management	43 C.F.R. 3100

Forest and Rangelands Renewable Resources Act of 1974 (RPA)
16 U.S.C. Sec. 1600 et seq.

Program	16 U.S.C. Sec. 1602; 36 C.F.R. 219
Assessment	16 U.S.C. Sec. 1601; 36 C.F.R. 219
Forest Plans	16 U.S.C. Sec. 1604; 36 C.F.R. 219
Timber Harvest	16 U.S.C. Sec. 1611; 36 C.F.R. 221
Minerals Management	43 C.F.R. 228

National Environmental Policy Act of 1969 (NEPA)
42 U.S.C. Sec. 4321, et seq.; 40 C.F.R. 1500

National Forest Management Act of 1976
(see Forest and Rangelands Renewable Resources Act of 1974)

National Historic Preservation Act of 1966
16 U.S.C. Sec. 470 et seq.

Public Land Law Review Commission Act of 1964
16 U.S.C. Sec. 1395-1400

Quiet Title Act of 1972

Recreation and Public Purposes Act of 1926
43 U.S.C. Sec. 869

Resources Planning Act (RPA)
(see Forest and Rangeland Renewable Resources Act of 1974)

Wild and Free Roaming Horse and Burro Act of 1971
16 U.S.C. Sec. 1331; 43 C.F.R. 4700

Wild and Scenic Rivers Act of 1968
16 U.S.C. Sec. 1271; 43 C.F.R. 8000; 36 C.F.R. 251

Wilderness Act of 1964
    16 U.S.C. Sec. 1131 et seq.; 36 C.F.R. 251, 293; 43 C.F.R. 19,
    3500, et seq.

BY RESOURCE

Coal

Mineral Leasing Act of 1920 (MLA)
    30 U.S.C. Sec. 201-210

Federal Coal Leasing Amendments Act of 1976 (FCLAA)
    30 U.S.C. Sec. 181, 201 et seq.
    43 C.F.R. 3410, et seq.

    Competitive Leasing   43 C.F.R. 3420
    Environmental Protection   43 C.F.R. 3460
    General Management   43 C.F.R. 3400

Surface Mine Control and Reclamation Act of 1977 (SMCRA)
    30 U.S.C. 1201 et seq.

    Environmental Protections   30 U.S.C. Sec. 1265;
                                 30 C.F.R. 700
    Areas Unsuitable   30 U.S.C. Sec. 1281;
                                 30 C.F.R. 700
    Surface Area Protection   30 U.S.C. Sec. 1304;
                                 30 C.F.R. 701

Minerals

General Mining Act of 1872
    30 U.S.C. Sec. 21 et seq.

Material Disposal Act of 1955 (Common Varieties Act)
    30 U.S.C. Sec. 611; 7 C.F.R. 15

Minerals Leasing

Mineral Leasing Act of 1920 (MLA)
    30 U.S.C. Sec. 181 et seq.

Acreage & Other Lease Limits	30 U.S.C. Sec. 184
Coal	30 U.S.C. Sec. 201–210
Phosphates	30 U.S.C. Sec. 211
Oil and Gas	30 U.S.C. Sec. 221–239
Oil Shale	30 U.S.C. Sec. 241
Sodium	30 U.S.C. Sec. 261–263
Sulphur	30 U.S.C. Sec. 271–276
Potash	30 U.S.C. Sec. 251–287

Mineral Leasing Act for Acquired Lands (1947)
    30 U.S.C. Sec. 351

Right of Way Leasing Act of 1930
    30 U.S.C. Sec. 301 et seq.

Oil and Gas

Mineral Leasing Act of 1920 (MLA)
    30 U.S.C. Sec. 221–239

Federal Oil and Gas Royalty Management Act of 1982
    30 U.S.C. Sec. 1701 et seq.; 43 C.F.R. 3100, 3110

Cooperative Agreements	30 U.S.C. Sec. 1732
Delegation to States	30 U.S.C. Sec. 1735
Funding	30 U.S.C. Sec. 1754

Other Resources

Land and Water Conservation Fund Act
    16 U.S.C. Sec. 460e-5a; 43 C.F.R. 17

Payments in Lieu of Taxes Act of 1976 (PILTS)
    31 U.S.C. Sec. 6901

Reclamation Act; Reclamation Reform Act of 1982
    43 U.S.C. Sec. 371 et seq.

Outer Continental Shelf

Outer Continental Shelf Lands Act of 1953 (OCSLA)
Outer Continental Shelf Lands Act Amendments of 1978 (OCSLAA)
    43 U.S.C. Sec. 1301 et seq.

Rights of States	43 U.S.C. Sec. 1311;
	20 C.F.R. 701
Coordination with States	43 U.S.C. Sec. 1345;
	30 C.F.R. 250
Environmental Studies	43 U.S.C. Sec. 1346;
	30 C.F.R. 250-251
OCS Leasing Program	43 U.S.C. Sec. 1344;
	30 C.F.R. 8252

Submerged Lands Act of 1953
43 U.S.C. Sec. 1301 et seq.

Surface Resources (see also General section)

Multiple Use Sustained Yield Act of 1960 (MUSY)
16 U.S.C. Sec. 528; 36 C.F.R. 212 et seq.

Public Rangelands Improvement Act of 1978 (PRIA)
43 U.S.C. Sec. 1901 et seq.

Grazing Fee	43 U.S.C. Sec. 1905;
	43 C.F.R. 4100
Cooperative Programs	43 U.S.C. Sec. 1906;
	43 C.F.R. 4100
Experimental Stewardship	43 U.S.C. Sec. 1908;
	43 C.F.R. 4100

Taylor Grazing Act of 1934 (TGA)
43 U.S.C. Sec. 315 et seq.

Bibliography

GENERAL

Anagnson, T. J. "Designing the Ideal Grant Program: Problems of Administrative Discretion and Implementation." Paper presented at the annual meeting of the Western Political Science Association, Sacramento, California, 1984.

Barnhill, Kenneth E. "The Role of Local Government in Mineral Development." Rocky Mountain Mineral Law Institute Proceedings. Mimeo, 1983.

Boldt, Robert. "Royalty Management I: Current Status." Paper presented at Public Lands Mineral Leasing: Issues and Directions Short Course, University of Colorado Law School, June, 1985.

Brubaker, Sterling, ed. Rethinking the Federal Lands. Washington, D.C.: Resources for the Future, 1984.

California. Senate Office of Research. "Seaweed and Sagebrush Robbery: State Revenue Losses From Offshore and Onshore Federal Lands." Prepared by Michael E. Shapiro. Sacramento, California, October 1984.

Clawson, Marion. The Federal Lands Revisited. Washington, D.C.: Resources for the Future, 1983.

Conlan, Timothy J. "The Politics of Federal Block Grants." Political Science Quarterly 99 (1984): 247.

Cope, Thomas F., "Leases for other Minerals: Recent Developments." Paper presented at Public Lands Mineral Leasing: Issues and Directions Short Course, University of Colorado Law School, June 1985.

Cowart, R., L. Wilson, and S. Fairfax. "State Sovereignty and Federal Lands: Strategies Beyond Sagebrush." Ecology Law Quarterly (forthcoming).

Dana, Samuel T., and S. Fairfax. Forest and Range Policy. New York: McGraw-Hill, 1980.

Fairfax, S., "PILTs—A Study of the Conceptual Basis, Legal Background, and Management Implications of the PILT Program." Paper prepared for the Council of State Governments, 1983.

------------. "Old Recipes for New Federalism." Environmental Law 12 (1982): 945.

------------. "RPA and the Forest Service. In A Citizens Guide to the Resource Planning Act and Forest Service Planning. Washington, D.C.: Conservation Foundation, 1980.

Fairfax, S., and B. Andrews, "Debate Within and Debate Without: NEPA and the 'Prudent Man' Rule." Natural Resource Journal 19 (1979): 505.

Francis, John G., and Richard Ganzel, eds. Western Public Lands: The Management of Natural Resources in a Time of Declining Federalism. Totowa, New Jersey: Rowman and Allenheld, 1984.

Ganzel, Richard, ed. Resource Conflicts in the West. Reno: Nevada Public Affairs Institute, 1983.

Gates, Paul. History of Public Land Law Development. Public Land Law Review Commission. Washington, D.C.: Government Printing Office, 1968.

Kroese, K. "Legal Aspects of the Upcoming Reallocation of Hoover Dam Energy: The Conflict Between Arizona, California, and Nevada." Arizona Law Review 24 (1982): 927.

Hays, Samuel P. Conservation and the Gospel of Efficiency. Cambridge: Harvard University Press, 1960.

Ingram, Helen. "Policy Implementation Through Bargaining: The Case of Federal Grants-in-Aid." Public Policy 25 (1977): 499.

Lamm, R., and M. McCarthy. The Angry West: A Vulnerable Land and Its Future. Boston: Houghton Mifflin, 1982.

Luce, Thomas, and Janet Pack. "State Support Under the New Federalism." Journal of Policy Analysis 3 (1984): 340.

Macdonnel, Lawrence. "State and Local Regulation Affecting Public Lands Mineral Lease Activities: What Are the Limits?" Paper presented at Public Lands Mineral Leasing: Issues and Directions Short Course, University of Colorado Law School, June 1985.

McGinley, Patrick. "Federalism Lives: Reflections on the Vitality of the Federal System in the Context of Natural Resource Regulation." Kansas Law Review 32 (1983): 147.

Markusen, Ann, Annalle Saxenian, and Marc Weiss. "Who Benefits from Intergovernmental Transfers?" Publius 11 (1981): 5.

Markusen, Ann, and Jerry Fastrup. "The Regional War For Federal Aid." The Public Interest 53 (1978): 87.

Marsh, W., and D. Sherwood. "Metamorphosis in Mining Law: Federal Legislation and Regulatory Amendment and Supplementation of the General Mining Law Since 1955." Rocky Mountain Mineral Law Institute 26 (1980): 209.

Masouredis, Linus, and Joseph Barbieri. "State Environmental Regulation of Private Mining on Federal Lands." Winter WNRL Commentary 27 (1985).

Muys, Jerome. "Environmental Considerations in Public Lands Mineral Leasing and Development, II." Paper presented at Public Lands Mineral Leasing: Issues and Directions Short Course, University of Colorado Law School, June 1985.

Nathan, Richard P., and Fred C. Doolittle. "The Untold Story of Reagan's New Federalism." Public Interest 77 (1984): 97.

Nelson, Robert H. "Seeking Alternatives to Federal Land Ownership: Addressing the Sagebrush Rebellion and the Privitization Movement." Paper presented at the American Society for Public Administration, Denver, 1984.

------------. "The Public Lands." In Current Issues in Natural Resource Policy, edited by P. Portney. Washington, D.C.: Resources for the Future, 1982.

------------. "Past and Projected State Revenues from Energy and Other Natural Resources in 13 Western States: Background Report." Office of Policy Analysis, Department of the Interior, September 1981.

------------. "An Analysis of 1978 Revenues and Costs of Public Land Management by the Interior Department in 13 Western States." Office of Policy Analysis, Department of the Interior, December 1979.

Nevada Legislative Counsel Bureau. State Sovereignty as Impaired by Federal Ownership of Land. Bulletin No. 82-1, Carson City, Nevada, January 1982.

Nothdurft, William E. "Renewing America: Natural Resource Investment and State Economic Development." Washington, D.C.: Council of State Planning Agencies, January 1984.

Peffer, E. Louise. The Closing of the Public Domain. Palo Alto: Stanford University Press, 1951.

Powell, John Wesley. Report on the Arid Regions of the United States. Washington, D.C.: 1879.

Public Lands News. 1976–present.

Sheldon, Karen. "Environmental Considerations in Public Lands Mineral Leasing and Development, I." Paper presented at Public Lands Mineral Leasing: Issues and Directions Short Course, University of Colorado Law School, June 1985.

Smith, R. T. Troubled Waters: Financing Water in the West. Washington, D.C.: Council of State Planning Agencies, 1984.

Stewart, Richard B. "Pyramids of Sacrifice? Problems of Federalism in Mandating State Implementation of National Environmental Policy." Yale Law Journal 86 (1977): 1196.

Stroup, R. "Private Use of the Public Lands." Paper presented at Fifth Annual Summer Program, Fleming Law Building, Boulder, Colorado, June 1984.

Swenson, Robert W. "Legal Aspects of Mineral Resources Exploitation." In History of Public Land Law Development. Paul Gates, principal author. Washington, D.C.: Government Printing Office, 1968.

U.S. Advisory Commission on Intergovernmental Relations Regulatory Federalism: Policy, Process, Impact and Reform. A-95, 1984.

------------. Payments in Lieu of Taxes on Federal Real Property. A-90, 1981.

--------------. The Federal Role in the Federal System: The Dynamics of Growth -- Protecting the Environment: Politics, Pollution, and Federal Policy A-83, 1981.

--------------. The Federal Role in the Federal System: The Dynamics of Growth. A Crisis of Confidence and Competence. A-77, 1980.

--------------. In Brief: State and Local Roles in the Federal System B-6. Washington, D.C., 1981 at 2 drawing upon ACIR, The Federal Role in the Federal System (B-4), 1980.

U.S. Commission on Fiscal Accountability of the Nation's Energy Resources. Report of the Commission. Washington, D.C.: Government Printing Office, January 1982.

U.S. Department of Energy. Energy Impact Assistance: Report to the President. Washington, D.C., 1978.

U.S. Department of the Interior. Minerals Management Service. Annual Report. Washington, D.C.: Government Printing Office, February 1983.

U.S. Department of the Interior. Bureau of Land Management. Public Land Statistics. Washington, D.C.: Government Printing Office, 1982-1983.

U.S. Department of the Interior. Office of the Secretary. "Information Memorandum: Assistant Secretary - Land and Minerals Management to Secretary, Subject: California Senate Office of Research Study -- Seaweed and Sagebrush Robbery" November 30, 1984.

--------------. Energy Resources on the Federal Lands. 1980.

U.S. General Accounting Office. Report to Congress: Private Mineral Rights Complicate the Management of Eastern Wilderness Areas. GAO/RCED-84-101. Washington, D.C., July 26, 1984.

--------------. Report to the Chairman, Subcommittee on Mines and Mining, House Committee on Interior and Insular Affairs. Possible Ways to Streamline Existing Federal Energy Mineral Leasing Rules. EMD-81-44. Washington, D.C., January 21, 1981.

--------------. Federal Leasing Policy -- Is the Split Responsibility Working? EMD-79-90. Washington, D.C., June 4, 1979.

--------------. Report to the Congress of the United States: Interior Programs for Assessing Mineral Resources on Federal Lands Need Improvements and Acceleration. EMD-78-83. Washington, D.C., July 27, 1978.

U.S. Public Land Law Review Commission. One Third of the Nation's Land: A Report to the President and to the Congress. Washington, D.C.: Government Printing Office, 1970.

--------------. Energy Fuel Mineral Resources of the Public Lands: Master Report/Volume I. Prepared by ABT Associates, Inc., published with revisions, National Technical Information Service, December 1970.

U.S. Office of Technology Assessment. Management of Fuel and Nonfuel Minerals in Federal Land: Current Status and Issues.

OTA-M-88. Washington, D.C.: Government Printing Office, April 1979.

Wallis, John. "The Birth of Old Federalism: Financing the New Deal, 1932-1940." Journal of Economic History XLIV (1984): 139.

Wurtzler, Gail. "Special Issues 1: Diligence Requirements." Paper presented at Public Lands Mineral Leasing: Issues and Directions Short Course, University of Colorado Law School, June 1985.

OIL AND GAS

Cwik, Lawrence J. "Oil and Gas Leasing on Wilderness Lands: The Federal Land Policy and Management Act, the Wilderness Act, and the United States Department of the Interior, 1981-1983." Environmental Law 14 (1984): 585.

Kite, Marilyn. "Readjustment of Federal Coal Lease." Paper presented at Public Lands Mineral Leasing: Issues and Directions Short Course, University of Colorado Law School, June 1985.

Lowenstein, Roger, and Andy Pasztor. "Abuses in U.S. Lottery for Oil, Gas Leases are Prompting Renewed Calls for Reform." The Wall Street Journal March 29, 1984: 29.

McDonald, Stephen. The Leasing of Federal Lands for Fossil Fuel Production. Baltimore: Johns Hopkins University Press, 1979.

Sierra Club. The Great Giveaway: Public Oil, Gas and Coal and the Reagan Administration, Sierra Club Natural Heritage Report No. 1. San Francisco: Sierra Club, 1984.

The State. "Interior Department's Sales Netting Less of Oil, Gas Leases." Columbia, S.C.: October 9, 1983.

U.S. Commission on Fiscal Accountability of the Nation's Energy Resources. Report of the Commission. Washington, D.C.: Government Printing Office, January 1982.

U.S. Congress. Senate. Committee on Energy and Natural Resources. Federal Oil and Gas Leasing Act of 1979. 96th Cong., 1st sess., October 12, 1979.

U.S. Department of the Interior. Office of the Secretary. "Secretary Clark Halts Oil Lease Subdivision to Prevent Fraud, Encourage Exploration." News release, March 15, 1984.

——————. "Interior Will Change Oil and Gas Leasing System." News release, January 31, 1984.

U.S. General Accounting Office. Opportunity to Increase Oil and Gas Exploration and Lease Rental Income. GAO/RCED-83-77. Washington, D.C., April 28, 1983.

U.S. Public Land Law Review Commission. Energy Fuel Mineral Resources of the Public Lands. Volume III: Legal Study of Federal Competitive and Noncompetitive Oil and Gas Leasing. Prepared by the Rocky Mountain Mineral Law Foundation, republished with revisions, National Technical Information Service, 1970.

COAL

Burford, Robert. "BLM's Role in Mineral Leasing on the Public Lands." Paper presented at the Public Land Law Conference, Missoula, Montana, May 1984.

Kolstad, Charles D., and Frank A. Wolak, Jr. "Competition in Interregional Taxation: The Case of Western Coal." Journal of Political Economy 91 (1983): 443.

Nelson, Robert H. The Making of Federal Coal Policy. Durham, North Carolina: Duke University Press, 1983.

U.S. Commission of Fair Market Value Policy for Federal Coal Leasing. Report of the Commission. Washington, D.C.: Government Printing Office, February 1984.

U.S. Department of the Interior. Office of the Secretary. "Secretary Clark Recommends Improved Framework for Federal Coal Leasing." News release, March 19, 1984.

------------. Review of Federal Coal Leasing. Response to Coal Commission Report, March 19, 1984.

U.S. Department of the Interior. Bureau of Land Management. Montana/Dakotas. Public Affairs Staff. "Questions and Answers on Federal Coal Leasing." April 1984.

U.S. General Accounting Office. Analysis of the Powder River Basin Federal Coal Lease Sale: Economic Valuation Improvements and Legislative Changes Needed. Washington, D.C., 1983.

U.S. Office of Technology Assessment. Environmental Protection in the Federal Coal Leasing Program. OTA-E-237. Washington, D.C.: Government Printing Office, May 1984.

------------. An Assessment of Development and Production Potential of Federal Coal Leases. OTA-M-150. Washington D.C.: Government Printing Office, December 1981.

OIL SHALE

Due, Mary Jane. "Oil Shale Problems and Issues." In Public Lands and the U.S. Economy, edited by George M. Johnston and Peter M. Emerson. Boulder, Colorado: Westview Press, 1984.

U.S. Department of the Interior. Bureau of Land Management. Draft Environmental Impact Statement on the Federal Oil Shale Management Program. Washington, D.C., February 1983.

------------. Colorado State Office. Final Supplemental Environmental Impact Statement for the Prototype Oil Shale Leasing Program. Denver, Colorado, January 1983.

U.S. Public Land Law Review Commission. Energy Fuel Mineral Resources of the Public Lands -- Volume V: Legal Study of Oil Shale on Public Lands. Prepared by the University of Denver College of Law, republished with revisions, National Technical Information Service, December 1970.

TAR SANDS

U.S. Bureau of Land Management. Richfield District, Utah. Utah Combined Hydrocarbon Leasing Regional Draft EIS: Volume I -- Regional Analysis. January 1984.

OUTER CONTINENTAL SHELF OIL AND GAS LEASING

California. Senate Office of Research. "Status of Energy Leasing Activities Offshore California." Sacramento, California: October 10, 1983.

Christopher, Warren M. "The Outer Continental Shelf Lands Act: Key to a New Frontier." Stanford Law Review 6 (1953): 23.

Greenberg, Eldon V. C., and Michael E. Shapiro. "Federalism in the Fishery Conservation Zone: A New Role for the States in an Era of Federal Regulatory Reform." Southern California Law Review 55 (1982): 641.

Miller, Daniel S. "Offshore Federalism: Evolving Federal-State Relations in Offshore Oil and Gas Development." Ecology Law Review 11 (1984): 401.

Shapiro, Michael E. "Status of Energy Leasing Activities Offshore California." Commentary: Western Natural Resource Litigation Digest. Winter 1984: 12.

U.S. Department of the Interior.   Bureau of Land Management. Final Supplement to the Final Environmental Statement Proposed Five-Year OCS Oil and Gas Lease Sale Schedule January 1982 - December 1986. vol. II.

U.S. Department of the Interior.   Minerals Management Service. "Outer Continental Shelf Lease Offering Statistics, Gulf of Mexico Region."   Report prepared by Eileen Swiler.   Metairie, Louisiana, February 13, 1984.

U.S. General Accounting Office. Congress Should Extend Mandate to Experiment with Alternative Bidding Systems in Leasing Offshore Lands. GAO/RCED-83-139. Washington, D.C., May 27, 1983.

--------------. Outlook for Federal Goals to Accelerate Leasing of Oil and Gas Resources on the Outer Continental Shelf. RED-75-343. Washington, D.C., March 19, 1975.

GEOTHERMAL

Futures Group. A Technology Assessment of Geothermal Energy Resource Development. Report prepared for the National Science Foundation, Contract C-836. Washington, D.C.: Government Printing Office, 1981.

U.S. FOREST SERVICE TIMBER

Clawson, Marion. "The National Forests." Science 191 (February 20, 1976): 762.

Craig, George A. "Are Changes Needed in Forest Service Timber Appraisals?" Journal of Forestry 82 (1984): 408.

Dennison, William N. "Purchaser Road Credit: A Tool in Need of Repair." Forest Industries 24 (November 1983): 24-25.

Dowdle, Barney, and Steve Hanke. "Public Timber and Wood Products Industry." In Forestlands: Public and Private, edited by Deacon and Johnson. Cambridge, Massachusetts: Ballinger, 1985.

Kadera, James. "Debate Over Forest Economics Heats Up." The Oregonian, December 16, 1984, p. C-1.

National Appraisals Working Group. "USDA Forest Service Timber Pricing in the West." Washington, D.C., Interim Report, July 31, 1984.

Nelson, Robert H. "The Future of Federal Forest Management: Options for Change." Paper presented at the National Forest Mission Symposium, San Francisco, 1984.

Obermiller, Frederick W., and Linda Wear, "National Economic Efficiency versus Local Community Stability Goals in Public Land Management: A Review of Relevant Literature." Mimeo, 1982.

Popovich, L. "Harvest Schedules: Parts I and II." Journal of Forestry 74 (September 1976: 559 and October 1976: 666).

Sample, V. Alaric, Jr. Below-Cost Timber Sales on the National Forests. Policy Brief. The Wilderness Society. Washington, D.C., July 1984.

U.S. Congressional Research Service. Testimony on H.R. 5425, The Idaho Wilderness Act of 1984. Report prepared by Robert Wolf. June 14, 1984.

U.S. Department of Agriculture. Forest Service. Washington Office of Information. The Role of Below Cost Timber Sales in National Forest Management. Mimeo, July 25, 1984.

U.S. Department of Agriculture. Forest Service. An Analysis of the Timber Situation in the United States 1952-2000. Forest Resources Report No. 23. Washington, D.C., December 1982.

U.S. Department of Agriculture. Forest Service. An Assessment of the Forest and Rangeland Situation in the United States. Washington, D.C., January 1980.

U.S. Department of Agriculture. Office of the Secretary. "Description of a Proposal to Revise the Manner by Which National Forest System Receipts Are Shared With the States and Counties." Western Timber Association Mimeo 11397, April 2, 1984.

U.S. General Accounting Office. Congress Needs Better Information on Forest Service's Below-Cost Timber Sales. GAO/RCED-84-96. June 28, 1984.

BUREAU OF LAND MANAGEMENT RESOURCE MANAGEMENT PROGRAMS

Arizona Law Review. "Symposium: The Federal Land Policy and Management Act of 1976." Arizona Law Review 21 (1979): 267-597.

Bureau of Governmental Research and Service. School of Community Service and Public Affairs. University of Oregon. The O&C Lands. 1981.

de Buys, William. "Overgrazing and Village Culture: A Double Bind for Service Range Managers in Northern New Mexico." Center for Natural Resource Studies. Berkeley, California, Mimeo, n.d.

National Research Council/National Academy of Sciences. Developing Strategies for Rangeland Management: A Report Prepared by the Committee on Developing Strategies for Rangeland Management. Boulder, Colorado: Westview Press, 1984.

Public Lands Institute. Public Lands Institute Newsletter 6 (May 1983): 1-4.

Scott, Valerie Weeks. "The Range Cattle Industry: Its Effect on Western Land Law." Montana Law Review 28 (1966): 155.

U.S. Congress. House. Committee on Appropriations. Surveys and Investigations Staff. A BLM Grazing and Management and Rangeland Improvement Program. Memorandum for the chairman signed by C.R. Anderson and R.W. Vandergrift, Jr. April 20, 1984.

U.S. Department of the Interior. Bureau of Land Management. Wyoming State Office. Rights of Way Handbook. Cheyenne, Wyoming, August 10, 1984.

Western Timber Association. Mimeo 3 11066, File 2.633 (August 2, 1983).

Wilson, Leonard, and Frank Lundburg. Cooperative Management on the Public Lands: Final Report. Washington, D.C.: Council of State Planning Agencies. n.d.

Zivnuska, John. "Timber Harvesting and Land Use Planning Under the National Forest Management Act of 1976." Address before the Committee of Scientists, Denver, August 1977. Cited in Dana, S. T., and S. K. Fairfax. Forest and Range Policy: Its Development in the United States. New York: McGraw-Hill, 1980.

OTHER PROGRAMS

Binder, M.A. "Payment in Lieu of Taxes Act: A Legislative Response to Federal Tax Immunity." Dickinson Law Review 85 (1981): 455.

EBS Management Consultants. Revenue Sharing and Payments in Lieu of Taxes on the Public Lands, Volumes I and II. Washington, D.C.: Public Land Law Review Commission, 1970.

Fairfax, S. K. "Coming of Age in the BLM: Range Management In Search of a Gospel." In Developing Strategies for Rangeland Management: A Report Prepared by the Committee on Developing Strategies for Rangeland Management. National Research Council/National Academy of Sciences. Boulder, Colorado: Westview Press, 1984.

Foss, P. Politics and Grass. Seattle, Washington: University of Washington Press, 1960.

Hammond, Kenneth A. "The Land and Water Conservation Fund Act: Development and Impact." Ph.D. diss., University of Michigan, 1969.

Harvey, J. Carol. "Federal Royalty Management on Federal Onshore and Indian Lands: Industry Concerns." Paper presented at Public Lands Mineral Leasing: Issues and Directions Short Course, University of Colorado Law School, June 1985.

Leshy, J.D. "Sharing Federal Multiple Use Lands - Historic Lessons and Speculations for the Future." In Rethinking the Federal Lands, edited by Sterling Brubaker. Washington, D.C.: Resources for the Future, 1984.

Manning, R. E. Preliminary Report on Taxes and Other In-Lieu Payments on Federal Property. Report prepared for the House Committee on Interior and Insular Affairs. 89th Cong., 2d sess. Committee Report 23, May 13, 1954.

U.S. Advisory Commission on Intergovernmental Relations. The Adequacy of Federal Compensation to Local Governments for Tax Exempt Federal Lands. A-68. 1978.

U.S. Congressional Budget Office. Current Cost-Sharing and Financing Policies for Federal and State Water Resources Development: Special Study. Washington, D.C., July 1983.

U.S. Department of the Interior and Department of Agriculture. Bureau of Land Management and Forest Service. 1985 Grazing Fee Review and Evaluation. Washington, D.C., 1985.

Also Available from Island Press

Hazardous Waste Management: Reducing the Risk
by Benjamin A. Goldman, James A. Hulme, and Cameron Johnson for the Council on Economic Priorities. $64.95 cloth; $34.95 paper.

Hazardous Waste Management: Reducing the Risk is a comprehensive sourcebook of facts and strategies that provides the analytic tools needed by policy makers, regulating agencies, hazardous waste generators, and host communities to compare facilities on the basis of site, management, and technology. The Council on Economic Priorities' innovative ranking system applies to real-world, site-specific evaluations, establishes a consistent protocol for multiple applications, assesses relative benefits and risks, and evaluates and ranks ten active facilities and eight leading commercial management corporations.

An Environmental Agenda for the Future
by Leaders of America's Foremost Environmental Organizations. $5.95 paper.

The chief executive officers of the ten major environmental and conservation organizations launched a joint venture to examine what goals the environmental movement should pursue now and on into the 21st century. This book presents policy recommendations to effect changes needed to bring about a healthier, safer living experience. Issues discussed include: nuclear issues, human population growth, energy strategies, toxic and pollution control, and urban environments.

> "... a substantive book addressing the most serious questions about the future of our resources."
> —John Chafee, Senator,
> Environmental & Public Works Committee

250

"While I am not in agreement with many of the positions the authors take, I believe this book can be the basis for constructive dialogue with industry representatives seeking solutions to environmental problems."
—Louis Fernandez, Chairman of the Board,
Monsanto Company

Water in the West
by The Western Network.
Vol. I: What Indian Water Means to the West. $15.00 paper.
Vol. II: Water for the Energy Market. $15.00 paper.
Vol. III: Western Water Flows to the Cities. $25.00 paper.

An essential reference tool for water managers, public officials, farmers, attorneys, industry officials, and students and professors attempting to understand the competing pressures on our most important natural resource—water. This three-volume series provides an in-depth analysis of the effects of energy development, Indian rights, and urban growth on other water users.

Community Open Spaces
by Mark Francis, Lisa Cashdan, Lynn Paxson. $24.95 cloth.

Over the past decade thousands of community gardens and parks have been developed on vacant neighborhood land in America's major cities. Community Open Spaces documents this movement in the U.S. and Europe, explaining how planners, public officials, and local residents can work in their own community to successfully develop open space.

Private Options: Tools and Concepts for Land Conservation
by Montana Land Reliance and Land Trust Exchange. $25.00 paper.

Techniques and strategies for saving the family farm are presented by 30 experts. Private Options details the proceedings of a national conference and brings together, for the first time, the experience and advice of land conservation experts from all over the nation.

The Conservation Easement in California
by Thomas S. Barrett and Putnam Livermore for The Trust for Public Land. $44.95 cloth; $24.95 paper.

The authoritative legal handbook on conservation easements. This book examines the California law as a model for the nation. It emphasizes the effectiveness and flexibility of the California code. Also covered are the historical and legal backgrounds of easement technology, the state and federal tax implications, and solutions to the most difficult drafting problems.

Building an Ark: Tools for the Preservation of Natural Diversity through Land Protection
by Phillip M. Hoose, Illustrations. $12.00 paper.

The author, The Nature Conservancy's national protection planner, presents a comprehensive plan to identify and protect each state's natural ecological diversity, and shows how plant and animal species can be saved from destruction without penalty to the landowner. Case studies augment this blueprint for conservation.

Land–Saving Action
edited by Russell I. Brenneman and Sarah M. Bates. $39.95 cloth; $24.95 paper.

The definitive guide for conservation practitioners. A written symposium by the 29 leading experts in land conservation. This book presents in detail land–saving tools and techniques that have been perfected by individuals and organizations across the nation. This is the first time such information has been available in one volume.

These titles are available directly from Island Press, Order Department, Box 7, Covelo, CA 95428. Please enclose $1.50 with each order for postage and handling; California residents add 6 percent sales tax. A catalog of current and forthcoming titles is available free of charge.

Island Press is a nonprofit organization dedicated to the publication of books for professionals and concerned citizens on the conservation and management of natural resources and the environment.